# SELF-SUFFICIENCY

# SELF-SUFFICIENCY

*The Science and Art of Producing and Preserving
your own Food*

John & Sally Seymour

*Illustrated by
Sally Seymour*

FABER AND FABER
3 Queen Square
London

First published in 1973
by Faber and Faber Limited
3 Queen Square London WC1
Reprinted 1973, 1974 (Twice) and 1975
Printed in Great Britain by
Headley Brothers Limited
The Invicta Press, London and Ashford, Kent

© John and Sally Seymour, 1973

**British Library Cataloguing in Publication Data**

Seymour, John, b.1914
    Self-sufficiency.
    1. Food supply
    I. Title    II. Seymour, Sally
    630                    TX353

ISBN 0-571-09954-8
ISBN 0-571-10635-8 Pbk

# Contents

1. What is it? Why do it?                                        7

2. Land                                                         14

3. Horse                                                        27

4. Cow                                                          42

5. Dairy                                                        55

6. Pig                                                          75

7. Bacon                                                        83

8. Poultry, Sheep, Goat, Rabbit, Pigeon                         97

9. Meat                                                        109

10. Grass                                                      121

11. Wheat and Bread                                            129

12. Barley, Beer                                               149

13. Other Field Crops                                          161

14. Garden Crops                                               172

15. Fruit and Nuts                                             186

16. Storage of Vegetables                                      196

17. Fish                                                       206

18. Bees, Wild Food, Wine, Wood, Smoke-house,
    Seaweed                                                    226

19. Last Word                                                  242

# I

## What is it? Why do it?

*How many a poor immortal soul have I met well-nigh
crushed and smothered under its load . . .*

THOREAU

What does being self-supporting mean? Robinson Crusoe, if we
except his raft-loads, got pretty near it, and many an African
tribesman, or Indian *ryot*, is not far away. I have lived in
African and Indian villages, and have seen a very high degree
of self-sufficiency in both, and also a very high degree of
happiness and true contentment. In every North Indian
village of any use there is a man who knows how to go out
into the country and cut down a *pipal* tree, and with it make a
plough to sell to his neighbour in return for wheat or rice or
other goods or services. There is a village miller, a *dhobi* or
washerman, a *tonga-wallah* or driver of a hackney-cart, carpenter and blacksmith, potter, and the people spin their own
cotton to give the yarn to the village weaver to weave their
cloth. If a man wants to build a house he and his neighbours
get to work and build it and that is that. Except at harvest
nobody works very hard.

There is one man in each village, though, or very often not
*in* the village but *of* the village, who does absolutely no good
at all, and who is a terrible burden on his fellow villagers, and
that is the *zamindar*—the land-owner. He probably consumes
more of the wealth of the village than all of the other villagers
put together, and in return for this he does absolutely nothing
at all. Remove the *zamindar* and at one stroke you more than
double the wealth and well-being of every other villager.

The Central African village has no *zamindar*, in fact it has
no landowners at all. The concept of land-ownership is

completely alien to the African tribesman. The *village* owns, or at least controls, such of the surrounding forest as it can hold from others, and the villagers till the land in common, each man tilling what seems to the Headman of the village a reasonable amount, and paying nobody any rent for it. The Headman tills (or at least his wives do) the same amount as anybody else, and everybody has enough, and could have more if he wanted it. Here, unless there is a famine (and in twelve years in Africa I never saw one), everybody gets enough to eat, and people who do not hanker after the flesh-pots of the white man live a very good life indeed.

Teach these people to read, though, and you immediately get a completely different situation. The children grow up no longer content with village self-sufficiency. They must have books, and books cannot be produced in the village (although I have seen paper being made in an Indian village in a mill; the chief constituent was a cow walking round in a circle providing the power), they wish to see the other parts of the world that they now become aware exist, they long for the sophisticated clothes, the machines, the gadgets and the other things that can only be produced by a city-based civilization. The Indians have two useful words: *pukha* and *kutcha*. *Pukha* means with a civilized finish on it. *Kutcha* means rough—made in the village without outside help. The man who has learnt to read, and been to town, comes back and wants a *pukha* house—one that makes use of glass and cement and mill-sawn timber and other materials that cannot be produced in the village: his old *kutcha* house is no longer good enough for him. He also wants white sugar instead of *gorr*, which is the un-refined sugar of his own sugar-cane, tea instead of buttermilk, white flour instead of his own wholemeal. He—and eventually his whole village with him—are forced into a money economy, crops are grown for sale and not for use, the village becomes part of the great world-wide system of trade, finance and interchange. In Africa what happens is that the young men of the village are forced to go and work in the white man's mines.

Now, the sort of self-sufficiency which I wish to treat of in

8

this book is not the old, pre-industrial self-sufficiency: that of the illiterate peasant or hunter who has never heard of anything else. That kind of self-sufficiency is, for better or for worse, on the way out. What I am interested in is *post*-industrial self-sufficiency: that of the person who has gone through the big-city-industrial way of life and who has advanced beyond it and wants to go on to something better.

If the findings of the National Academy of Sciences and the National Research Council of the United States are correct (see their report *Resources and Man*—W. H. Freeman and Co., San Francisco), we will be forced into this kind of self-sufficiency whether we like it or not. For, according to these findings the fossil fuel supply of the earth will be exhausted long before we can possibly develop atomic or solar power to take the place of more than a tiny fraction of the motive power that our big-city civilization requires to make it work, and there are, apparently, insuperable obstacles to the really widespread global development of atomic power. After all, the existing electricity-producing power stations of the earth, no matter how they are driven, could not power a tiny fraction of the road, sea and air transport of the world, and if the latter ground to even a partial halt the whole great fragile edifice of global interdependence would collapse.

If this does not happen though, and if—as most people are in the habit of thinking—'they' find a way to keep a hundred million motor cars roaring along the roads after the oil has dried up (whoever 'they' are), there is still a case for far more self-sufficiency of communities and individuals. If there is fast and cheap land transport it is not necessary for a jeweller to live in Birmingham, a potter in Stoke-on-Trent or a cutler in Sheffield. Such craftsmen can live, if they wish, right out in the country, and practise their crafts in their own homes. Their raw materials can be got to them cheaply, and cheaply they can send their finished articles away. With unlimited cheap transport the whole need for crowding people into industrial cities fades away, and more and more city people will leave the big cities (which will become more and more unendurable anyway as more and more ignorant people try to crowd *into* them) and set up their workshops in pleasant places, and many of these people will eventually get the idea of being at least partially self-supporting.

There is no good economic reason why they should be self-supporting: a craftsman living in the country need not even grow a cabbage if he doesn't want to—he can simply produce enough of the produce of his own industry to buy the food he needs. But a surprising number of such craftsmen find that they *want* to be at least partially self-supporting. A surprising number of the more intelligent people who have passed through the big-city-industrial stage are reacting against it: they *want* to advance to a more interesting and self-sufficient kind of life. After all, specialization may be economic, but it is terribly *boring*. I am a writer, but if I wrote enough hours a day to buy everything I and my family need I would write myself into the ground. I would quickly become bored and unhealthy. As it is, I write for half my working day, and during the rest of my time work mostly out of doors, growing and producing much that we eat and use, thus keeping happy and fit. Economics is a great science, but it falls down flat on its face when it tries to equate all good with *money*. It is inefficient, any agricultural economist will tell you, for me to hand-milk a cow. But what if I *like* hand-milking a cow? What is the economist going to say about that? Has any economist ever tried to measure the 'efficiency' of playing golf? And what if a couple of gallons of milk a day derive from my activity of hand-milking a cow? Does that make it in any way less 'efficient' than if I spent the time playing golf? When economists try to measure things like that they quickly get themselves in to very deep water.

So more and more people, in all the highly industrial societies, are trying partially to opt out of the big-industry set-up and become less specialized and more self-sufficient. These people are not anachronistic, or ignorant or stupid, but are in fact drawn from the most intelligent and self-aware part of the population. The list of 'intentional communities' in

the United States of America is long and getting longer with
an increasing momentum. In this country there are several
hundred such communities, and the army of 'hippies' and
'drop-outs' wandering about the roads like the pilgrims of old
contains many individuals who would *like* to be self-supporting,
but haven't the faintest idea how to set about it.

For the last eighteen years Sally and I have been probably
as nearly self-supporting with food as any family in north-west
Europe. We have a very good idea of what it is like and what
it involves, and therefore I feel qualified here to utter a solemn
warning.

It is beyond the capabilities of any couple, comfortably, to
try to do what we have attempted. If a married couple settled
down on five or ten acres of good land, in the British climate,
and devoted their entire time to being self-supporting in food,
clothes and artifacts; and if they knew how to do it, and had the
necessary stock and equipment, already paid for, they could
succeed. They would be working just the fifteen hours a day,
three hundred and sixty five days of the year, that is, if they
were to maintain the standard of living, and variety of food
and of living, that they could maintain in a town. They would
be very *healthy* doing this, they would not be *bored* (because
they would never be doing the same job for long and would be
doing a great variety of tasks), but they might sometimes wish
they could sit down.

Thoreau, when he lived at Walden and wrote his famous
book about it, lived almost exclusively on beans, and he didn't
work very hard at all. He spent a very large part of his time
there wandering around in the woods, peering into the depths
of his pool, thinking and dreaming and meditating. I think he
was a very sensible and enviable young man indeed. But he
didn't have a wife and a family to bring up. Personally, I
would not be prepared to live for two years and two months
(which is the time Thoreau spent at Walden) on beans.
Sally certainly wouldn't either, and we would be very hard
put to make the children do it. We have, in fact, lived for
eighteen years on the fat of the land: we have probably eaten

and drunk better than most other people in this country: our food has been good, varied, fresh, and of the very best quality. We have never been self-supporting—but we have been very *nearly* self-supporting. We have lived extremely well on a very small money income, and the tax-eaters have not done very well out of us. We have not contributed much to the development of the atom bomb, nor to the building of *Concorde*. When the latter breaks the sound barrier over our heads, and scares the wits out of our cows, we have to endure it, but at least we have the satisfaction of knowing that we haven't *paid* for it.

We started our life of partial self-sufficiency with no stock, no land, no tools, and no money at all. Therefore, we have always had to work at money-bringing jobs, Sally at potting and myself at writing; and we have had to do the self-supporting work in our spare time. We have both had to work harder than people should have to work. But supposing there had been a small handful of *other* effective 'drop-outs' in the vicinity? Supposing, instead of having to keep both cows and pigs, we had only to keep cows? And swapped milk for bacon? Whenever we have been near another 'self-supporter' we have immediately found our task lightened considerably. We could share tools and equipment, 'know-how' (I apologize for borrowing a word from the culture that I have opted out of), and partially specialize: for example, trade asparagus for globe artichokes, mutton for salt fish, pottery for wooden vessels.

This, you may say, is the beginning of specialization, and the beginning of the road back to Birmingham. I do not think it need be. I believe that if half a dozen families were to decide to be partially self-supporting, and settle within a few miles of each other, and *knew what they were doing*, they could make for themselves a very good life. Each family would have some trade or profession or craft, the product of which they would trade with the rest of the world. Each family would grow, rear or produce a variety of goods or objects which they would use themselves and also trade with the other families for their goods. Nobody would get bored doing their specialized art or craft, because they would not have to spend all day at it, but there would be a large variety of other jobs to do every day too. This partial specialization would set them free for at least some leisure: probably more than the city wage-slave gets, after he has commuted to and from his factory or office. A more organized community than this—such as the Americans call an intentional community, or the Israelis a *kibbutz*—might work even better. There is room for endless experiment. The New England village community of the eighteenth century, if you forget the witch-hunting, must have been a very good place to live in.

I can imagine, one day in the future, a highly sophisticated society, some of the members of which would live in towns of a humane size, others scattered about in a well-cared-for countryside, all interdependent and yet in some ways very independent, the towns contributing to the country—the country to the towns. This would not be a very mechanized or industrialized society, but a society in which the real arts of civilization are carried on at a high level, in which literature, music, drama, the visual arts, and the crafts that lead to the good life, are all practised and appreciated by all the people. This would not be 'going back', whatever that means. It would, if you like to think in terms of such imaginary progressions, be 'going forward', and into a golden age. Periclean Athens wasn't such a bad place, give or take a few slaves. If we could find a way to achieve the same result without slaves, we would have achieved something very worth while.

# 2

# Land

*To live well, to enjoy all things that make life pleasant,
is the right of every man who constantly uses his strength
judiciously and lawfully.*

WILLIAM COBBETT

Give any man, anywhere in the world, his fair share of the
earth's surface, and—if he survives one harvest—he and his
family need never be hungry again.

There are 860 people per square mile in England. There
are 640 acres in a square mile, so this makes something like
two-thirds of an acre for every man, woman, child and baby.
But Eire has only 105 people per square mile, and Wales and
Scotland are pretty under-populated too so the figures are not
as bad as they seem, and the British Isles is one of the most
highly populated places in the world. I travelled in a train
over a thousand miles in southern Africa, from De Aar to
Outjo in Namibia, and hardly saw any human dwellings at all,
and yet nearly all of the country over which I passed was
potentially very fertile. The Israelis would make it blossom
like the rose. According to last year's June the Fifth Returns
there is about half an acre of farm land per human soul in
England and Wales, plus of course some rough grazing,
mountain grazing and woodland, and, again, England is one
of the most populated countries in the world.

Cobbett says you can keep a cow alive and productive on
half an acre by feeding her on Swedish turnips and cabbages.
Plenty of commercial farmers nowadays are keeping a cow on
half an acre *plus* a considerable amount of bought-in fertilizer
and food. Personally I should want to see at least two acres
per cow if I was buying nothing in from outside: no hay, no

dairy cake or corn, and no fertilizers. There would be plenty of room on those two acres for other things as well as the cow though: you can run a sheep with every cow without starving the cow and the products of the cow could help substantially towards feeding a pig which need take up hardly any land at all. Sally and I reared our family of four children for eight years on five acres of very poor land, and the only things we had to buy in any quantity in the food line at least were wheat-meal for bread, sugar, tea, coffee and certain spices: there was lighting of course (in our case paraffin) and anthracite for the Aga. We cut most of our fuel, though, from the surrounding forest. It is true that we bought some foodstuffs from outside for our animals, but it is also true that we exported a lot of animal products: our exports of calves, weaner pigs, fat chickens, ducks and geese more than paid for our imports of feeding stuffs.

I would say, then, from my own experience, that a family with four children could live very well on five acres of good land, buying very little from outside, but only if they managed their affairs very carefully. Of course, if they lived like Thoreau did, on beans, or like Punjabi peasants do, mostly on wheat, they would have no trouble at all and would have a surplus for sale. Without any artificial fertilizers you should grow a ton of wheat on an acre, and it takes a child a long while to eat his way through a ton. But I am thinking of a rich, full and varied diet.

Balance is all important in this, and to achieve this balance is very difficult. It would make the problem immeasurably easier if there were even one or two other families, within easy walking distance, doing the same sort of thing. For example, if a family keeps a cow she will not give them milk all the year round because she will be dry for part of the year. So the family must keep two cows. The two cows will then be in milk for most of the year together and the family will have far more milk than it needs. If there was another self-supporting family nearby though, either one family could keep two cows and keep both families in milk, or each family could keep one cow and supply the other family when *their* cow was dry. Again, if you kill a pig or a sheep, and have not got a deep freeze, you cannot eat all the meat unsalted before it goes bad. If you share this meat between two families you can, at least in the winter-time. If there were four families you could eat all the meat in the summer-time too, at least in the case of a sheep or a small porker. There are all sorts of ways round this, of course: you can turn milk into cheese and pork into bacon; but for the rich full and varied diet, without an excessive amount of labour, a little specialization helps enormously. If you wish to mechanize, and grow your own hay and your own wheat, you will need either to own or to hire both a binder and a grass mower. If you have a neighbour, he can grow the hay for both of you and you can grow the wheat. You each need half as much machinery. The road back to Birmingham? There is a lot of difference between growing only hay and not wheat, and putting on Nut No. 365872 a thousand times a day on some machine. There is specialization and specialization.

The answer to the question of how much produce you can grow or rear on a given piece of land varies enormously. A countryman, or a good gardener, will grow a great amount on a small area of land while a beginner, or somebody who does not have enough time to devote to the job, will grow practically nothing worth while at all. I have a half-acre plot at this very moment which I planted with brassica (plants of the cabbage family) in the spring, and it was well cultivated, manured and fertile. It is now nothing but a mass of weeds and rubbish, and the slugs and pigeons have destroyed what little there was of the brassica plants which had survived the weeds. This was because I was forced, by circumstances, to spend most of my summer away and was just not able to keep down the weeds. Cobbett says: 'you ought to depend more on the spade and the hoe than on the dung heap'. Suffolk men say: 'A good hoeing is worth a shower of rain.' Bad land will yield a fair crop if that crop is kept constantly hoed and weed-free: the best land in the world will yield nothing if it is not. It is far better to have a small acreage of land and really 'do' it well, than have a large acreage and scratch over it. It takes very little land to grow the vegetables for a family, if that little land is 'farmed' to the utmost.

So it is very hard to say what is the minimum amount of land needed for a family which wishes to be either wholly or partially self-supporting in food. Do the children want to keep ponies? Will they keep a horse or two for ploughing, or will they use machines? Or will they confine themselves to the spade? If they have machines they will not be self-supporting, because they will use oil. But if they use machines they will have more time to devote to their cash-getting craft or profession, and will be able to pay for the oil and for the machines. Maybe, though, they don't approve of machines. Maybe they think it is immoral to use machines that have to be made by unhappy people in huge factories which they themselves would not consider working in even for one moment. Maybe they don't care. I've got a tractor myself—and I wouldn't spend one minute of my life working in a tractor factory. But I've got horses, and horse implements also, and know very well how to use them.

But if a family controls an acre of good land for every member of that family, that is very well indeed. If the family has access to a little common grazing, or can collect wood in a forest or woods held in common, or catch fish in the sea, or derive wealth in fact from outside the borders of its holding, so much the better. If the family holds more land than that, then that family ought to be exporting a surplus of food for feeding townspeople, who cannot grow any food at all.

Now comes the question of what to grow and what animals to rear and fatten and otherwise exploit on the holding. Nothing is more boring for the farmer or worse for the farm than monoculture, or only growing one crop. Most of the commercially farmed arable land of England now is devoted to monoculture, barley being the crop. The same crop can be grown year after year on the same land by the addition of larger and larger amounts of artificial fertilizers, and larger and larger amounts of pesticides, fungicides and chemical weed killers. As the years go by the one crop always takes just the same elements out of the soil, and the pests, fungi, bacteria and weeds that like to infest that particular crop become more and more strongly established and the farmer has to call in the chemist more and more to combat them and farming becomes hydroponics and not true husbandry at all. The modern agri-businessman is dealing with an inert sterile soil, rendered lifeless and barren by monoculture and inorganic chemicals, but made to grow crops—and large crops too—by the addition in an inorganic form of the chemicals that the crop needs. Whether this process can continue for ever nobody yet knows: certainly it has already continued long enough for many people to have made large fortunes out of it, and for large urban populations to have been fed. It is not true farming at all because the soil itself is contributing nothing to the growth of the crop except holding it up: all that the crop needs is coming from the phosphate and potash mines of various parts of the world, and the giant factories that extract nitrogen out of the air. When the fossil fuel of the earth is exhausted this process will stop of course, and men will have to get back to real farming.

But we are not considering this kind of farming at all, for we are not concerned with growing cash crops on a large scale to sell to the urban masses, but with producing subsistence crops of high quality to eat ourselves or perhaps trade with our immediate neighbours. Therefore variety is what we must strive for. Firstly, because growing a variety of crops, and keeping a variety of animals, is more *fun*. (That is the most important thing of all.) Secondly, because it is better for the soil: each crop takes something different out of it, the pests and diseases of each crop die of starvation the next year when another crop occupies that piece of ground, the plants feed the animals and the animals feed the plants, for the two kingdoms to which these creatures belong are completely complementary.

At the Broom, which is the name of the five-acre holding on which Sally and I spent our first eight years of trying to be self-supporting, we never brought in any fertilizers of any kind at all, and yet as the years went by we found our land growing better and better crops. We used no sprays, hardly any, if any, insecticides, fungicides or herbicides ( I do remember once or twice squirting some stuff over the apple trees, but I don't believe it did any good) and yet we never seemed to suffer any trouble from pests or diseases. The reasons were that we had a great deal of animal manure, we never grew the same crop twice running on the same bit of ground, and we grew such a large variety of crops that no single pest or disease could ever get any sort of a hold at all.

Another advantage of growing and keeping a multiplicity of crops and animals is that in this way you can spread your labour load right round the year. The agri-businessman has a huge investment in sophisticated machinery to enable him to cope with his one huge crop all at the same time, and that with practically no labour at all. There is a man in Cambridgeshire who farms *ten thousand acres*, growing nothing but barley, with the help of three men. I have seen his land—it is a desolation and an affliction to the soul, but it grows an awful lot of barley. (Not a very high yield *per acre* but an enormous yield *per man*.) But if you are working by hand you cannot deal happily with large amounts of any one crop. By diversifying you always have something to do but never too much. Your harvests, and planting times, and all the other work-load peaks, come at different times.

And now we come, inevitably, to the great question of animals or no animals. Are we to be vegetarians or not vegetarians?

The world can support a certain number of vegetarians, but for reasons that I shall now set forth I don't believe it can support a population which is all, or nearly all, of this persuasion. The non-vegan vegetarian I think we can discount, that is if he is a vegetarian on moral or ethical grounds alone. If he just doesn't eat meat because he doesn't like it that is his own business entirely: after all plenty of people don't like boiled turnip and nobody else worries about it. But the man who takes a high moral attitude about not eating meat, and eats eggs, drinks milk or eats butter or cheese, wears shoe leather or wool, just does not have to be taken seriously at all. A cow won't give milk unless she has a calf every year, and every other calf she has, on average, is going to be a bull. What do you do with the bull? Let it starve to death or feed it until it dies of old age? If you do the latter your five acres soon aren't going to be supporting anything else except bulls—and it won't support them for long. We have only to go to the parts of Hindu India where they really don't kill cattle, and have no export outlet for them, to see what happens there. The children starve while walking hat-racks wander about picking up any bit of stick they can eat and eventually provide the vultures with poor pickings indeed.

You can't hatch eggs to provide yourself with hens to lay more without hatching out as many cocks as hens. What do you do with the cocks? If you keep sheep to shear your sheep will breed, unless you are very careful—or would you allow castration, vegetarian?

As for the vegan (a vegan will eat no milk or eggs besides, of course, no meat), a vegan world cannot really suffer any large animals to live at all. If I become a vegan what would I do with the two sows I have got in my sty now? Do I feed them until they die of old age—not letting them breed of course? Or do I turn them loose to roam the roads and get what living they can? If I do that somebody's crops are going to suffer— if enough people do it there won't be any crops left at all. Man has a part to play in the balance of nature, and if he fails to play it that balance gets off-balance and nobody benefits at all. The only possible way in which, in a vegan country, we could suffer large mammals to share the same country as ourselves and go on flourishing would be to import large predators to control them. If we just let loose all the cattle, sheep and pigs that we have now, what does any vegan think would happen? What is the alternative to letting them loose? Well, kill them all, or castrate all but one or two of the males and let all but a few zoo specimens die out. I have never heard any answer to any of the above arguments and I am quite sure I never will, because there are no answers. As for the non-vegetarian whom the self-supporter is bound very often to meet who, with his legs under your table, a knife and fork in his hand, and tucking away happily into his share of a shoulder of mutton, says: 'Ugh! How on earth can you bring yourself to kill a poor sheep!'—well, the only answer to him is to take his plate away.

The good husbandman is not the tyrant of his piece of land, but should be the benign controller—and *part of the biosphere himself. He* is an animal, and the fellow of his sheep and his pigs—and of his grass and his cabbages too: hasn't it now been proved that all life on earth derived from one cell? Take a five-acre piece of wilderness, or a five-acre stretch of a barley-prairie, and there is really very little life on it at all—very little of the higher forms of life at least. Give that five acres to a true husbandman, to live and rear his family on, and you will soon find it supporting a very rich flora and fauna. The application of the intelligence that only man has is beneficial to the other life forms, but for this man must be free to harvest and control, not only among the plants, but among the animals too.

So while I would never try to persuade any vegetarian to become a carnivore I would never become a vegetarian myself. The vegetarian cannot share his holding with other large mammals. I don't think I have the right to be so exclusive.

Once you accept animals, then the greater variety of them that you have on your land the better. Each species draws something different from the soil, and puts something different back. The parasites that afflict one animal die when ingested by another. If you have nothing but, say, sheep, you will get a build-up of sheep-infesting worms on your land. If you have cows too, and alternate the two species on the various parts of the farm, the cows will ingest the eggs of the sheep parasites and these will die, and vice versa, and the animals of both species will be the healthier for it. Any vet will tell you this, and any commercial farmer who has any sense. Also, the cows will eat the coarse grass that the sheep won't touch, and the sheep, which crop much closer, will come behind the cows and crop the very short grass that the cows can't get. A cow grazes by curling her tongue around the grass; the sheep (like the horse) nips it off with her teeth very close to the ground. Thus put your calves first into a clean piece of pasture, follow them with your adult cattle, and follow these with your sheep and horses.

Geese, too, are an important grazing animal and, except for that merry fortnight when they are being fattened for the table, they can live on nothing but grass. They fit very well into your ecology. Ducks are one of the few animals that will eat that revolting thing—the slug—and therefore are very useful for patrolling your land to keep these down. You can let them wander in your garden, within reason, and although they will nibble the lettuces they will also eat the slugs and the latter would do far more damage. And, after all, you can eat the ducks can't you?

Hens will thrive in woodland, or any rough ground if it is not too wet (if it is wet then what are your ducks and geese for?). If moved across pasture they do great good to it, scrapping out the matted grass, eating thistle seeds and other weed seeds and manuring it. Put on stubble after a corn harvest they save from waste the spilled grain and also scrap out wireworm and other monsters. Run behind larger animals they help by spreading their droppings, and help themselves (and you) by eating any undigested grain.

The pig is a noble and magnificent animal. He will eat not only the food that grows on the top of the soil but will mine deep down and munch up the roots of docks and nettles, wire worm and leather jackets, and derive only the pig knows what health and benefit from what lies underneath. He is your best ploughman. On light land I have seen a pig completely bury herself—a huge sow with only her tail sticking up above the level of the ground. Keep pigs on a small area of rough useless ground, until they have dug it over and over and manured it again and again, and that land will have been turned into an easily-worked and fertile part of your holding. A *small* area per pig though—let Old Mother Common

Sense say how big. But don't keep pigs there too long. Like other animals, they will eventually build up parasitic infestation if left too long on the same piece of land, but we will discuss all that in Chapter 6.

As far as crops are concerned, if you have plenty of animals, and use the plough or the spade and the hoe enough, you will have no difficulty growing the finest crops in the world and you won't have to spend a penny on fertilizer. There is a benign cycle—vegetable–animal–vegetable and so on *ad infinitum*—that will progressively increase, and not decrease, the health and fertility of your holding. I personally have nothing intrinsically against artificial fertilizers. I don't believe myself that you can *really* taste the difference between a cabbage that has had a pinch of sulphate of ammonia shoved on it and one that has not. If my land lacks phosphate I put some slag on it, if I can afford it, and find it very good stuff. But I have to admit I don't like *paying* for slag—or any other 'artificials'. I am mean. And if by good husbandry I can keep my land fertile enough not to *need* to import 'artificials', that I would far rather do. And I believe that the richer the micro-flora and micro-fauna you have in your soil the healthier the plants and large animals that live off that soil will be; 'artificials' suppress the micro-flora and micro-fauna, while 'organic manure' (droppings of animals plus rotten vegetation) encourages it.

Rotate your crop by all means: never grow crop after crop of the same species year after year on the same land. Of course with perennials, like fruit bushes or trees, asparagus or globe artichokes, you can't rotate, but consider—all those things need great quantities of muck or compost. You practically renew their soil every year by the addition of manure. But annual crops should never be grown twice on the same land. Rotate your crops and rotate your animals above the crops and neither will suffer from any disease.

As for the initial fertility of your land, I would advise anyone taking over a holding to have the soil tested by a man from the Ministry of Agriculture, and if he says it lacks lime—lime it, phosphate—slag it, or potash—potash it. If the land is in very poor heart (as it certainly will be if your predecessor has been an agri-businessman) then you may have to use some nitrogen for a year or two, until your animals have made you enough fertility to put the heart back into the soil. If you insist on farming with no animals then you will always have to buy nitrogen, even if you make vegetable compost, and if you make the latter you will have to get vegetable matter from outside because there just won't be enough on it to make enough compost to increase fertility. A man can't *really* hoist himself up by his own boot-laces, nor can a farm.

Another question we must consider before we leave the subject of the land is drainage. Much land is dry and self-draining, and if it is we don't have to worry about this aspect at all. But if land grows sedges, rushes, heavy tussocks of grass, or mare's tail, then it will probably want draining, and won't be any good until it is drained. Wet land cannot support aerobic micro-organisms, therefore old vegetation cannot rot down properly into it (it turns into peat instead); few crop plants will thrive in it and it is almost impossible to cultivate. It will grow poor, coarse grass for grazing sometimes, and this may be welcome in a dry season, but whether you grow grass on it or arable crops, it will be far more productive if it is drained. And a factor against grazing wet marshlands is the almost certain danger from liver fluke. Both sheep and cattle will suffer from this, and man will himself too—if he eats, for example, watercress from flukey land. There is no excuse, really, for any husbandman to have ill-drained land on his holding unless he is keeping it for a nature reserve. Some marshes, indeed, ought to be preserved for this, for marshy flora and fauna can be very interesting, and have as much right to exist as we do.

But if you have wet land, and wish to drain it, in Britain you had better send for the drainage officer of the Ministry of Agriculture, Fisheries and Food. For not only does that gentleman know a lot about drainage, but also he can hand out certain very useful subsidies: the government will pay half the cost of drainage schemes at the moment, and at times this subsidy has gone up as high as 75 per cent.

If you wish to do it yourself, though, and on small holdings it is better sometimes to keep the government men as far away as possible, and in other countries but Britain there may not be a subsidy anyway, there are certain principles that must be borne in mind.

The first is (and this the non-farming layman often finds very hard to understand) that a ditch dug along the contour of sloping land drains the land *below* it and not that above it. The layman says 'How can this be? The water in the land won't run uphill—how can it get into the ditch to drain the land?' The answer is that the contour ditch above the wet field stops more water running into the field. The water already in the field is going to work its way downhill anyway, and by the time it had got to a contour ditch dug at the *bottom* of the field it would have been on the point of leaving the field anyway. The rain that falls on a field is not enough to make it boggy: it is the water working its way underground from higher land that does this, and it is this water that is intercepted by the contour drain.

Open ditches drain very efficiently, but they must be fenced against cattle or the latter will break their sides down, and they must be cleaned out from time to time, which is a laborious process. It can be done by hand, or else by tractors fitted with power-arms, such as the McConnell. Underground drains may not drain quite so freely but they require no maintenance: cattle cannot break them down and you don't have to clean them out. They may not live for ever though. There are two sorts: piped drains and mole drains. Mole drains are merely opened in the soil by a mole drainer pulled behind a tractor: the moler looks like a little torpedo stuck on the bottom of a steel blade. There are plenty of contractors who do this work. Mole drains stand up well in clay soil, less well in lighter soils, and if there are too many big stones or boulders underground you can't make them at all. In good cases they last about eight years.

Piped drains are the other sort of underground drain. A narrow ditch is dug, either by hand or by machine, and a pipe is laid in the bottom of it. Formerly the pipe was fired earthenware, in lengths of from a foot to eighteen inches: now it tends to be of long lengths of plastic. The plastic has holes in it to let the water in, the earthenware pipes let the water in where they join. In either case loose stone or gravel is poured in on top of the pipe and then earth filled in on top. Piped drains may last a very long time. I dug a ditch in heavy land in Suffolk and thus revealed the carefully-bricked outlet of a piped drain with a date on it: 1880. When we cleared the mouth of the drain, water immediately began to run out of it and it was working perfectly.

You can also drain by digging a ditch and putting bushes in it and burying them (the Romans did this) and I have experimented by putting down brushwood and then laying half-sheets of rusty corrugated iron on top of it and filling in the soil. What happens when the iron rusts right away I don't yet know. You can split the sheets easily with an ordinary mattock—standing over them and cutting them down the middle. It is a very good way of getting rid of unsightly old pieces of corrugated iron.

But whatever sort of underground drains you use they have got to come out somewhere, and that will probably have to be in a ditch. The ditch will have to be either running down the slope at one side of the field, or else running along the contour at the bottom of the field. You can often drain a field by simply digging a ditch along the top contour, as I have said, but if the field is very large, or very wet, you will need underground drains too. On sandy or gravelly soil, or soil with a porous subsoil, such as sand, gravel, limestone or chalk, you won't need any drainage at all and you can heave a sigh of relief.

# 3

# Horse

*Come all ye honest ploughmen,*
*Old England's fate you hold!*
OLD SONG

In spite of the teachings of the no-digging and no-ploughing school of husbandmen, people still go on digging and ploughing, as they have done ever since Neolithic times, and my guess is that they will go on digging and ploughing as long as men live on this earth. For there is really no other way of effectively growing arable crops—at least, without the impracticable use of enormous quantities of compost.

Cobbett says, in *Cottage Economy*: 'As to the act of making bread, it would be shocking indeed if that had to be taught by means of books.' I would like to paraphrase that: 'as to the act of digging'. The only thing I will say about it, realizing that the flight from the cities is likely to include people who have practically never seen a spade, is that you should nearly always dig a trench: that is, remove one spit of soil (a spit is the wedge of soil cut by the spade) out in a furrow right across your piece of ground and dump it, then turn the next row of spits upside down into the furrow you have left. Thus you always have an open furrow in front of you to invert your spits into. When you come to the end of your piece you should, in theory at least, load the first lot of spits you dug out and dumped into a wheelbarrow and cart them back to fill up the empty furrow that has been left.

One way is to split your work down the middle and dig from alternate ends. You can then throw the first spit of each long narrow strip into the last furrow of the other. It is often admissible, however, to dig by inverting the spits *in situ* and not 'digging to a trench' when you are digging land over for the second time, or just loosening the soil around soft fruit bushes, or digging with a fork. But the serious self-supporter is likely to be more interested in growing food than in such counsels of perfection. But, in my experience at any rate, the more you dig the better, and it is better to dig badly than not dig at all.

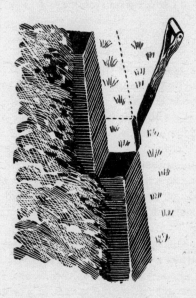

If we wish to grow food on a larger scale, then there are three things we can do effectively. One is to buy an agricultural tractor. The other is go in for one of those little garden cultivators: either a rotovator or a mini-plough. The third is to plough by horse.

## TRACTOR

In comparing these different methods of cultivating I will merely draw on my own experience. We have now a Ferguson diesel tractor which cost us £70·00 together with a fore-end loader, a link box, and a mounted spring-tine cultivator.

For £70·00 we could not have got much of a garden cultivator which you can comfortably lift off the ground with one hand. We can always borrow from a neighbour a two-furrow plough to fit on the tractor (a good second-hand one from a farm sale would cost us about ten pounds), and we could certainly plough very deeply and well five acres in a day (if we were willing to spend a whole day doing one job, which we are not). This tractor will break up rough ground and bury any amount of rubbish as it ploughs; if it hits a boulder in our boulder-strewn glacial deposit of a farm, it just stops the tractor, and if the boulder is no bigger than I am it will lift it right out of the ground with its hydraulics. The spring-tine cultivator covers a lot of ground, therefore it is easy to make many passes with it, and it will pulverize the roughest soil and make a seed-bed. Or almost make a seed-bed—it is generally desirable to haul a set of light harrows, or a ring-roll, over the land after it, to make the tilth fine enough for small seeds. The tractor will work in a small garden—both with the plough and the spring-tine cultivator—so long as the garden is quite empty of crops and unencumbered. It becomes difficult when there are patches of crop left which must be undisturbed, for the tractor takes room to manoeuvre.

I must explain here that Harry Ferguson revolutionized tractor work when he invented the three-point linkage (which has now been adopted on most tractors), and for the first time made it possible to use tractors in confined areas of ground. Hitherto a tractor hauled a set of ploughshares mounted on wheels—like a kind of cumbersome gun-carriage being dragged along behind the tractor. The ploughs could (in some cases) be lifted out of the ground by locking the carrying bar to the wheels so that the turning of the wheels lifted the ploughs up into the air, and then the tractor could be turned fairly easily. But even so it was difficult to plough the headlands, impossible to plough into the corners, and impossible to plough right up against the hedge.

The three-point linkage changed all this, and made the big tractor a possible implement for using in small gardens.

The plough was now mounted on three arms which stuck out of the back of the tractor, two of them activated by the hydraulics. Wheels are dispensed with, and the equipment is compact in the extreme. By pulling a lever the driver can whip the ploughs right out of the ground when it is easy to back the tractor into any odd corner and plough right up into the hedge. Most other implements can be three-point mounted too, and thus used with the same ease and manoeuvrability. The three-point linkage undoubtedly saved what was left of the hedges of England, for it made it easy to plough right up to a hedge. In the old dragged-plough days ploughing small fields was intolerable, and farmers were bulldozing out their hedges to knock small fields into bigger ones as fast as they could. Now this process has been slowed down at any rate, if not stayed.

As to the costs, and general bother, of the big tractor, I have sorrowfully to report that my machine has cost me over its purchase price already in repairs. Being a diesel it is hard to start: if not used frequently its batteries get flat and the high-compression engine is very hard to turn. I either have to leave it on top of a hill and run it down to start it, or else use a jump-lead from my car battery, and it canes that. Alternatively I take the tractor batteries out (and they are very heavy!) and put them on charge with a trickle-charger (yes, we now *are* on the electric mains). As for fuel oil for the diesel, to run it economically, in Britain at least, you will have to use duty-free oil. To obtain this you will either have to have your own large storage tank, or else buy at cost price from neighbouring farmers. Diesel fuel you buy in garages is taxed, and nearly twice the money. But our tractor has many uses. It ploughs both field and large garden, it harrows the pastures, it hauls firewood from the forest, it cuts grass for hay, it turns and tedders the hay, it carries the bales, it pulls a muck-spreader that we borrow from a neighbour when we have a lot of muck to spread, or when we have a little it carries that little in its link-box—a kind of scoop that fits on to the three-point linkage. The fore-end loader has a fork attachment which will load muck into a muck-spreader very quickly indeed, or a dozer attachment which can be used for levelling land.

If you have anything over an acre of arable land it might well pay to get a big tractor, if you can buy one cheap. It might well pay to get a petrol-paraffin, or 'T.V.O.' one, for these are much easier to start (you can swing them by hand) and if they do cost a little more for fuel, well how much fuel will you use anyway on a small place? In using a farm tractor on a small-holding you are using a sledge-hammer to crack a nut, but if you can get a sledge-hammer for the price of a nut-cracker —and it does the job equally well or better—then maybe it is worth it. Our present holding is seventy acres, so, in the absence of *time* to do our work with horses, we need a large tractor.

## GARDEN CULTIVATOR

Garden cultivators are a different thing altogether. The kind that pull ploughshares—unless they are very heavy ones— I would discount. They plough but I don't believe they plough very well. The rotovator kind are of two types. One, like the Howard, pulls itself along by its wheels and stirs the soil by means of the rotovator. Others, like the Merrytiller, have no power-driven wheels while they are rotovating, but shove themselves along with the rotovator itself. The latter are harder work to handle but I believe they do a better job if you are comparing machines of the same size. The Merrytiller type of machine is excellent for inter-row cultivation, for keeping land clean between soft fruit trees, and for the initial clearing of small areas of ground. It is nimble, handy and cheap. The bigger wheel-propelled machines like the Howard are better for working large areas of land. The consumption of fuel for all these machines is almost negligible, but the amount of ground they can get over in a day is comparatively small. To use them on a field scale is tedious beyond belief, and they make an awful lot of noise. If you like to hear the birds sing while you work (and for me that is very important) they are not for you.

# HORSE

And so we come to the horse, and here many people who have
not worked with horses, or seen them working, will say 'how
absurd! You might as well go back to ploughing with oxen!'
Well I have ploughed with oxen, and would very much like
to do so again and may one day. There is nothing wrong with
ploughing with oxen at all. And as for horses—they have a great
deal to be said for them.

*Ploughing.* With two good horses it is possible to plough an acre
of moderate land in a day. Your fuel need cost you nothing
(at least nothing that has to come from outside the farm),
you can hear the birds sing as you work, and will not be working
in diesel or petrol fumes, and, if you have a good *rapport* with
your horses, ploughing can be a delight. I don't believe there
is a more entrancing occupation. And there is one little thing
that a horse can do that a tractor can't, and that is to have
another horse. A mare can work in chains (although not in
shafts) to within a few hours of foaling. She foals in the spring,
so can work the winter through, which is when you want to
do your ploughing. After she has had her foal she must rest for
six weeks at least, and then only come into her work gradually.

Now *one* horse will not plough an acre a day, nor will he
plough very deep, or plough very rough ground. Nevertheless,
one horse can very well do the cultivations of a smallholding.
If the ground is too rough to put the plough into it, put pigs
on it. They will pioneer the way for your one-horse plough
for you. A horse will plough land very well that has not been
allowed to go too far, but long tussocky grass, tough old pasture
too coarse for sheep to graze down properly or rough grass
between apple trees, your one-horse plough will not manage.
Pigs are your answer to such problems, and if you can't use
pigs, then get a contractor in with a big tractor. And *then*, when
your land has been initially bust-up, *keep* it bust-up—by ploughing and ploughing with your one horse, or dragging through it
such harrows and cultivators as you can lay your hands on.

Keep 'pulling of it about': *grass* is the enemy of the plough: don't let it come back.

The kind of horse plough that we use nowadays, when we do use a horse plough (and one is very useful for row-crop work even if you have got a tractor), is the Brabant. We bought ours in Spain. This is a wheeled turning plough, or one-way plough, with no handles. You don't have to hold it, it steers itself as long as the horse walks in the furrow. All you have to do is turn it round at the headland and swing the shares over, so as to turn the furrow the other way. As the plough is also turned the other way that means that you go back ploughing the *same* way. Ploughing with a one-way plough, whether by horse or by tractor, is much easier and demands less skill than ploughing with a fixed-furrow plough. But if you try ploughing with a fixed-furrow plough you will see the difficulty immediately, and have to set about finding a way round it. You must plough a furrow, then turn round and plough another furrow against the first. You then go round and round this, each time ploughing another furrow *towards* your first two furrows: *gathering* the stetch as ploughmen say. When you think you've gone far enough you can start another stetch by laying out another *top*—in other words, going to one side into unploughed ground and ploughing two more virgin furrows leaning up against each other. *The Horse in the Furrow*, by George Ewart Evans (Faber and Faber), is the best book I have ever found dealing with this complicated subject, but no book in the world can beat half an hour's instruction from an old horseman. Good ploughing with horses is a highly skilled and technical job, and it takes years to learn to do it properly, but anybody can scratch away with a plough well enough to turn his land over somehow or other. Perfection will come with time.

Other implements you can pull with a horse are many and various. A ring-roll or Cambridge roll is a very good thing to have; the rings can be bought separately and made up to any width required. Cultivators, scufflers, expanding horse-hoes and steerage hoes come in great variety. An implement I like is the old-fashioned hoop-hoe, which any blacksmith

can make. The spring-toothed harrow is a marvellous implement. A tractor normally tows a gang of these: a horse will
easily pull just one member of the gang and you can adjust
the depth at which the tines go down into the soil. These
spring-toothed harrows are easy of draught and marvellous
at pulling down clods and getting a seed bed, and you can
often get them at farm sales.

Digging by hand, or hoeing by hand, are immensely slow
and laborious jobs. Cobbett, writing in 1820, claimed that a
man could dig with the spade twelve rods a day. A modern
man could not dig anything like so much, and I am fairly
certain that no man reared in a city could do a quarter of it.
A one-horse plough might very well do half an acre in a day, or
eighty rods. That is the difference. As for hoeing, the difference
is far greater: what would take a week to hand-hoe can be done
in an hour or two with a horse-hoe. But mark, you will also
have to hand-hoe your row crops in the end no matter how
many times you horse or tractor hoe them. This is because no
mechanical device can get in between the plants in the rows,
nor tell the difference between a weed and a plant. But a
working horse lightens the job of husbandry enormously;
he really enables you to get on top of your holding.

As to where you can get all these horse implements: well, up
to now, farm sales have been the answer. Up until 1970
anyway you could get practically any horse implement you
wanted, in Britain at least, for a few shillings. Now people are
beginning to buy up horse ploughs to stick up outside pubs
and the market is wearing thin. Ireland, incidentally, is a
richer source of old horse tools than is England, and in France
or Belgium you can still get anything you want in this line new:
although God help you when you try to get it through the
British customs.

*Harness.* One thing you have to have with a horse, of course, is
harness. This you used to be able to buy up at farm sales for a
few pennies or sometimes get for nothing; now if it is any good
it is snapped up and hung on a pub wall. You can get good

harness, new or second hand, on the Continent still, or in Eire, and Spain makes some of the best harness in the world, and the cheapest. The imagination boggles at trying to get past the British customs though. If you can use a needle you can do a lot in the way of repairing old harness, but if the leather has perished then it is useless. Harness hung up on pub walls for a year or two is ruined: one thing leather can't stand is drying out. Harness must have oil: not too much but enough. In South Africa we used to use mutton fat, and it worked very well. In Britain people generally use neat's foot oil. You should oil or grease the *grain side*—that is the rough inside of the leather, but wash the polished outside of the leather with water and saddle soap. It seems a general rule that animal fats and oils are better for animal products, vegetable for vegetable (e.g. linseed oil for cricket bats) and mineral for mineral (e.g. mineral oil for motor cars). Wet is the enemy of leather, but oil keeps it out. Heat is a worse enemy: to dry harness on a radiator is to kill it stone dead.

You must get somebody to show you how to put the harness on the horse. There are certain principles that have to be considered. Forward power is transmitted from the horse by the *tugs* (see figure). If the horse is working in chains (i.e. pulling a plough or such instrument) the chains go straight to the collar, from a whippletree. The latter is a 'spreader' of wood or iron that keeps the chains apart so that they don't pinch the horse. A back-strap can go over the horse's back to keep the chains from sagging and getting under his hind legs when he stops. This strap should be long enough to allow the chains to be straight when the horse is pulling. When the horse is in shafts the *ridge pad* (like a saddle) supports the *ridge chain* which holds the shafts up and also takes any weight which is on the shafts owing to a two-wheeled cart being front- heavy. The *girth strap* goes under the belly of the horse to prevent the cart falling over backwards if it is back-heavy. The britchin goes round the horse's buttocks and is chained on to the shafts to keep the cart back if the horse is going down-hill, or to back the cart. So with shafts there are just three

35

chains to hook on one side of the horse, and two the other. The order of hooking them on ('*shutting the horse in*' or '*putting him in*') is: go to the off side (right side) of the horse, hook the tug on, throw the ridge chain over, hook the britchin chain on. Go to the other side—hook the ridge chain on, then the

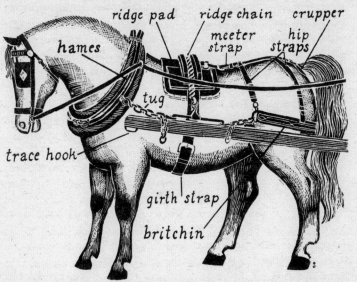

*ridge pad*    *ridge chain*    *crupper*
*meeter*    *hip*
*strap*    *straps*
*hames*
*tug*
*trace hook*
*girth strap*
*britchin*

britchin. See that the britchin is not too tight so that it worries the horse, but is not too slack either, for if it is the front of the cart will shove against the horse's backside when you go down hill and annoy him. See that the shafts are a comfortable height and length and don't pinch the horse, or poke him in the face when you are turning. If the tugs are correctly adjusted you should be able to produce an imaginary line from them, going backwards, and this line should pass through the hubs of the wheels. I don't think anybody should try to harness a horse unless they have been shown how to, but if you have to, remember that you must take the hames off the collar, or at least loosen them, and put the collar on upside down, and then reverse it and put the hames on. Generally you must do this with the bridle off the horse, or the collar won't go on over it.

*Feeding and Management.* With the little work you will have
to do on a very small holding, if the horse gets plenty of
grass, you will hardly have to feed him at all. When the horse
is not working he will live on grass alone, and don't give him
too rich grass either (particularly if he is a pony) or he will
get ill. In the winter, if grass is short, you must give him more
or less hay according to how much grass there is. If you work
a horse at all hard you must give him other things besides
grass. Hay is better than all-grass for a working horse. Grass
makes a horse soft. Hay keeps him hard. The hay must be good
if you feed it to horses: dusty or mouldy hay is dangerous.
All-clover hay is bad too, except for nursing mothers. Oat
straw can be a substitute for hay, and I have fed horses most
successfully on oats in the sheaf: that is one sheaf a day of
unthreshed oats. They eat it straw, corn, and all. O.M.C.S.
(Old Mother Common Sense) will tell you to take the string out.

If the horse is working hard though you must pay him
with oats, crushed maize or other corn. A big plough horse,
working a full day, needs as much as 20 lbs. of oats or other
corn a day. For light work perhaps half that. A cob, say of
15 hands, would do with perhaps three or five pounds for light
work, ten for heavy continuous work, plus hay, and/or straw.
Bran is also good. Eight to ten pounds of hay is about right,
with no grass: less with grass. Feeding should be at least three
times a day, and the horse should be given plenty of time to
eat: at least a full hour. A working horse should be groomed
once a day. When the horse is not working he should not have
corn, or if he does only a very little. If you rest a hard-working
horse you must knock off his corn, otherwise he will get ill.

You must shoe your horse about once every six weeks,
whether you are working him or not. If you turn him out to
grass for a long period you had better pull the shoes off him:
if you leave them on his feet will go on growing under the
shoes and he will go lame. Shoeing is a highly skilled job and
no unskilled person should tackle it. The demand for the service
of shoeing smiths is now insatiable, in Britain at least, and this
is a very good and profitable profession for a young man to

go in for. You get two pounds per horse, and should easily be able to do ten in a day: twenty pounds a working day and no rat-race is not to be sneezed at: see if you can earn that by getting a degree in philosophy.

*Breeding.* The profitability of the smallholding horse can be increased enormously if she is a good mare, and used for breeding as well as work. Your mare may do any work for the first six or seven months of pregnancy: then she should only work in chains, for the shafts are uncomfortable for her. She can be worked, with advantage to her health, right up to foaling: many a mare has dropped her foal in the field in which she has been ploughing, with no ill results.

After foaling the mare should be pampered a bit: a nice warm bran mash for example, some oats, and she should be turned out on to good fresh grass: if possible on which no horses have been grazing for some time. She should not be worked at all for at least six weeks, and then only be given very light work for a few hours a day up to the time of weaning. Before weaning she should not be kept away from the foal for more than two or three hours. Weaning can be at four months, but the later the better for the foal. When you wean the foal you must keep him out of hearing of the mare, on very good pasture, and then start working the mare as hard as you like to help dry her milk off. Good summer grass is ample for the foal, but when the first winter comes you should give him perhaps a couple of pounds of crushed oats and three or four pounds a day of good hay. If you want a gelding get the vet, or a wise man, to come and castrate him at about a year old, when the weather has become milder after the winter but before the flies are about. Foals on pasture should have their hoofs rasped down every so often, so that the frog (the soft bit in the middle) justs rests on the ground.

The sooner you halter-break the foal the better. Get a rope halter on at a few days old, and teach the foal to be led and not be afraid of people. Get him used to having his feet lifted. You can begin to break him for work in his second summer (one assumes he was born in the spring). Breaking should be a gradual but firm process. Keep him in for a time (nothing tames a horse, or gets him used to humans, so much as being kept inside), handle him a lot, get him used to wearing harness, trotting round on a leading rein (if you are going to ride him he should have a mouthing bit and a breaking harness for a week or two), then try him in chains in front of something that doesn't matter, such as a set of harrows.

*Pasture.* Horses living out don't want very good fattening pasture. It is bad for them. The wider range of grazing they have the better, and they do not thrive on land where only horses are kept. They do far better running out either with, or after, cattle. A horse kept out all the time and worked occasionally and lightly is most unlikely to get ill. One worked hard and continuously must be stabled and fed 'high', and it takes a skilled horseman to keep him fit and working. You are being forced to keep him unnaturally, i.e. on food that is richer than his digestion was evolved to cope with. But a horse out on grass should give you very little trouble, if any at all.

*Buying a Horse.* There is no mystery about this. If you want to do really heavy work, perhaps till a farm of fifty or a hundred acres or more with horses, you will have to buy proper heavy horses, Shires, Clydesdales, Percherons or Suffolks. Personally I should never have any hesitation—I should plump for Suffolks. They are the kindest, most noble, and most beautiful animals that ever walked. But if you just want to pull a one-horse plough get a good strong cob. Go to a horse sale and buy one, or to a good dealer who won't cheat you. Have a vet look at him first if you feel like it. At a reputable horse sale animals are 'sold sound'—that is you have a come-back if there is anything wrong with the animal. Do not, until you are an expert, buy a horse from anybody but a man with a reputation to lose unless you have the animal vetted. If you are a beginner buy a fairly old horse already broken and trained. You don't want *both* to be learners.

If you have a good horse, and are kind to him, and work a lot with him, you will get very fond of him and he will of you. He will be a source of great pleasure to you. He will be pleased to see you and will try to please you. And he will cultivate your large garden or small fields as well as any tractor and better in many ways.

To compare the pros and cons of these three main sources of power on the smallholding, farm tractors, garden cultivators and horses, we end up with this: A second-hand farm tractor is immensely good value for what it is, because a tractor that is too old for a full-size farm is not too old for doing occasional odd-jobs on a smallholding, and also that sometimes the government subsidises farmers who buy new tractors whereupon they sell their old ones long before they need to. It will cope with any of the cultivation jobs in the field, will cultivate even in fair-sized gardens, but is not as good as either garden cultivator or horse at doing row-crop work or working in confined spaces. Any fool can use it.

The garden cultivator may cost as much, new, as an old farm tractor, and beware of getting an old garden cultivator unless you know that there is a very good reason for its being for sale. They wear out. It is infinitely slower than a farm tractor, won't really plough (unless it is a very big one), is fine for row crops, no good for transporting things, and any fool can use it.

The horse costs about as much as the second-hand farm tractor or the new garden cultivator. If you have enough land you can feed him for nothing, and if she is a mare she may give you foals. These can be a very valuable export item. A horse will cover ground much more slowly than a farm tractor but much faster than a garden cultivator. He is very good for row crops and for transport. Working with a horse can be a delight but the horseman must be a sensitive and intelligent man. The horse is no tool for fools, and no fool can use him.

# HORSE

Come all ye honest ploughmen
Old England's fate you hold
Who labour in the winter time
In stormy winds and cold
To clothe our fields in plenty
Our farmyards to renew
That bread may not be wanting
 Behold the painful plough!

The townsman in his turmoil
The gentleman at ease
Forget the gallant sailor
Who ploughs the raging seas
But we do give him sustenance
And this he knows be true
He sails upon the Ocean
 By virtue of the Plough.

# 4

# Cow

*When you have got the cow, there is no more care about manure.*

WILLIAM COBBETT: Cottage Economy

The cow should be absolutely central to the economy of a smallholding. When you get a cow you immediately find the pace of all your other smallholding activities will be forced on. To feed the cow you will have to grow fodder. To use up the manure from the cow you will have to dig or plough more land. To use up milk by-products, such as skimmed milk or whey, you will have to keep other small stock—probably pigs. Your pigs will then produce even more manure and you will feel like ploughing more land. Besides, you will need to grow crops for the pigs. You will have calves to dispose of—what will you do with them? Your cow will go dry one day and you will need another cow to fill in the gap. Then the time will come when both cows are in milk. Unless you are part of a community you will then have too much milk. What do you do then— put the two calves on one cow and milk the other? Whatever you do you will find the purchase of a cow will push on the pace of your other self-supporting activities. It will save, at a stroke, possibly more money than anything else. Butter and cheese go up and up in price.

But think hard about it. A cow is the biggest tie in the world. You will have to milk her twice a day and you will be very lucky to find somebody to stand in for you. Very few people in this world *can* milk. I would say that, unless you are fully determined to spend all of your life at home, or only go away at rare intervals when you can either get somebody else to look after your cow or else board her in their herd ('meat for manners'—in other words—they keep her and they get the milk), or unless you are part of a community, you should think loud and often before getting a cow

But a cow is a very gentle, beautiful creature, and you can get very fond of her and derive much enjoyment from her. And you and your children can also derive much help. We have never been without a cow, in milk, these last fifteen years.

*Feeding.* A cow can theoretically be kept on an acre of grass, but I would far rather have two cows on five acres. By flogging grass with nitrogenous fertilizer I think you could keep a cow on an acre during the summer time, but you would not be able to cut hay on it as well.

A cow needs at least a ton of hay every winter. You might get this off half an acre. If you can't grow it you can buy it. There is something to be said for buying in your hay and straw, if you have to buy anything. Farmers say when a man buys hay he buys land, and this is so in two ways. One way is that he thus spares his own land to feed animals or grow other crops. The other is that to buy hay is to buy fertility, and the best sort of fertility too: the kind that improves the land permanently, and brings you returns year after year. For every ton of hay or straw that comes on to your land stays there, in the beneficent form of muck, and improves the humus status of your soil. So if you wish to keep cows but have not got enough land, remedy this by buying in hay from other people. If you have weatherproof storage for the hay you can best buy it straight from the field, just after it has been bailed. That is when it will be cheapest.

In the summer the cow will live, and give you plenty of milk, on grass, and grass alone. That is provided she has enough grass and it is of good quality. In the winter though she will need supplementary feeding or she will not give you very much milk. A dry cow or a bullock may very well live out all winter on good grass without any supplementary feeding except a little hay if it snows, but a cow in milk needs food, and her milk yield will reflect very sensitively how much food she is getting. The aim of the modern agri-businessman is to get the highest milk yield possible, and he feeds his milking cows on a very rich diet, mostly of bought-in cake. The self-supporter may not wish to get so much milk out of his cow or cows, and will be content with a lower standard of feeding. His cows will be the healthier for this: it is the 'steaming up', or very high-level feeding, to exact bigger and bigger milk yields, that causes so much disease in modern dairy cows. The nearer you can keep to nature—that is to the conditions for which cattle were bred by natural selection when they were in the wild state—the less disease you will have. You must depart from nature to some extent or you won't get much milk, but it is a matter of departing from it in moderation.

The traditional way of feeding dairy cows is to give each cow a maintenance ration, which is calculated to be enough to keep her in fit bodily condition but not to produce any milk, and then on top of that a production ration according to how much milk she will give. Thus twenty pounds of good hay are considered a production ration for a Friesian cow for a day (less for a Jersey), less hay plus some roots will do, or some of the hay can be replaced by good oat straw supplemented by roots. Thirty to fifty pounds of roots a day, plus perhaps ten to fifteen pounds of hay, would be a maintenance ration.

Your production ration is generally given in the form of concentrates: that is corn or 'cake'. Cake is nutritious matter made by compounders in huge mills and comes in paper sacks and is very expensive. If you allow three and a half pounds of a good average cake per gallon of milk that your cow is giving in the winter you will not be far wrong. But to be truly self-supporting you will not wish to buy in cake. The only thing you can do then is to grow plenty of fodder crops (roots and brassica), and corn and beans. A mixture of ground oats, barley and field beans, with possibly a sprinkling of some proprietary mineral mixture, or seaweed meal if you like (which has all the necessary mineral), fed at the rate of three and a half pounds per gallon, would not be far off. But the temptation for the overworked man on a smallholding is to buy cake and pay up and look pleasant—and hope to pay the mill bill with money got from the sale of calves or surplus stock. And this should be feasible.

*Breeds.* Now for the question of what sort of cow to get, and how to get her. Jerseys are beautiful and very docile (ours came in the house one day and ate a number of corn dollies that Sally had been making for sale). They would happily live in the living room with you, if you allowed them. In India cows of course do, with mutual benefit to the cows and the people. Jerseys give superb milk: the richest in the world, averaging five per cent butter fat. They have one big disadvantage for our purpose: their bull calves are almost worthless. The heifer calves can be reared up, of course, and sold for dairy herd replacements, or taken into your own herd. The bull calves however are not worth rearing up, commercially at any rate. The fat of the Jersey is yellowish and the animals do not put much meat on. If you serve your Jersey cow with an Angus* bull you will get a slightly better 'butcher's animal' but the butcher can still spot that it is half Jersey and will not give you much for it at any age. We keep a Jersey or two and what we do is to rear up one bull calf a year, keep him until two years old, and then send him off to the slaughterhouse to be killed for our own use; but more of this in the chapter about meat. The meat of the Jersey is very good incidentally—and what if the fat does look slightly yellow? Who are we to be colour prejudiced?

The Guernsey gives a little more milk than the Jersey, slightly less rich, is slightly hardier, and the bull calves are slightly less objectionable to the butcher. They still bear the stigma 'Channel Island' though, and won't fetch much.

The Friesian is the most widespread breed in the Western world today, and almost the only breed beloved of agri-businessmen. It gives an enormous amount of milk of low quality and crosses very well indeed with the Hereford bull, or bulls of other breeds (nowadays often Charollais) to make an ox beloved of graziers and butchers. Most of the beef eaten

*A Charollais is even better.

in the Western world today comes from this source: the steers are a by-product of the milk industry. Even a pure-bred Friesian, although a dairy breed and not a beef breed, makes a very acceptable butcher's animal. The Friesian is big, and eats a lot more than, say, a Jersey, but gives a lot more milk.

The Ayrshire is something like the Friesian, although smaller, and with slightly more butter fat in the milk. She is very hardy. Not a good butcher's animal.

The Welsh Black is a fine animal, and one I should say ideally suited for the self-supporter. Crossed with the Hereford she throws a fine beef calf, and she gives a fair amount of good milk. She is superlatively hardy, and most unlikely to go wrong.

The Shorthorn is a fine dual-purpose animal, hardy, quite good milk, good beef or beef cross. The Dairy Shorthorn has, alas, almost died out in Britain, and the Beef Shorthorn is not as widespread at it was. But occasional Shorthorn-type animals can be bought from small farmers, and very good they are too.

Of the beef breeds, the Hereford is supreme, for he impresses his coloration (the famous white head) and configuration on other breeds of cow, and the butchers love him and his progeny. The Hereford bull, incidentally, is the gentlest of creatures. The Jersey bull, in sharp contradiction to the Jersey cow—that sweetest of animals—is a little sod. Many a man has been killed by a Jersey bull.

The Aberdeen-Angus is also a fine beef breed, producing, with the Galloway, most of the fine beef that comes out of Scotland. It is a little animal, and thus fine for crossing with the Jersey. Its progeny are slower-maturing than the progeny of the Hereford.

The Charollais I know little about. It is said to be quicker maturing than our beef breeds, and to make very fine beef animals, with a big proportion of expensive meat to cheap. Here in Pembrokeshire it does not seem to be so popular, and much of the hullabaloo which heralded its appearance in the U.K. has died down. It was to make millionaires of every one of us.

*Breeding and Calves.* To get your cows in calf, you either borrow a bull, have one of your own, unfortunately leave the gate open (by mistake) so that your neighbour's bull unfortunately gets through it and serves your cow (in which case you hide your delight and chide your neighbour for not keeping his bull under control), or you get the 'A.I. Man'. A.I. is artificial insemination. It is cheap (£1.25 at the moment), easy and effective. If you have only a handful of cows it is a very good way. The calves are no better and no worse than calves got by any other method, except that they are better in so far as A.I. is able to afford the best bulls in the world.

The disadvantage of A.I., though, is that if you have a number of cows and they are running out loose, you can't always 'spot' them when they are bulling, or on heat. A cow shows that she is bulling by mounting other cows in a lesbian fashion, or standing while they mount her, by bellowing, and by discharging at the rear. She must be caught immediately and served the next day. Immediately you see her you must telephone the 'A.I. Man' (Milk Marketing Board). He will come next morning. But if you are not constantly vigilant you can miss a cow, in which case you will have to wait exactly three weeks, when you hope she will shows signs of bulling again. Having your own bull guards against such delay: your bull will know if a cow is bulling or not. But a bull would only be justified if you had quite a large herd of cattle: certainly not less than a dozen.

The cow gestates for 280 days, or about nine months. In this, as in many other things, she resembles the female of *Homo sapiens*. We like our calves to be born out of doors, in clean pasture, winter or summer. We leave well alone unless the cow has serious trouble and we *have* to interfere. Don't interfere until the cow has been in labour herself for several hours. Then, if you must, roll your sleeve up, douse your hand and forearm with carbolic oil, and gently dive in to see what is wrong. The calf may be wrongly presented, in which case you must move it about in the womb until it is rightly presented: preferably with its fore-legs poking out first with its nose between them

47

(the normal way) or, at a pinch, a 'breech' presentation—arse first. If the presentation is normal, fore-legs first, but if the cow simply cannot get rid of the calf because he is too big, gently pull his fore-feet out, tie a cord on to them, and pull gently but firmly—and pull *only* when the cow is straining. Sometimes you end up by having to pull pretty hard, but don't pull harder than you have to. The above advice applies to sheep or horses too, incidentally. But if animals are kept as naturally as possible, running out in the open, not too fat or overfed, you should have no trouble at all. Generally what happens is that you go out to look at the old girl in the morning and there she is—standing up with a dear little calf sucking from her and she is licking its tail.

Don't be afraid of her. She may look worried but if she knows you she won't butt you. Pick the calf up and carry it gently in front of the cow, stopping to let the cow smell the calf at frequent intervals, and the cow should follow you, and get them both into the shed.

There are now many schools of thought as to what you should do next. Some people say take the calf right away from the mother and never let the two animals see each other again. We have never been able to bring ourselves to do this. The proponents of this method say that the cow will settle down to being milked by human or machine much quicker, and will forget the calf very quickly. Well, if you do this, you don't have my blessing.

Another way is to leave the calf and cow together for three or four days, or a week, not milking the cow yourself so that the calf gets a 'good start', and then separate them. When you do, both cow and calf will make the welkin ring with their bellows for two or three nights, and the cow may kick a bit when you milk her, and may not be too keen to let her milk down. Persevere.

Yet another method is to keep the cow away from the calf most of the time, then let the calf suck when you bring the cow in for milking until his belly is full, then take him away and get the rest of the milk out yourself. You may have trouble but on the other hand some cows don't mind it at all: I have a neighbour who milks with the calf sucking away on one side and himself squatting down milking on the other. Our cow is now having her fore-teats milked by the calf and her hind by us, and it is working perfectly.

Another way is to let the calf suck, say, once a day and you milk at the other end of the day. Again, you may possibly have psychological troubles with the cow, on the other hand possibly no trouble at all.

Probably to remove the calf altogether after a week is the best method. After a day or two of unsettlement the cow then settles down to the regime of being milked very nicely, and you get all the milk.

Then what to do with the calf. Well, you have got to feed the calf either on milk, reconstituted milk powder, or milk substitute for at least three months, and he will need about a gallon and a half a day when he gets a little older, perhaps a gallon a day to start with. Offer very very good hay to the calf when he is old enough to want it, and try him with a little concentrates, either ground corn or calf cake bought from the mill.

The moment you take the calf away from the cow your are going against nature, and you may have to pay the consequences. The calf may get ill. He will probably show this by *scouring*— that is having diarrhoea. If he has nasty smelly white droppings or blood in his droppings, send for the vet and no messing. If he just has pretty stinky diarrhoea, smelling like babies, take him off milk immediately, make him drink warm water, or warm water with a little glucose in it, and keep him warm and dry. Shove some antibiotics into him too: there are several pills and tablets you can get from the chemists. If you don't, he will probably die. He will live without milk for several days, with a little glucose and water, but use common sense, and when he seems to be better let him have a little milk diluted with water, then a little milk.

Calves should be kept out of draughts, but with fresh air passing above them, on clean bedding, be gently and kindly treated, and the apparatus you use to feed them should be clean and sterilised. The milk you give them should be body-temperature and fresh. A calf just let to suck naturally from his mother will almost never go wrong, particularly if left out of doors. Cows calve high in the mountains in the bitterest winter and lose hardly any calves. A calf taken from his mother and fed from a bucket is very likely to go wrong. The calves that you see at every cattle mart, or market, being thrown out of the backs of vans and lorries, dragged about by their tails, flung into dirty and contaminated pens where they stand in mess and draught for hours on end with other frightened little animals, to be auctioned, flung into the back of some-body's old banger, driven back to a farm, dragged into a stuffy shed: these calves are fighting for their lives and often don't bother to fight very hard. I have a neighbour who buys calves thus, perforce for he has to rear beef for a living, and I asked him how he got his replacements. 'Buy them in the mart on Monday', he said, 'put them on antibiotics on Wednesday, and bury them on Friday.'

We've done the same, although Sally is an absolute genius at nursing little things back to health. But it is a fight, and the whole system of selling little week-old calves in the open market should go the way of the slave-trade—out. It is monstrously cruel and extremely inefficient. There is a law that these calves should have a week of their mother's milk before they are sold. Without the protection of the colostrum—the medici-nal first-milk of their own dam—they are doomed anyway. But many milk farmers just do not observe the law. How can anybody know if they have? Dairy farmers want rid of their calves—quick. They don't want them. This is why they are taken to the mart, to be sold to specialists, or smallholders' wives who like to rear a calf or two, and brought up on the bucket. There should be agencies set up all over the country, working by telephone, to put such dairy farmers in touch with calf-rearers—on the same principle as agencies to supply *au pair* girls. The buyer could then go and get the calf straight from the farm where it was born, make sure that it had been properly treated, cary it carefully to a nice warm car, drive it quickly home, and then nurse it. You see, many of the buyers want to get the calf to put on a cow of their own who has just calved, on the principle known as multiple suckling, which we shall deal with in a moment. Such buyers need a calf, or more, immediately: just when their cow has calved. If they introduce the calf to her foster mother immediately after the latter has calved she is far more likely to take to him.

To teach a calf to suck from a bucket we have a thing called a 'little mother', which is a stainless steel or aluminium bucket which hangs on the wall and has rubber teats hanging down from it. When the calf is very young they must be scrupulously cleaned. The more usual method is to teach the calf to drink straight out of a bucket. You do this by grabbing the calf's nose, poking two fingers in his mouth so that he starts to suck, and forcing his nose into the milk. After a time he discovers that thus he can suck milk besides your fingers. It may be a struggle at first, and women have got much more patience with small animals than men, not unnaturally. The great advantage of 'little mothers' is that they satisfy a calf's desire to suck. If a calf sucks his milk from a 'little mother' he will not suck other calves. If he gollops his milk up from a bucket he will have an insatiable desire to suck—anything— the navel of another calf (which can lead to disease), an old dirty rope-end, baling twine, or the poisonous lead paint off the gate of his stall.

When the calf is weaned you can either put him out onto good clean grass, if it be summer time, but go on feeding him some concentrates for several weeks, or else keep him on indoors (you must in the winter time, and probably should if it's his first summer) and feed him on roots, good meadow hay, and perhaps four pounds of concentrates a day: more the older he gets.

The reason why one is worried about letting him out to grass is because of husk (or hoose). In many parts of the country the grass is infested with the lung worms of cattle, and these, if ingested by a young calf, give him the disease of husk. It makes him cough, he loses condition, and eventually dies. Why don't calves running out with their mothers get husk? Well they do, but they acquire such immunity from their mothers that it does them little harm. Whatever happens, if you are ever going to let your calf out of doors to mix with older cattle, he is going to get husk. The trick is to let him pick it up slowly, when he is older, in good condition, and well fed. He will then get an immunity to it before it gets him down. If you have really clean pasture, that is pasture on which no older cattle have grazed at least since it was last ploughed up and re-seeded, put him on that. We tether calves in our orchard, there is no husk there. Can't be—no big cattle ever go there. If you turn callow young animals straight out into husk-infested pasture you are heading for very big trouble. You will have to get the vet, get the animals injected, get them indoors again and probably keep them indoors, well fed, for another year. I know—I've had it.

While on the subject of calves, there are three other ways of rearing up calves, and any of them might be useful for the self-supporter as a source of money income. After all, the rest of the world has to eat too.

The first is single-suckling. You simply let a herd of cows out onto grass, or rough pasture, with a bull at the right time of the year. The bull, and the cows, will do the rest. Take the calves off the cows at six months of age and sell them in the nearest 'suckled-calf sales'.

The second is outdoor multiple suckling. This is very applicable to the smallholder. Your cow has a calf. You don't want to milk her. Rush to a neighbour and buy another new-born calf, put him on your cow with your calf. Keep watch on them both for a few days, indoors, to make sure that she has accepted her foster child and is letting him suck, and then turn them out and, after a little more vigilance, forget them. She will rear two fine calves for you, instead of one. This is a very profitable performance.

The third method is multiple suckling indoors. It is one way of cheaply building up a herd, but it requires the patience of

Job. When your cow has calved go and buy two or three new-born calves. Keep them indoors, bring your cow in twice a day, tie her up, and *make* her allow the four little calves to suck (her own and the three others). She will kick. She will butt. But she can't kick if you hold her tail up tight in the air and if you put a rope tightly around her belly and loins, to pass just in front of her udder. Maybe she'll get tired of it all before you will. After three months of this, wean those four calves and put, say, three fresh ones on her, or two, depending on what condition she is in. After three months wean those and put one on her. Then dry the poor old thing off and give her a rest before she calves again. Ain't it a beggar, said the Queen of Spain. We've done it once but we'll never do it again.

As to the small matter of actually milking your cow—you do it like this. Pinch the top of a teat between thumb and forefinger so that the milk cannot escape from the teat back up into the udder. Then squeeze in a downwards direction with the rest of the hand.

# 5

# Dairy

*If the butter do taste a little of the Swedish turnip, it will do very well where there is plenty of that sweet sauce which early rising and bodily labour are ever sure to bring.*

WILLIAM COBBETT: Cottage Economy

## MILK

Milk is one of the most complex organic substances that one could possibly imagine, and the extraordinary things that it will do, and that can be done with it, are legion. Long before the word 'plastics' was invented people were making knitting needles and spectacle frames out of it.

If you leave fresh milk alone in the summer time it curdles. This is because the lactic acid bacteria (*Streptococcus lacticus*) feed upon the lactose which is one of the constituents of milk (its sugar in fact) and change the lactose sugar into lactic acid. As the milk becomes more acid the isoelectric point is reached and at this point the particles of the milk no longer repel each other, but come together into what we call curd. Milk curdles best in warm weather or in warm climates (at about 77°F. or 25°C.). We consume a great deal of naturally curdled milk: it is acid in taste, but mildly acid and very good and digestible. In South Africa it is called *dik melk* and is a major article of diet. The South Africans have a refinement of *dik melk* which they call *calabash*. It is made in this way: milk is put inside a hollowed-out calabash and allowed to curdle. Every day some of the curdled milk is taken out of the calabash and some more fresh milk put in. Before it is taken out the calabash is shaken like a cocktail shaker. As the weeks go by the taste of the stuff that comes out of the calabash gets stronger and stronger until it is simply delicious. You must never

55

'starve' it, or it will turn bad: every day some must be taken out and some put in. I have drunk from a calabash which had been kept going thus for *six years*, and I kept one going myself for a year. I know somebody who does it in Wales, but in a bottle.

You can cause milk to clot immediately, that is form curds, by adding rennet. Rennet is stuff that is taken from a calve's fourth stomach (see Chapter 9). Presumably you could obtain it yourself if you killed a young calf, but we buy it in splendid little stoneware bottles from R. J. Fullwood and Bland, 25 Bevenden Street, London N.1.

Milk contains all the vitamins known to man, and no less than sixty fatty acids have so far been identified in milk, which gives an inkling of its enormous complexity. Lest it be thought that drinking or eating all these fatty acids will lead to coronary thrombosis, let us remember the Borana of Northern Kenya and Southern Ethiopia, and the Turkana their sworn enemies, who live on nothing else but milk except for an occasional gorge on meat when they ritually slaughter an animal. No Borana has ever been known to have coronary thrombosis. I knew these people very well and they were very healthy. The only element that milk is short of, from a dietetic point of view, is iron.

If you keep milk at a higher temperature than 77°F. (25°C.), say at 95°F. (35°C.), and inoculate it with the right bacteria (*Bacillus bulgaricus*), you will get not *dik melk* but *yoghourt*. *Bulgaricus* likes more warmth than *S. lacticus* and can tolerate much higher acidity. The way to make yoghourt is to boil your milk (to kill rival bacteria), cool it to 95°F. (35°C.), inoculate it with live yoghourt, and keep it at that temperature. It will keep quite well owing to its acidity.

Pasteurizing is done to all commercial milk nowadays: it kills T.B. and brucellosis bacteria and makes the milk keep a long time. It can only be done with special equipment, and the self-supporter will never wish to do it: his cows haven't got brucellosis or T.B. and he doesn't want his milk to keep for long periods. In any case, pasteurized milk is only fit for townspeople, who have got to the state when they don't know anything better.

To pasteurize milk by the Holder Method keep it at from 145°F. (62°C.) to 150°F. (65°C.) for 30 minutes.

To pasteurize by the Flash Method heat to 158°F. (70°C.) quickly and cool immediately.

## CREAM

If you want cream you can get it by 'setting' the milk, as soon as it comes from the cow, preferably in the cool, whereupon the cream floats to the surface. You can get it off with a 'fleeter' or skimmer (a little metal dish with holes in it), or by setting it in a wide slate trough with a hole in the bottom, the hole bunged up with a stick. When the cream has risen pull the stick out; the skimmed milk will run through the hole and leave the cream sticking to the bottom of the trough. You can also put the milk, fresh, through a separator. This is a centrifuge, and separates the cream from the milk by whirling both round and round whereupon the heavier milk is flung outwards and the lighter cream is forced inwards. We have a separator. It is very good, but as it takes some time to clean and reassemble we only use it if we have a lot of milk to deal with. It is more efficient than 'setting'. Set cream has 20 per cent butter fat; separated cream has 35 per cent. The milk left over after separating is naturally very thin (practically no butter fat at all) but is still rich in vitamins and minerals, and marvellous for all young animals and for pigs.

To make Devonshire cream, set your fresh milk for 12 hours, scald to 187°F. (92°C.), cool for 24 hours and then skim.

## BUTTER

Butter is made by bashing cream about after it has 'ripened', which means after the lactic acid bacteria have got to work long enough to turn some of the lactose, or milk sugar, into lactic acid. Commercially the cream is pasteurized and then

inoculated with a pure culture of lactic acid bacteria. This is why shop butter is so reliably uniform, and so reliably dull. We make butter by keeping the cream for at least 24 hours (twice a day we add some more to it—but the *last* lot to be put in must be left in for at least twelve hours before churning) and then churning. Nowadays we have a small glass churn with an electrically driven paddle which revolves in it. It takes about five minutes at the longest—often not more than one minute. In theory the cream should be ripened at 68°F. (20°C.), but we can't be so theoretical.

Before we had the electric paddle we used a variety of churns. If you have plenty of cream, say the cream from three cows, you can usefully use one of those beautiful varnished wooden butter churns, that turn end-over-end. A wooden cylinder open at the top, with a plunger in it that was worked up and down, was one way of doing it. A 'blow' churn, which is a glass jar with a hand-operated paddle turning in it, is very good if you can get one. Anything that gives the cream a good bashing will do. The whole secret is to get the cream properly ripened first. If you have trouble try keeping it at a higher temperature, and try adding some existing sour milk or cream as a 'starter'. If all else fails send off for a pure culture of lactic acid bacteria, but I never met anybody who had to do that. If the butter won't 'come', don't go on churning hopelessly for hours. Put it in the warm, if it is too cold, and wait a few hours, and try again. Don't get it *too* warm though: 68°F. (20°C.) is about right.

When the butter 'comes' a dramatic thing happens. Suddenly your cream separates into butter milk, and a mass of little yellow pellets as big as Number Six shot. If it is too hot the pellets will be larger, and soft: if too cold they will be smaller.

Drain the butter milk out, and put it to one side. It is a most noble drink, and if I had enough butter milk to drink I don't think I would often drink anything else.

Now put plenty of cold water in your butter, churn again and drain. The whole purpose now is to *wash* the butter, to get every drop of milk out of it. The cream you made the butter from was quite sour. The butter milk is beautifully sour. But the butter must not be the least bit sour. Therefore, if you want your butter to keep well and not go rancid, wash and wash again. Wash until the water comes out quite clear. Squodge the butter up in the cold water as much as you like. Squeeze the water out of it again. Dump the butter out on to a clean board—wash and squeeze—wash and squeeze. The old-fashioned wooden butter-maker was a wonderful tool—I wish I had one.

Sprinkle salt on, according to taste, squodge the butter about hard, taste a bit. If it's too salt wash some salt out with fresh water and taste again. If it's not salt enough add some more salt and squodge again. Obviously you must squodge until the salt is evenly mixed right through the butter. If 2·5 per cent of the whole butter consists of salt (in other words if it is pretty salty butter) the butter will keep for a long time. Unsalty butter won't keep for so long unless you keep it in the deep freeze. Always wrap butter—light and air oxydize the unsaturated fatty acids called oleic and linoleic and cause rancidity. Rancidity is caused in wrapped butter by the decomposition of butyrin into butyric acid.

If you heat butter you drive off the volatile fats which cause rancidity, and your butter then does not go rancid. Nor does it taste any more like butter, because you have lost the very elements that make it so taste. But the Indians turn this into account by making *ghee* (*samli* in East Africa). If you want to preserve butter in a glut, and have no deep freeze, you can do the same. Put the butter in a pot over the fire and let it simmer for an hour. Skim the scum off. Pour it into a sterilized container, cover from the air, and it will keep many months. It won't taste like butter but it will be very good to cook with: part of the glorious flavour of Indian food comes from the *ghee* in which it is cooked.

But in our cooler climate you can store well-salted butter in barrels right into the winter. The barrel (or earthenware tub) should be scalded, dried in the wind, and the butter should be flung hard into it to exclude all air, each layer sprinkled with salt and banged down with the closed fist. All air must be driven out. If the butter is too salt when you want to use it you can always wash the salt out again.

A word here about the cleaning of all dairy implements. If you want all your dairy produce to keep well, and not taste tainted, scrupulous cleanliness is necessary in the dairy. From the hands that milk the cow, through the milking pail, 'setting' pans or separator, butter churn, 'Scots hands', butter worker or draining board on which the butter is washed, cheese-making bowls, chessits, followers, cloths: everything must be clean. All untensils must be cleaned of any matter sticking to them, then scalded thoroughly in boiling water, washed well in cold clean water (and it must be clean), put upside-down to rinse and, if a wooden implement, put out in the clean wind to dry. *Never* use a 'tea-towel' or dish cloth to dry dairy untensils. Such rags are laden with germs. If your milk starts going sour too soon you are not sterilizing something properly. Remember the sequence: scour thoroughly (you don't have to use any beastly detergent, which will make your septic tank foam and stink), scald with boiling water, rinse immediately in clean cold water, turn upside down to drain—in the wind if possible. *Store* upside down so dust doesn't settle inside.

## CHEESE

Cream cheese is terribly easy to make, but as it won't keep long there is no great advantage in making it, except in so far as it can be very pleasant to eat. When milk goes thick on you (as it often will) simply pour the curds and whey into a muslin and hang it up to drip. The whey will run out, for the pigs. The curd will turn into cream cheese. You can flavour it with salt and herbs and all sorts of things. I've heard of wrapping it in hazel leaves, then cloth, and burying in the garden for three days.

But it is the making of hard cheese that is important to the self-supporter, or the self-supporting community, for here we have a way of storing the summer flush of milk (which we can take as being free because it is all made from grass) for the winter, when milk is scarce and expensive. For a non-vegan vegetarian community I would say that the manufacture of cheese was absolutely essential, but for any homesteader it is an enormous asset. A pound of cheese has 2,000 calories of energy in it. Meat from the fore-quarters of an ox has 1,100 calories. No wonder the navigators who dug the canals all over England, and later built the railways, made cheese the greater part of their diet. Good cheese from unpasteurized milk and honest wholemeal bread gave them the strength to move mountains.

To make cheese you will need some equipment. You will need a cheese press (unless you make Stilton, which is un-pressed), a chessit and a follower. The chessit is a cylindrical barrel open at the top and with holes in it to let out the whey. The follower is a piston which goes down in it and presses the cheese: just a round wooden board, in fact. The press is an arrangement of levers, heavy weights and gears capable of putting, in some cases, up to two tons of pressure on the cheese, by means of the follower inside the chessit. You can still buy old cheese presses in the countryside, but as more and more 'self-supporters' come about they are getting very scarce. It should not be beyond the wit of man to make one. A car jack is capable of exerting enough pressure but it would be hard to measure this pressure. Maybe O.M.C.S. (Old Mother Common Sense) would have to be brought into play again. You can get cheese presses from Messrs. Clares (Wells) Ltd., Somerset.

The making of good, and consistently good, hard cheese is a very difficult and extremely complicated operation. Many an old farmer's wife, in the days before acidimeters and pure cultures of this and that, and all the rest of the scientific stuff were invented, turned out fine cheese year after year: probably much better than most of the cheese that is made today under the most scientific conditions. But one must remember that the farmer's wife in question had inherited her dairy from her mother or mother-in-law, had been taught to make the local cheese as a child, and had developed what was almost an instinct to tell her just when to do each separate operation with the same precision as the modern cheese-maker with his thermometers and acidimeters. That craft and that skill have now died out: killed by the onslaught of shiploads of factory-made cheese from over the seas, and two world wars which made real farm cheese-making illegal, like spying for the enemy, and which killed by stupid legislation, so many of our inherited country skills and crafts. Sally and I sailed a boat to Holland once, and tied up on a canal at a remote farm, and there found the farmer, his wife, and no less than sixteen children. The cowshed was attached to the dwelling house (an excellent arrangement) and the farmer milked sixteen cows. I asked him, in my foolishness, if he had a milking machine. He pointed to his children and said: 'What do I want with a milking machine?' He turned all his surplus milk into cheese: huge cart-wheel cheeses, some of which were *nieuw kaas* or new cheese, and eaten after two months, and others *oud kaas*, which was soaked in brine and then kept in the great cheese cellar for a year. We tried both, and they were both delicious beyond any telling of it. We bought a whole *nieuw kaas* and it kept us in marvellous cheese for six months, and the last slice was as delicious as the first. This cheese was made completely traditionally, with no scientific instruments at all, and *Meneer* van de Poel told me they never had a bad cheese.

The Dutch cheese (Gouda and Edam) that is sent to England is specially made for the English market out of pasteurized separated milk in big factories. The Dutch themselves will not eat factory-made cheese. Much Dutch cheese is sent to France, and the French will not buy factory-made cheese. Only farm cheese is sold to the domestic market in Holland and to France. Only the English will take the factory-made stuff.

Let us get back to our self-supporter's cheese: the self-supporter is not starting with an inherited lore of cheese making, and therefore he must use every aid available to him. The main aids are a thermometer and an acidimeter. Sally has been making cheese for the last fifteen years without the use of the latter, and I will describe the way she does it with, perhaps, a few flourishes of my own. I am not going to pretend that every Sally cheese from the year dot has been a prize-winner because that is not the case. I know a woman who makes cheese by more or less this method (without an acidimeter) and for many years she made the most splendid cheese in the world. You could not have found better cheese had you searched the Earth to the Antipodes, and it was a standing invitation to gluttony. But suddenly her cheese lost its fine quality, although she did not alter her methods in the least degree. Why? A change of bug? No one knows. I think that she should now turn to the acidimeter, and perhaps also starter too, and then perhaps she would discover the reason for her falling-off.

But this is more or less the way in which Sally makes cheese. Because she generally only milks one cow, and in the summer there is a big demand with us for fresh milk, she generally has to save up several days' milk to get enough for a cheese. Well that in itself is wrong. What should happen is that you keep the evening's milk, and in the morning you dump the morning's milk into it. Then you make your cheese. This sounds trivial, but in fact it is very important. But before you dump the morning's milk in with the evening's milk you have to go through a little rigmarole with the *cream* of the evening's milk, for if you don't the cream won't mix back again with the milk (it has all come to the surface in the night of course) and you will lose the cream in the whey which you give to the pigs and have 'thin' cheese. What you do is to fleet the cream off the evening's milk (skim it), raise its temperature to 85°F. (30°C.), and dump it back in the milk again. Then stir it well in. *Then* dump in the morning's milk.

If you have starter put it in now. I will discuss starter, and how to use it, later on. Sally has never used it, but that does not mean to say that it would not be better if she did.

Raise the temperature of the milk to 90°F. (32°C.).

Put 1 teaspoonful of rennet in a cupful of cold water and

put it in. (Rennet from R. J. Fullwood and Bland, 25 Bevenden Street, London N.1.)

Stir for about five minutes with your hand. As soon as the milk begins to cling to your fingers when you pull them out stop stirring. Another test is to drop a drop of water in the milk. If the water just disappears go on stirring. If it stays on top in a globule then stop. This again sounds trivial, but it is very important to get it right. The thing is, if you don't stir you will lose the cream from your milk and your cheese will be thin. Now as soon as you can no longer go on stirring begin to stroke the top of the milk with the fleeter (the fleeter is a slightly curved metal disc with a handle with holes in it, used for fleeting, or skimming, cream off milk) in order to 'send the cream down'. Do this for a few minutes.

When the curd no longer sticks to your hand, but feels firm when you press it, i.e. in about fifty minutes from when you stopped stirring, *cut the curd*. You will have by then curds and whey. Cut the curds (which don't take much cutting), either with a knife or, if you have them, with a pair of American curd knives. The latter are multi-bladed knives, one with vertical blades and one with horizontal. Your aim is to cut the curd into cubes about ¾ inch square. So with curd knives you will obviously make one pass with the horizontal blades and two, at right angles to each other, with the vertical. No more. If you just have to use an ordinary knife cut diagonally from one side of the receptacle, then diagonally from the other two sides, trying to achieve cubes ¾ inch square. You don't have to *measure* them of course—it's not that critical.

Warm the curds and whey *very slowly*—not quicker than a rise of one degree in three minutes—to 100°F. (38°C.). While this warming is going on stir the curds and whey very gently with the hand. If you stir too hard you will lose cream which is the one thing you want to avoid. This particular heating is called the *scalding*. It is not done for every cheese, Stilton for example. If you have a water-jacketed cheese vat this raising of the temperature of course is easy: if you have not the best way to do it is to scoop a saucepanful of whey out, put it on the stove, heat it, and put it back again. Go on repeating this until you have got the whole to 100°F.

The next operation, which is a non-operation, is called *pitching*. All you do is leave the stuff alone. The curd just soaks in its whey, and you don't stir it or anything, but what you do do is keep testing for acidity. For the idea of the pitching is to give the lactic acid bacteria time to work and attain a certain degree of acidity, and it is *most* important that this acidity should be *just right*. If you do not use an acidimeter the way to test for acidity is to take a piece of curd, touch it on a hot iron (the hot stove-top will do) and draw it away. If the acidity is just right threads of just half an inch long will come off from the curd before they break. If they are shorter than this leave to pitch longer.. If they are longer than half an inch you are going to have a dry acid cheese and there's nothing you can do about it. So when the threads are just half an inch— *drain off the whey*. Into the pig bucket with it. It has done its work of raising the acidity of the curd.

Now comes *cheddaring*. This is the process of wrapping the curd into bundles about nine inches across in cheese cloth and leaving them on a sloping surface so that the whey can gently drain out of them. Turn the bundles from time to time.

Then *milling*. If you haven't got a curd-mill (and why should you have?) get some of those guitar-playing friends of yours, see that they wash their hands carefully, and exhort them to break the curd up into pieces as big as walnuts.

And *salting*. Chuck an ounce of salt in to every 4 lbs of curd and mix well through.

Now take your chessit, which is a cylinder of wood or metal, line it with a cheese cloth, and load your walnut-size pieces into it. Wrap the cloth over the top of it all and put it in your cheese press. Apply about a couple of stone of pressure. In other words very light.

After say six hours pull the cheese out, take the cloth off it and wring it out in warm water, wrap the cheese up in it again, turn the cheese, and return it to the chessit. Apply half a cwt. pressure.

Leave it thus for two days, turning it once. Then give it half a ton pressure for a couple of days, turning it once.

Take it out, paste on clean bandages with flour and water, put it on a clean shelf (very important) in a well-ventilated store with a temperature of about 55° to 60°F. (13° to 16°C.), turn it every day for a week, then turn about twice a week; always brush mould off it and suffer not cheese mites to exist. Contrary to general belief they are *not* a good thing. Some people dip the whole thing in wax after a week or two's drying and I think this is a very good idea.

If you try the above method and find it not satisfactory just try the following process. Omit the scalding. Instead take the ¾ inch cubes of curd out of the whey as soon as you have cut them, and go straight in to your cheddaring process, tightening the cloth from time to time. After twenty minutes start doing the hot iron test. When you get your half-inch threads, *mill*.

If this still does not please you try scalding as before, but to a higher temperature, say to 107°F. (42°C.).

There are two things to remark on: (1) don't try to make cheese in the winter: it's economically crazy anyway and furthermore much more difficult; (2) the bigger cheeses you can make the better. You should get about 1¼ lbs. of fresh cheese from a gallon of milk, and about 1lb. when it is fully ripened. If you can get, say, ten gallons together with your morning and evening milking, and can cope with this quantity, you will have a decent sized cheese. Personally I would not go to the trouble of making cheese from the milk of just one cow, but in this Sally would disagree with me.

*Starter*. The purpose of adding starter is to ensure a rapid development of the sort of bacteria you want—lactic acid bacteria. The way to do this, obviously, is to put in a lot of lively lactic acid bacteria, and that is your starter. Many cheese makers do not use starter, but you may find you have to. You can buy pure cultures of lactic acid bacteria (from Messrs. Harsens Lab., Reading, or The Somerset Farm Institute, Kennington, Bridgwater, Somerset, amongst other places) but you can also make your own starter. You can only do it in the summer time.

Take a quart of clean milk from a healthy cow. Do not include the first few squeezes of the cow's tits—these are heavily infected with bacteria: in any case they should always be given to the cow-shed cat. Milk with clean hands into a sterilized bucket (boiling water—then cold water—then upside down). Strain the milk through a sterile pad of cotton wool into a sterilized bowl.

Place the bowl in your dairy. Keep the windows open. Now I am assuming that your dairy is *clean*, for this is essential. The air of a dairy is teeming with lactic acid bacteria, which are the chaps you want. Keep the quart of milk as near as you can between 70° to 75°F. (21 to 24°C.). The quart of milk will curdle.

Now we are only half way there. Take some milk (fresh milk that has been through the separator is best because it is better without the butter fat: *but* the milk must be fresh—not long from the cow). Pasteurize it by scalding it to 185°F. (85°C.) and keeping it there for 10 minutes and then cooling it quickly (by standing the saucepan in cool running water) to 70° to 75°F. (21° to 24°C.).

Skim the top off your quart of curdled milk and give the skimming to the cat (or eat it yourself). Then dump the rest of the curdled milk into the pasteurized milk. What you are doing now, you see, is heavily inoculating *sterile* milk with lactic acid bacteria. Cover with a muslin cloth and keep between 70° to 75°F. (21° to 24°C.). Keep thus for 24 hours. Skim the surface off and what is left is your starter, and can be added to the milk from which you are going to make your cheese.

You can keep this starter *going*, by, every day or so, adding some of it to more pasteurized milk. The use of starter takes some risk out of cheese making but remember the best cheese in the world is made without it.

Is this trouble worthwhile? Well, if you are making a lot of cheese for 'export' (I mean to sell off the holding), or if you are the cheese-making brother or sister in a fair sized community, then I would say it is. You will get more consistently good cheese. And really it takes longer to *read* this than it does to do it. Once you have done all these cheese-making operations half a dozen times, so you don't have to look at the book, you can really do them quite quickly and easily.

Assuming that you have to make a large quantity of cheese and wish to do it at least semi-professionally, and have not inherited a dairy, complete with all the right bacteria with a pedigree of a million generations on the same soil, and ten human generations of skill from your maternal grandmother, I will describe the way in which Cheddar cheese is made on the few farms which still make it. I have chosen Cheddar because it is a straight-forward cheese which will *keep*. A full sized Cheddar should weigh near on 100 pounds, should not be cut into for six months at least, is better after nine months, and if properly made and carefully kept it will be good the second winter after it is made. Do not be put off by the word 'Cheddar' remembering all the dull 'Cheddar' mouse-trap you have bought at the shops. Factory-made cheese, from pasteurized milk, can never be anything else but fuel for the masses.

In the first place you will need a means of testing the acidity of your milk and whey and curd. In the second place you will need a cheese vat. The vat should be an oblong box, lined ideally with stainless steel but wood will do (if it doesn't leak). The advantage of metal though is that it can be either heated or cooled by hot or cold water or steam passed round it in a jacket. Professional cheese makers will want one of these because they represent an enormous saving of time and labour. Old-fashioned cheese ladies just used a wooden tub. It is an advantage if the vat can be lifted up at one end so that the whey can drain downhill away from the curd. There should be a tap at the bottom at one end. If you don't get a water-jacketed vat make do with a plain rectangular bin—of wood or metal— and raise your temperature when need be by the laborious process of dipping out whey, heating it on the stove, putting it back again, taking out some more from the other end, etc. Professional vats can be got from Messrs. Clares (Wells) Ltd., Wells, Somerset.

*Acid.* Milk cannot be made into cheese until the acidity of the milk has been raised by the action of bacteria. There are a number of bacteria which can do this, but the most beneficial from the cheese-maker's point of view is *Bacillus acidi lactici*. These little creatures convert one molecule of lactose into four molecules of lactic acid thus:

$$\frac{C_{12}H_{12}O_{11}}{\text{lactose}} + H_2O + \text{bacteria} = \frac{4C_3H_6O_3}{\text{lactic acid}} + \text{bacteria}.$$

These bacteria eventually kill themselves with their own pollution. Like humans on this planet they eventually reach such numbers that their 'planet' (the milk tub) is not big enough to support them and, by their excessive numbers, they pollute their environment (by turning it too acid) to such an extent that they die, and other bacteria, which can withstand and exploit this situation, take over. These latter are putrefactive bacteria and they turn milk bad. There is all the difference in the world between sour milk (which is delicious and highly beneficial) and bad milk, which is not beneficial at all.

The *mystique* of cheese making consists entirely of doing all the operations *at exactly the right degree of acidity*. The *kind* of cheese you make, and the quality of that cheese, depends entirely upon this factor of the correct acidity. The correct acidities of the material at the various stages in the making of Cheddar, in the summer time, are as follows:

| Operation | Acidity |
|---|---|
| Putting milk into vat | 0·15 to 0·16 |
| Adding rennet | 0·19 to 0·20 |
| Cutting the curd | 0·14 to 0·145 |
| Pitching | 0·17 to 0·18 |
| Drawing whey off | 0·21 to 0·22 |
| Milling curd | 0·75 to 0·95 |

The manner in which you *test* this acidity is much simpler than it sounds. Take 10 cc of the milk or whey. Add to it three or four drops of phenol phthalein solution. Put a measured amount of N/9 solution of caustic soda in a burette. That is fill the burette up to the level indicated on it. Drip the caustic soda solution drop by drop into the whey or milk, stirring and watching carefully. As soon as the whey or milk gets a pink tinge, stop. Read off how much caustic soda solution you have used. As you use a burette which is specially measured off for you you can read the acidity of the sample straight off on the burette. To *do* this takes much less time than to read about it. You can buy a Dairy Acidimeter from: Astell Lab. Service, 172 Brownhill Road, Catford, London S.E.6. It consists of the burette on a stand, a bowl, a bottle of phenol phthalein, a bottle of N/9 (or Standard) caustic soda, a pipette for measuring the milk or whey, and glass stirring rods. You do not have to be a Ph.D. Chemistry to use it; any good cook-general could learn to do it in five minutes.

*Farmhouse Cheddar.* Cool your evening's milk (if the weather is hot) and leave overnight. Skim the cream off in the morning—heat that cream on the stove—pour it back again. You do this to mix the cream back with the milk. Dump in your morning's milk.

Add ½ gallon starter (optional) to 100 gallons milk. Stir.

Test for acidity. When 0·19 add 4 fluid oz. rennet per 100 gallons. The milk should be 84°F. (30°C.) when you do this.

Deep-stir for 4 to 5 minutes. Then top-stir only. You know when to stop deep-stirring when the milk clings to your hands.

About ten minutes after the rennet has gone in coagulation occurs.

The acidity goes down as it coagulates. When it is exactly 0·14 cut the curd. You will have to have American curd knives to do this effectively.

Stir by hand—very carefully and gently. Don't bash the curd about or bruise it or you will lose cream.

Slowly (1 degree F. every three minutes—not quicker) raise

71

the temperature to 90°F. (32°C.). Heat a little quicker (1 degree F. every two minutes) to 100°F. (38°C.). Stop heating.

Stir by hand until a handful of the curd feels firm and springy. Keep stirring until acidity is 0·18. Then pitch, i.e. leave the curd to soak in its whey. Keep testing for acidity. When whey squeezed from a handful of curd is 0·21 acid drain off the whey.

*Cheddaring.* This is the process of wrapping the drained blocks of curd into cloths and leaving them on the dry bottom of the sloping vat so that the whey keeps dribbling out of them, turning them occasionally until the acidity has reached 0·75 to as much as 0·95. If you have not got your acidimeter here you can test by the hot iron test (on the stove top). You should be able to draw threads off your hot iron in your whey at least 1½ inches long.

Then mill. You can buy a cheese mill or you can get all your communiteers around (*after* they have very thoroughly washed their hands) and break the curd up by hand to the size of walnuts.

Add 2¼ lbs. salt to 100 lbs. curd (say from your 100 gallons milk). Thoroughly mix the salt with the milled curd.

Cool to 75°F. (24°C). (You can see the advantage of having a vat with a cooling jacket.)

Put the curd cloths in chessits which should be 15 inches high and 15 inches in diameter. This will give you a 100 lbs. cheese, which is a cheese worth having.

Put in press and press lightly until the whey begins to run, then give it 10 cwt. for three or four hours, pull out, turn, rinse cloth and chessit with warm water, then give it 25 cwt. Next day remove and bathe cheese in water at 130°F. (54°C.) for 30 seconds, return to press and give it 40 cwt. Third day pull it out again, rub all over with lard or butter, bandage with clean calico and press again at two tons.

On the fourth day remove from press, bandage again and this time sew bandage on (some people don't bandage but rub with lard oil every day for a week). Write date on it, put it on the shelf, turn it every day for a month and then every other day for another month. Some people soak it in brine for three days. The store should be airy and 60° to 80°F. (15° to 25°C.).

All this is a lot of work, but consider, to buy 100 lbs. of cheese would cost you, at 25p a pound, £25! For the value of three cheeses you can buy a cow. And you won't get cheese at that price now and if you did it would have nothing like the quality of the cheese you can make for yourself.

I am not suggesting that the lone homesteader should make cheese on this scale, unless he intends to make it a major item of his foreign exchange trade. After all, to get 100 gallons of milk in two milkings he will need from twenty to twenty-five cows in milk. But for communities this might well be the scale on which cheese would be made, with one specialist in charge of the making, and perhaps two cheeses a week being made and butter being made on other days. But the lone homesteader could well use the same scientific care with his temperatures and acidities with his cheeses made from say ten gallons of milk. Sally keeps milk from more than two milkings to make up enough for a cheese. If she used the acidimeter test she could do this far more reliably. And milk kept over from more than two milkings would certainly not need starter added, it would reach the required acidity (0·19) without that.

When one kind of cheese has been mastered no doubt the enthusiastic cheese maker will want to experiment. Gruyère, and the other holey cheeses, are made with *fresh* cow's milk (straight from the cow) with no starter, curdled with rennet, and kept at 86°F. (30°C.). The acidity here is mostly caused by *Bacillum bulgaricum* and a gas is formed which causes the holes. Stilton *should* have extra cream added (I wonder how many Stiltons do nowadays!) and should be inoculated with *Penicillium roqueforti*. (Buy a small Roquefort cheese to get this.) But when the cheese maker gets to this stage he will wish to get some more literature on the subject anyway.

If you want to make yoghourt, get a good live yoghourt, put some in milk warmed to about blood heat, keep it in a closed container not too far from the stove, use a little every day, and add a little fresh milk every day, and go on as long as it keeps pleasant.

A 'Poor Man's Cheese' described in *Food in England* and apparently once made in Scotland, which has the advantage of being a 'one cow' cheese, is made by putting milk in a pot over a slow fire. Let it curdle, leave in the whey that night, drain the whey off next morning, cut the curd up and salt it, tie tightly in a linen cloth, hang to drip all day, retie tightly and hang up for four weeks. If you hang it in a net it will have a nice pattern. At the end of the month it is fit to eat. If some butter be worked into the curd and the cheese kept for three or four months it will be very good. I have never tried this but at least it sounds simple. Any method of preserving the summer milk for the winter is good.

# 6

## Pig

*A couple of flitches of bacon are worth fifty thousand
Methodist sermons and religious tracts.*

WILLIAM COBBETT : Cottage Economy

If you have a cow you will ultimately find yourself making
butter, and perhaps cheese, and then you will have skimmed
milk and whey and what are you going to do with these? You
can, in fact, fatten ducks or chickens on milk products, but the
best use to which you can put them is to feed them to the pigs.
Also, your fields and garden will by now be yielding you much
waste that you cannot eat yourself. There is very little that a
pig will not eat. True, you can compost vegetable waste, but
show me a better way of composting anything than putting it
through the guts of a pig!

There are several ways in which you can have pigs. For the
individual or community seriously intent on being self-supporting the obvious purpose of the job is to have pigs to kill for meat.
There is nothing wrong, though, in having a surplus to sell,
or to trade with other people for other produce. Other con-
siderations are: the fewer pigs you have the more completely
you will be able to feed them on the waste products of your
farm. A gallon of skimmed milk a day will go a long way to
fattening a pair of baconers, but spread among a dozen its
effect is not so noticeable: in fact you will have to feed them
primarily on other food, the high protein part of it probably
bought in. You are thus getting further from the idea of being
self-supporting. But, say you only want two pigs, how are you
going to get them? To be truly self-supporting you must breed
them yourself. So you must have at least one sow. Now she
will give you, say, twenty to as many as thirty piglets in a year

(ours always used to give us twenty-four, never more, never less). You need two pigs to kill for your family. But of course you can always sell the others as weaners (that is at eight or ten weeks old, straight off the sow). But all this forces you to be in pigs in a bigger way. Then from where do you get the boar? You can't afford a boar to serve one sow. There are 'boar walkers' though, who go around carrying a boar in the back of a van, and who will come when you telephone them, provided you can catch your sow when she is on heat, which is not always easy. But this boar problem is a problem. One answer is to have enough sows to pay the wages, as it were, of a boar. My belief is that if you have six sows, or even as low as four, and they pay you really well, you can afford to support a boar. But again it drives you into a bigger and bigger commitment in pigs. From a man wanting a couple of baconers for his family you now become a pig farmer.

Of course the whole problem is eased if you are part of a like-minded community. Either the community can keep the boar in the centre, as it were, and lend him out to the communiteers, or else one member of the community can do all the sow keeping, and swap weaners for other produce. I say weaners; this is ecologically a sounder method than that the one pig keeper should fatten the pigs too, and simply trade pig meat with the other people. The pigs do better, and more good, and are fed more cheaply, if they are spread out among everybody.

But if you are on your own, and don't want to go into all the intricacies of sow keeping, you can simply buy a pair or more of weaners. I will personally have no part in suggesting to anybody that they should buy *one* weaner. I have made the point that the husbandman is a benevolent ruler and not a tyrant, and a benevolent ruler does not keep anybody in solitary confinement. But you can buy weaners, at this day and age, for from five to ten pounds. My advice is, if you have milk by-products, to buy the cheapest weaners you can. Normally weaners are sold at from eight to twelve weeks, and the older they are the dearer they are likely to cost. But if you have milk you can buy them very young—and thus get them cheaper.

Let us deal with this plan of buying weaners and fattening them first. The countryman who used to keep a pig at the bottom of the garden (all too often alone, I fear) used to show him to you and say: 'I'm only a "growin" on him now o' course.' He meant that he was not feeding him a fattening ration, but just enough food to keep him growing, in good lean condition. When the time came in would go the barley meal and the pig would be fattened. 'That's no good a "fattenin" on him twice,' the owner would say. So when you first get the weaners you should feed them well, with plenty of milk, until they get over the shock of being weaned from their mother, and then feed them on a lower diet, and keep them active and happy, until they are fully grown. Then you should confine them in a warm place and simply push the food into them.

When I worked on a farm in Gloucestershire, as a boy, we fattened a hog until it was enormous: twice as big or bigger than any baconer that is killed today. We turned this pig into bacon and the bacon was nearly a hundred per cent fat. There was hardly a streak of lean in it. This bacon was never fried, but boiled. It was boiled in great chunks, and every morning the cold chunk of fat was put on the table for breakfast and we ate slices of it with dry bread and a boiled egg, and mustard. To have eaten it with butter would have been revolting, but as it was the stuff was perfectly delicious, marvellously digestible, and it kept us working at very hard manual labour, out of doors in the severest winter England had had for many years, for many hours a day. This is how pigs used to be eaten. Cobbett says: 'Make him quite fat by all means—the last bushel does the most good if he sit to eat it.' He goes on to say that if the pig can walk a hundred yards he is not fat, and that lean meat is only fit for wasters and drunkards.

Nowadays apparently we have a population of wasters and drunkards because the only baconers the market will accept are—like Cassius—lean and hungry pigs—such pigs are dangerous. The fact is, of course, that people who live hard and out of doors can relish fat bacon, and it does them good. We all know the executives' nursery rhyme:

*Ring a ring a roses*
*Coronary throm-bo-ses,*
*A'seizure!*
*A'seizure!*
*We all fall down!*

Animal fat only gives seizures and coronary thrombosis to people who do not get enough exercise. When this nation was fed on fat bacon and fat beef and mutton the disease was unknown. Now, as meat gets leaner and leaner until it nearly fades away, thrombosis is increasing faster than any other disease except lung cancer. It is idleness that causes diseases of the heart. True manual workers never get coronary thrombosis, and nor do self-supporters. But it's all a matter of taste. I like fat bacon—boiled, mind, not fried in yet more fat. If you don't, well don't have it—kill your pigs when they are lean.

If you want good fat bacon buy your weaners in the spring and kill them just before Christmas. At Christmas you should be eating hams killed the Christmas before; hung a year they are so much better. And it's nice to have some fresh pork at Christmas anyway.

I do not like to see pigs kept indoors all the time. If you let confined pigs out of their confinement it is pathetic to see them snort and gallop and leap about in their happiness to be free at last. During the last month or two of fattening a pig keep him indoors by all means, he seems to get his pleasure then from the thing a pig likes, after all, to do more than anything else—eating. But until this fattening stage—when you are 'a "growin" on him', let him out. Of course you can't let him run anywhere or he will do endless damage. And this is where we draw on the resources of the modern world. The electric fence is your answer. You can keep pigs in with pig netting, with a strand of well-strained barbed wire at the bottom, but it's a running battle. Electric fence is the thing, either two single strands or the new electric netting which is very good. If you use single strands and find they don't work try erecting wire netting behind them, for its psychological effect. Pigs are tryers. In a world with no electric fencing I would say, tether your pigs. A rope or leather harness with one strap in front of the pig's fore-legs and another behind them will do the trick. Incidentally, if you want a quiet life never try to keep prick-eared pigs, like the Large White, out of doors. The flop-eared pig is far more likely to stay behind a fence, for his ears hang down over his eyes.

But while we have electricity let us use it, and part of your garden thus fenced off, and well pigged, will benefit enor-mously. It is the way to bare-fallow land. If you like you can grow a fodder crop (see Chapter 14) and put the pigs into that, or you can put the pigs into your potato patch after you have harvested it (the pigs will find the last potato) or you can just bare fallow. On a *small* enough area the pigs will destroy every weed, if you leave them there long enough even the horrid perennial weeds like spear grass or twitch. They will bring valuable elements up from the subsoil, they will heavily manure the land, and they will leave it twice as valuable as it was before. Don't ring them. Let them dig. Don't expect a couple of pigs to do much good to half an acre though, concentrate them.

Meanwhile you have got to feed them something as well as what they can find for themselves. While they have plenty of milk (skimmed milk is just as good for them as whole milk would be) milk mixed into bran or other wheat offal is all they need. Milk and barley meal are very good too, but unnecessarily expensive, if you can sell your barley or have to buy it. In the fattening stage milk and barley meal is the finest food you can give them. If you can't give them milk then you will have to buy in some protein. The easiest thing to do is to give them pro-prietary cake; 'outdoor pig nuts' are the easiest. They are big and won't get trodden into the ground easily. Just throw them down at half the rate recommended on the bag and let the pigs hunt for them. Or you can buy fish meal and mix it with any kind of meal at the rate of about ten per cent fish meal. Or twenty per cent beans in a mash will give them enough protein: feed them as much as they can clear up in twenty minutes and squeal for more.

You can give the pigs all your small or misshapen potatoes. You can often buy 'stock feed' potatoes at very little a ton, or spoiled carrots (but if these have been washed they won't keep) or other spoiled food. Kitchen swill is always fine for pigs. I know a man who buys tons of stale bread from a bakery and his wife has to spend hours pulling the wrappers off sliced loaves. (Ugh!) Fodder crops you can grow specially are fodder beet, carrots, potatoes, kale and greens of all sorts and, most important on light land anyway, Jerusalem artichokes. The latter are marvellous; they grow in the roughest and most weed-infested land, their foliage smothers everything, and the pigs thrive by rooting them up. Take the pigs to the artichokes though, not the artichokes to the pigs. Let the pigs do the work. Or plant a special pig field, a field you want to 'pig' anyway, to clean it and fertilize it. Plant, say, a strip of Jerusalem artichokes, one of fodder beet, one of kale. Give them a little of all three. Then, when they have cleared that up, move them on. Variety is the spice of life.

Always keep a pig bucket in the scullery. When we have a pigless period we don't know what to do. What do we do with that lovely greasy rich washing-up water? Criminal to throw it down the sink. What do we do with the celery tops, the potato peelings, the carrot tops, the waste food? Out in the garden what do we do with the bean and pea haulms, the sweet corn tops, the scythed nettles, the pulled-out weeds? If we have pigs they will either eat it or tread it into the soil as good compost.

As for how much concentrated food to give your pigs, give them as much as they will clear up quickly. If there is any left after half an hour give them less next day. Keep them a little hungry for concentrates.

As for housing, if pigs are running out of doors they will need the minimal, but they will need some. They will need a dry place and some shelter from the rain. That is all. What form it takes every man must decide for himself as long as it is the cheapest and easiest, and the most mobile, for you will be dragging it around with the pigs. You *can* buy Pigloos.

Now for sows and pig breeding. I will say very little about this, only that sows thrive out of doors, provided they are not over-stocked on the same land for too long. At a high rate of stocking I like to move pigs on to fresh ground at least once every six weeks, otherwise a worm infestation builds up and the pigs suffer. Let loose in a wood pigs do wonders. If you give them two pounds of pig nuts a day when they are dry that will do them. After they have farrowed though you must give them from six to eight, depending upon how much other food they can get and how many piglets they have. All this business of feeding animals is common sense really. You can find pages of complicated instructions and tables and starch equivalents and all the rest of it in the text books but if you just *keep* animals, and watch them carefully, and note whether they are growing or not, are hungry or not, and use your common sense, you don't need a whole lot of scientific gobble-de-gook.

As to housing and mangement of breeding sows, there must be a shelter—no matter how rough (and it doesn't matter) but more or less waterproof—available for a sow, for her sole use, when she farrows. That is all. The books will tell you to put no litter in a farrowing pen. We put as much litter in as the sow thinks she needs. Throw straw or bracken or what have you outside if you like; before the sow farrows she will carry as much as she needs in herself in her mouth. We then leave the sows completely alone. Don't go near them. We have never worried about farrowing rails (although there's nothing wrong with them) nor infra red lights, or any of the rest of it. In eight years at the Broom we kept sows all the time, up to six of them, and our losses of piglets were as nearly nil as it was possible for them to be. In eight years I seem to remember burying two piglets. Once you start to interfere with nature, with sows, you've got to interfere more and more. Keep them too confined and they get worms—so you have to confine them even more, on concrete. Keep them on concrete and they can't get iron, so you have to inject the piglets with it or they get anaemia. Farrow them in a confined space with plenty of straw and they get confused and smother the piglets. So you give them no straw. They then lose their natural chain of instinctual actions—nest-making and all the rest of it—so they lay on, or eat, their piglets. They are mixed up. So you confine them in a farrowing crate where they can't move at all and attract the piglets away from them with a warm infra red light. And the piglets get virus pneumonia. So you go in for embryotomy. You kill the sow and take the piglets out of her belly in aseptic conditions and bring them up in sterile boxes. This is actually being done on a large scale in America and more and more in England. Pigs are now being kept, all their lives, in total darkness except when they are fed, and in tiny wire cages like battery hens. Where do you go from there?

Right back, I should say, to keeping sows under the most natural conditions possible, allowing their proper chain of instincts to work itself out. We used to get a pound a head more for our piglets than other weaner producers because the fatteners knew they would never get virus pneumonia. They had spent their lives running about in the open air, and getting what minerals they wanted straight from the soil, and they were as tough and hardy as wild boars.

# 7

# Bacon

*Meat in the house is a great source of harmony.*

WILLIAM COBBETT : Cottage Economy

*Slaughtering.* In most parts of Britain at least there is a public slaughterhouse somewhere in the vicinity; although these get fewer and fewer and further and further as the great philosophy of the twentieth century—Bigger Means Better—has its sway. Where at one time a bullock was quietly walked a mile or two to the village slaughterhouse, rested in the butcher's paddock for the night, and knocked on the head next morning, now he is crammed into the back of a huge cattle truck with thirty others, banged and lurched, terrified, over up to a hundred miles of roads, forced bellowing into a blood-reeking meat factory and eventually slaughtered. All in the sacred name of Progress.

However, if there is a slaughterhouse not too far away you can send your pig, or pigs, there and have them slaughtered for a fee. You have to get them in there though, pay for the job to be done, and go and fetch the meat back again. You make, in other words, four journeys. It is therefore very much better, if you can, to slaughter them yourself.

In most real country districts there is at least one man who will kill you a pig for a small fee. He makes it part of his living. Or perhaps there is a friendly village butcher who will do it for you. If you can entertain such a man with friendship and home brewed beer he will do it the more willingly, and be the more likely to come and do it again. Pig killing may seem to the townsman to be a brutal and grisly business, but in fact the occasion can have a kind of boozey, bucolic, charm.

I kill my pigs with a .22 rifle which I claim is the most humane method there could be. I have killed three pigs a year for sixteen years and only once (when I first began) did I have to use a second shot. I lure the pig quietly out of his sty into the cow shed with a little food in a bucket (he has had no supper the night before) and put the food into a dish. As the pig starts to eat the food I shoot him in the brain. Anywhere in the head will stun him actually, but I always shoot him in the brain. Draw a line with your imagination from his left ear-hole to his right eye, and from his other ear-hole to his other eye, and where the two lines cross, shoot him. You could not shoot him thus with a humane killer because he would not stand still for you. As soon as you put the humane killer near his head he would move away. Therefore if you use a humane killer you will have to *rope* your pig (getting a slipping noose in his mouth and round his snout) and he will squeal and struggle, and his last moments will be violent and unhappy and not perfectly peaceful as they should be. The .22 is by far the kindest way to kill a pig. One moment he is happily eating—the next moment he is in Heaven.

*Immediately* you have shot him stick him in the front of the neck. The place to stick seems easy to see in practice. Suffice to say that you should use a shortish knife (6 inches is long enough), stick it two inches in front of his breastbone at an angle of 45 degrees from the horizontal line of the pig and *keep it dead central*. You can easily feel the breastbone if you are in doubt, then remember, insert the knife two inches in front of it and at an angle of 45 degrees up towards the back of the pig. Thus will you cut both the carotid arteries and the jugular vein. Two things will happen. One is that blood will gush out in great quantity and now is the time for your wife to be at hand to catch it in a basin if she wants to make black pudding and has a stronger stomach than most people's wives (our blood goes down the drain I am afraid), and, secondly, the pig will begin to kick as though it is trying to win the Grand National. Let it kick, and remember it can feel nothing—its soul is in Heaven playing a porcine harp. If your wife has caught the blood, incidentally, she must stir it or whip it immediately otherwise it will clot.

We thereupon haul our pig up on a tackle, to make sure that all the blood drains out. Most people don't bother.

*Scalding and Dissecting.* Some people drop their pig into a huge half tub containing scalding water. We used to but now do not. We went through a phase of pouring methylated spirits over the pig and lighting it and letting it burn like a Christmas pudding but have given that up too. Now we do what all the local Pembrokeshire people do around here, we let the pig lie on the concrete floor and pour the scalding water over the pig. The object of this is so that you can scrape the bristles off the pig. Now great skill is needed for this, and this is one of the arts that you had better learn from your local expert.

The water must be from 145° to 150°F. (63° to 66°C.) and no more. If it is too cold it won't get the bristles out; if it is too hot it will 'fix' them and you'll never get them out. The local wise man will know whether the water is right by looking into it (as a brewer does). If he can see his face in it it is right. Or he will put one part of cold water into three parts of boiling water. That is as good. You must have plenty of hot water ready—ten gallons is not too much.

Pour some of the scalding water over part of the pig—slowly—then keep plucking at the bristles. Suddenly they will come out easily in your fingers. Now is the time to start scraping. Don't scrape with a knife, the lid of a tin is ideal, or a tin coffee-pot lid. Don't cut the skin. Just scrape until the bristles come out and if the pig started off by being a black pig, it will end up as a white pig. Colour, in pigs as in humans, is not even skin deep. Meanwhile your wife/mistress/home-brew-drinking neighbour is busy pouring more water on a different place. Scrape away. Put each trotter right into a jug of scalding water, pull it out, scrape it, and yank the horny hoof off with a pair of pincers or a hook. In a very short time the pig will be clean. Do his head too—every part of him. Suffer not a bristle to remain and mar his beauty. Besides hot water you need plenty of home brew to go with this operation.

Now 'hock' your pig, or ham string him, that is cut behind

the tendons (gam strings) at the back of his hind legs just above the hoof. A glance at a pig carcase in a butcher's shop will show you how to do this. This tendon, although slender, is amazingly strong. Put the ends of a gamble through these tendons. A gamble is a spreader: a metal or wooden stick, maybe fifteen inches long, hung from its middle by a block tackle, and with flattened out and curving ends for hanging a pig on. See them also in any butcher's shop. Now split the breastbone of the pig with knife and chopper. Do this immediately. Haul the pig off the ground with the tackle.

We always cut the head off at this juncture. I think it simplifies things to do so. Some people leave the head on and split it when they split the pig, but you cannot do this until next day. We cut the head off at the first vertebra and put it where no flies can get to it (but normally we kill pigs in the winter when there are no flies, and I do not recommend killing them in the summer anyway) and now we gut it. This takes skill, and common sense. Get on a chair behind the pig and encircle its anus with the point of the knife. You do this so that the bowel will drop out when you get the guts out and not tear, leaving the anus behind where you don't want it and spilling excrement all over the place. You very carefully cut the actual anus, or arse-hole, of the pig right round so as to separate it from the rest of the pig. Before you cut the last bit you grab it with one hand, cut it away completely, haul the bowel out a few inches and get a friend (it seems a little indelicate to ask your wife) to tie a piece of string round it. This is, as I hope you have guessed, to stop any excrement coming out of it. Now you let it go and the weight of the rest of the bowels pulls it down inside the pig.

This grisly business over you get down, and round to the belly of your pig, and you very carefully insert just the point of your knife in the middle of the belly just about where our solar plexus would be. Only let the knife *just* cut through the skin—you are not Jack the Ripper. Then insert your forefinger in along the back of the knife and move the knife upwards (i.e. towards the tail of the pig) with your forefinger acting as a guard to prevent that unforgivable happening: shoving the knife point into the pauch or guts and thus fouling your meat. Cut right up to where the two hind legs join. Dissect out the penis and urethra and bladder if a male pig, and bladder if a female. Now as you open the belly the paunch and guts will try to get out. You now see why you were told to split the breastbone while the pig was on the ground: if you had not done so the guts would be hanging down out of the pig and you wouldn't have been able to.

Let the guts flop out into a tin bath.

Carefully remove the *pluck*. This is the liver, heart and lungs, with a few oddments, all hung together on the windpipe or trachea. Cut the gall bladder out, very carefully so as not to splash gall over anything at all, and throw it away. Stick a hook through the windpipe and hang the pluck up in a fly-proof place.

We always chuck a couple of buckets of cold water into the eviscerated pig to wash the blood out of it. Some experts might tell you that this is not a good idea. I think it is though.

Then go and finish the rest of the home brew. You deserve every drop of it, you and your companions. About the only part of the pig that is fit to eat for supper that night is the liver.

Next morning go back to your pig. He has been hanging up all night, we hope, in a nice cold draught, where neither rat nor cat can get at him. Cut a score down his back, through all that back fat, from his tail to where his head used to be, right along the central line. You can feel this for part of the way with the finger, but much depends on a good eye and judgment. Next take a light sharp chopper—not one of your vast axes such as beheaded Mary Queen of Scots—and chop the back-bone right down the middle. Split your pig right in half. Now obviously when you pull one half of that pig off the gamble the latter will tip up and deposit the other half on the floor. You must allow for this either by tying the other half up, or getting somebody stronger than your poor wife to take it off while you take your half off. And half a large baconer is very heavy indeed let me tell you.

Lay your half on the table and cut it into suitable joints for curing. Our plan is to lay the side skin-side down, put the knife in under the tail (or where the tail should be) and with the blade slanting towards the head end of the pig cut a good generous curve until you hit bone. Then start at the belly side of the pig and do the other half of the proposed generous circle until you hit the bone again. Then a few strokes of the meat saw (or any old saw) will cut through the bone and complete the job. Like this, as you started *under* the tail, you miss the spine of course. You now have what looks very much like a ham. Cut the trotter off but *below* the first joint, so that you have plenty of leg to hang the ham up by.

Cut the pig straight across, at right angles to its back, about nine inches from the tail (at the point at which the spine suddenly curves upwards). This odd bit of meat, which is good, we use as a roasting joint in due course. It is an awkward shape for salting though.

Now inside the side of the pig is the belly fat, which makes the finest lard, and this we rip out. All fat is cut into little pieces and put into a big crock, with a little water, and put into the *slow* oven. Do not overheat it as it will burn. From time to time pull it out of the slow oven and pour the liquid fat off it, and put it into basins; but more of that anon.

Now pull the kidney out, and then carefully cut out the tenderloin: that strip of lean meat inside the carcase near the kidney. This should be baked in due course draped with the caul of the beast: that thin membrane with dollops of fat all over it on which the small intestines were hung. With onions it is quite delicious.

Separate the forequarter from the side. To do this cut right across the carcase between the 4th and 5th ribs, just behind the shoulder blade.

You will now have a ham, a forequarter and a side. The side is a big one. Maybe you will prefer, for ease of handling, to split it right down the middle, sawing through the ribs, so as to leave a back and a belly. The belly will be poor tack: a thinnish sheet and mostly fat. We used to roll this and put it in a wet pickle, but it is good for sausages. You can dry salt it, only don't leave it in the salt for more than a week. You also have a couple of good roasting joints from where the loin was. You can cut the forequarter into joints and roast it too if you like, or you can salt it like the ham. First cut the blade bone off if you like, and use that fresh as a joint.

*Curing.* There are scores of methods of curing ham and bacon, but I will give you the simplest and most widespread, in England and Wales at least. I will just describe what we do, and what most of my neighbours do (or such as still cure their own bacon).

We have a big slate salting bench. We dump some dry salt on this (you will need at least forty pounds of salt to do a pig in comfort. If you wish to be more economical with salt you will have to be a lot more careful and take a lot more trouble. We just use a lot of salt and bury the pig in it). Lay a ham on the salt. Sprinkle as much saltpetre as you can hold between your finger and thumb on the cut end of the ham. Take a handful of soft brown sugar and shove that on the cut end of the ham. Rub it, and the saltpetre with it, in hard. Then rub salt in, and rub in hard. Then treat the skin-covered part of the ham the same. Now I know that all the books tell you to weigh the saltpetre, and mix it thoroughly with the salt, etc., but once you have to start messing about weighing dribs and drabs of this and that the meat will go bad while you are fussing. The method I have described has worked for perhaps a hundred hams with me and they have all been excellent. Bury the ham in salt. Do the same with all the other joints. Add enough saltpetre just for the merest sprinkling. The saltpetre is supposed to preserve the colour of the meat. I have a shrewd suspicion that if you didn't use it at all the ham would be just as good but I don't know. You needn't use sugar, but most people do, particularly for the hams. It makes them sweeter. Squeeze the hams hard and a gout of blood will come out from a certain vein. See how much of this you can squeeze out.

Then every day, for three days, take the joints out and rub

them hard with salt. See that they get dry salt in contact with them all over, and put them back again, probably upside down. After three days just leave them be in the salt. Take the bellies out in a week, the sides out in a fortnight, the forequarters out in a fortnight to three weeks depending on how big they are, and the hams out in three weeks to a month (three weeks if they are just ordinary sized hams). Rinse the salt off them and hang them up in an even temperature somewhere and let them dry off for a week or two. We hang ours straight in the *simnai fawr*. The *simnai fawr* is the big chimney over our fireplace open to the sky. There is a bend in this chimney so part of it is not exposed to the rain, and there are pipes up there as a rack. I hang the meat up there, high above the fire, where it gets the smoke and does not get too hot. It must not get too hot, or the fat goes rancid. It wants to be a good ten feet above the fire. If you haven't got a *simnai fawr* you can build a smoke-house, and this I will describe in Chapter 18. Smoke for a week or a fortnight, depending how often you have the fire alight, and then take down and store. Smoking preserves meat and gives it a fine flavour but it is not necessary. Plenty of people round here don't smoke.

We store ours by just hanging it up. Many people bandage their hams and hang them up or, better still I believe, wrap them well and store them down in a chest buried in dry ashes, or dry bran or oats, but you must watch for mice or mites with the latter. This prevents the hams from drying out. If hung it should be hung in the dark, and in fresh air.

When you need a bit of bacon, cut a big slice off one of the sides, bone it (troublesome—but watch a grocer do it one day), and slice it as you need it. But it is saltier than shop bacon (which is not meant to keep) so soak the slices in fresh water for up to half an hour before frying it. If you wish to boil a lump of it soak it for twelve hours first.

Keep the hams, if you can, a full year. Scrub well, soak all night, put in water with plenty of pepper and simmer (not boil) for 25 minutes for every pound of ham. Let it cool in its own liquor. Eat cold.

There are plenty of sweet pickles for hams. These generally involve plunging the fresh ham into a brine made with such things as beer or cider mixed with treacle, sugar, spices and salt. Keep turning it in the pickle for, say, a month. Here is a typical cure, such as one of our Suffolk neighbours used to recommend:

| | |
|---|---|
| 1 quart old ale | 1 quart malt vinegar |
| 1 lb. brown sugar | $\frac{3}{4}$ oz. saltpetre |
| 2 lbs. salt | 1 oz. cloves |
| 1 oz. pepper corns | |

Boil it all together, cool it, soak the ham in it for a month. I tried this but found I needed a lot more pickle. The ham was very good though.

Curing bacon and ham is much simpler than people think, and if you follow the above simple instructions for the ordinary dry cure you will have no trouble and not go wrong. (But don't blame me if you do—and don't try it in the summer!)

Now what has your faithful wife been doing while all this has been going on?

Why, the very first day she has taken the stomach and large intestine, hereinafter called the *chitlings*, down to a clean brook if she has one, or in the sink if she hasn't, opened them and carefully washed the excrement out of them. She has then cut the large intestine into six-inch lengths (if she doesn't want it for sausage), put it and the stomach, also cut up, into a clean bowl, taken them back to the house, scalded with boiling water, washed in cold water, and then filled the bowl with brine. She changes and charges the brine every day for a few days, then she boils the stuff for two hours, lets it cool, and fries it with onions when it is perfectly delicious.

Another fate waits the small intestines, and maybe the large too. These, as soon as the pig is killed or at least the next day, are separated from the fat that clings to them and unravelled. One end is put on the cold tap and the tap turned on, whereupon they writhe about like a snake, but eventually all the excrement is washed out of them. They are then turned inside out on a smooth stick, which is easier than it sounds. They are then laid flat on a board and scraped with the back of a knife. This gets the gut lining off them. They are then coiled down tight in dry salt and put away until they are needed as sausage casings.

The bladder is washed out well. A small funnel can be poked into it and hot lard poured in. The lard cools and the thing is hung up as a storage vessel for lard. As for the rest of the fat, as the days go by you will render out more and more beautiful white lard which you can pour into sterilized jars or bottles, cover well, when it will keep for some time. If you have a deep freeze put some of it in that to keep longest. You will have free cooking fat for a very long time indeed.

Now for that grisly *memento mori*, the head. As soon as you have time, that first day, shove it in a big crock and fill it with brine. Let it soak for two or three days or more until you have some leisure. Then the bath chaps (which are the cheeks) can be cut off separately and hung in the smoke and cured. They are very delicious boiled and eaten cold with plenty of mustard. Whether you do this or not shove the head, with or without its cheeks, in a large boiler together with the trotters and any other gristly bits and simmer for four hours or so. Pull it all out and take all the meat off the bones. Cut the meat up small (you can mince it if you like), mince six large onions, put plenty of pepper and other spices on the meat (the more the merrier in my opinion), skim the fat off the soup that you boiled the meat in, put the meat back into the soup and simmer for two hours, or until the liquor is reduced to what common sense tells you it ought to be. Pour the stuff hot into basins and let cool. You now have a delicious brawn, which will keep for a month or more in a cold winter, and for ever if you bag it and put it in the deep freeze. Or you can pour it boiling into kilner jars, boil the jars for 20 minutes, and seal.

*Sausages.* English and Welsh home-cured bacon and ham is as good as any in the world, but there is one thing that the

British have never cottoned on to, and that is the Continental-type sausage. The whole idea of this is that it is a way—and a delicious way—of preserving meat. Our English sausages are fine to eat fresh, or to keep in the deep freeze, but it is an enormous advantage to be able to make a big glut of meat into sausages that can be hung up from the ceiling, and left for months, and one hauled down whenever you feel like it, and sliced and eaten raw. If you have bread and butter and that kind of sausage you always have a sumptuous meal waiting ready for you.

We have tried dried sausage (if one can call such a delicious thing by such a pedestrian name) with casings from the small intestine of the pig, and these are fair enough but are too small to keep moist for very long or to provide conditions necessary for producing that succulent thing, a true, smoked, spicey and garlicky Continental sausage. To make such a thing you need the large intestine of the ox, if you can get it, or the sheep if you can't, or large intestine of the pig, which you must treat in the same way as I have described for treating the small intestine above. You want to produce a sausage as thick as your wrist.

There are a hundred different recipes for producing what I must call, for want of a better word, Continental sausage. Some of them are contained in a very useful book: *Charcuterie and French Pork Cooking* by Jane Grigson (Michael Joseph). All such recipes call for an ounce of this and half an ounce of that and it all sounds terribly complicated, and of course by making small adjustments in the ingredients you can make small differences to your resulting sausage; but the principles of the thing are simple enough, and if you keep the principles in mind you can make what sort of sausages you like, and very good they will be too.

You need some lean meat and some fat. The lean of course will be from the 'cheapest' cuts of your pig. You can put beef in too if you like. We used to use 1 part lean pork, 1 part lean beef and 1 part belly fat of pork. Two parts of lean pork and one part of fat are a good mixture. Bacon fat will do too.

For every three pounds of lean-and-fat you need:

> 1oz. salt
> 2 teaspoons of pepper
> 2 or 3 cloves of garlic
> As much spice of whatever sort you have
> Some people like a tablespoonful of brown sugar
> If you haven't marinated the meat in wine a glassful of any kind of wine is useful, or liquer.
> A big pinch of saltpetre

Mince the lean meat and cut the fat into small dices (it is the latter which gives the cut sausage that white-speckled appearance). We have always marinated the lean meat for twelve hours in elderberry wine and it works very well. You should really, of course, use grape wine. Or you don't need to marinate at all. Try both.

Whether or not you marinate mix the whole lot up together and stuff it all, raw as it is, into your casing. Tie the long casing off into sausages of the length you fancy, hang up in a warm dry place—this is important—not warmer than 70°F. (21°C.). A steady 60°F. is what you should aim at. If you have an Aga that never goes out nearby that is ideal. Now if you have a big open chimney, or any other kind of smoking device, hang the sausages up in it after say a week of drying and smoke them for a day and a night. Take them down and hang them in a well-aired dry place and forget them for six months. They will grow a white mould over them. Hooray. Give them at least six months (if you can wait) to mature. Eat them raw.

But the meat will shrink a lot, and if you use large casings you will have to squeeze the meat down hard into one end of the casing once or twice during the drying to keep it tight. Then tie the skin off to keep it tight. It is a good thing also, with big sausages, to tie them round with string like Malvolio's cross garters, and to tighten the strings from time to time to keep the sausage compressed. I have seen fine sausages made like this using the pig's bladder, and I think this would be a very good use for the bladder, rather than filling it with lard or blowing it up like a balloon and giving it to the children to clown about with.

If you don't like so much fat don't use so much. If you don't like garlic don't use it. The casing is important: you can't use plastic, for the reason that it cannot breathe and the meat could not dry out. Bacterial action of a benign sort takes place within the sausages also and that needs the controlled transpiration that natural animal membrane can give. Remember—nothing is cooked. It is all raw. It may seem an insuperable obstacle that you have got to find animal large intestines, but if you go to any slaughterhouse they will give you guts galore, and all you have to do, remember, is turn the guts inside out, scrape the lining off with the back of a knife, wash well, and pack down in dry salt until you need them. Pack down close and away from air.

Our getting a deep freeze, and a bigger farm, put paid to our Continental sausage-making activities. It is so much quicker to shove everything into the deep freeze. But there is nothing to touch well spiced and smoked and well matured Continental sausage: it is perhaps the most delicious food there is. And next time you see some in a shop just enquire the price of it—*per ounce*—let alone per pound! And it is very easy to make after all; the biggest trouble is mincing the stuff and for that you must have a good mincing machine. Kenwood have a mincer plus sausage-filling attachment.

*Fresh Pork.* Your true porker is a much smaller pig than your baconer. A baconer can be nearly a year old, a porker say four months. If you have a deep freeze, to kill a porker is all very well (you do it in exactly the same way as you do a baconer), or also if you make Continental sausages. But it is better to take your pigs on to bacon weight and then get what pork you want out of them before baconing or making sausages of the rest. Pork, like all other meat except offal, should be hung in a cool draughty place for several days before either cooking, or putting in the deep freeze.

*But about this time it is more than possible that the Methodist parson will pay you a visit. It is remarked in America that these gentlemen are attracted by the squeaking of pigs, as the fox is by the cackling of the hen.*

WILLIAM COBBETT: Cottage Economy

# 8

# Poultry, Sheep, Goat, Rabbit, Pigeon

*He who can deliberately inflict torture upon an animal . . .
is an abuser of the authority which God has given him,
and is, indeed, a tyrant in his heart.*

WILLIAM COBBETT: Cottage Economy

## POULTRY

And that rules out, completely and absolutely, Belsen houses
of whatever nature they be: battery houses or broiler houses.
To confine, whom nature has given the urge to scrap, to perch,
to flap her wings, to take dust baths, in a wire cage in which
she cannot do any of these things, is revoltingly cruel and
I cannot bring myself to talk to anybody who does it, nor
would I, on any condition, allow such a person inside my
house.

Let your hens run outside, so that they can suffer, as we do,
the heat of the sun and the bite of the frost. No animal was
meant always to be kept at the same temperature. Let them
have a house in which they can perch at night away from the
foxes and the rain, although hens do very well indeed, in our
climate, just perching in trees. Give each hen a handful of
grain every evening and a handful or two of high protein food
in the morning, and any scraps you can spare. They will eat
a lot of grass and a lot of earwigs. If they want to go broody,
let them go broody. They will hatch you out a clutch of pretty
little chicks, which you can eat when they get less pretty, or,
if pullets, introduce into your laying flock. Keep them out of
your garden or they'll play hell with it. A dozen, or a couple of
dozen, hens kept like this will keep you and your family in eggs
most of the year, at times you will have some to give away, at

97

times you may be without any but if you have plenty of bacon hung up that won't kill you.

If you want to go in for hens in a larger way, say because you are the hen specialist in a community, or because you want to make eggs part of your export trade, then I would recommend the method used by that doyen of poultry keepers, Mr Jim Worthington. Keep hens on free range and give them whole grain in one self-feed container and protein in another. Let them have as much of both as they can stuff, and this won't be much, as a matter of fact, because they will balance their own diet. If they are not on free range give them green food, household scraps and anything else they will eat. The self-feed hoppers you can make yourself by hanging oil drums down from the roof with holes knocked in the bottoms of them enough to let the birds peck out the grain. If you feed protein mash in one you should stand it in a tray, with holes knocked in the bottom of the drum so that any spillage is caught in the tray. Raise it up to keep out mice and rats. You will find by this method that you have very little work to do, and you get your eggs very economically, and your hens stay fit as well.

Always keep a cock among your hens—hens like having it off as much as we do. Also, all animals thrive better if they can live in their natural social groups, which in the case of chickens means a harem of hens around a cock.

If you can let the hens run right out into the fields and woods so much the better. You will lose a few eggs from out-laying—but what does it matter? They will be getting so much free food that that will make up for a few clutches of eggs, and surprisingly often you will see a hen, apparently long-lost, come waddling back from who-knows-where with fourteen fine little chicks at her heels. Why go in for incubators and brooders and all that nonsense when hens will do all that work for nothing for you? And they know so much more about it than we do.

If you haven't got much space you will have to have a semi-intensive method of keeping hens. The best I have ever seen was the hennery of Lady Eve Balfour, the founder of the Soil Association. In her garden in Suffolk she kept her hens under the following arrangement. The hens lived in a henhouse. The house was surrounded by a wire fence, and inside the wire fence much straw or other litter was put. Lady Eve claimed that each hen made, with this litter, a ton of manure a year to go on her garden. Next to the straw pen were two small pens planted with grass and clover. Lady Eve used to let the hens into one of these two pens every day for a fortnight. She would then close that pen and let the hens into the other pen for a fortnight. Thus the grass and clover got a chance to rest and recover, and you saw none of that awful scratched-earth policy that you see with most semi-intensive henneries— all dust and holes and old tin cans and bunches of nettles. The hens do all their scratching in the straw yard, for that is where you throw their grain down for them. They thus only go into the grass and clover pen to peck grass and clover. If you had three grass and clover pens I believe it would be even better, for you could give the grass a longer rest, and if you rotated by grazing with ducks, geese, sheep or calves it would be excellent, for you would thus keep internal parasite infection at a minimum.

All poultry need access to grit: insoluble grit such as crushed flint for use in their crops and, if they are not running on limestone or other calcareous land a calcareous grit such as crushed sea-shells. It is a good plan to throw your used egg shells in the slow oven of the stove and then every few weeks pull them out and crush them up to powder and feed to the hens. The protein component of the mash can be a high-protein concentrate from the mill, or a mixture of, say, fish meal, meat meal, bone meal and soya bean meal in about equal proportions (although it doesn't matter). Boiled fish offal is excellent and if you can get plenty of it, or meat offal, this is the cheapest answer. You will get some eggs from grain and household scraps alone, but not many. If hens are really to produce eggs they must have some protein. The eggs of England derive largely from the trawling grounds of the Atlantic Shelf.

Sally has bought hens from the Belsen houses sometimes. Hens in batteries will only live about a year (we have had a hen laying at ten years old and laying really well). But before their first year is out battery hens are sick, like to die, and cannot be kept alive in the wire cages any longer. They are therefore sold for 'scrap', at prices as often as low as ten new pennies. Sally has bought them thus for half a crown, brought them home in the van, and turned them loose. Always some fail to survive the journey. It takes them two or three days to learn to *walk*—at first you have to carry them about. Within a week they have learned to do something they have never done before: that is scrap, or scratch about for food. Within a month they are new hens. The feathers grow back on their chafed and naked necks (they had worn the old feathers off on the wire), the sores and callouses on their breasts have healed, they learn to flap their wings, run, chase earwigs, and it does the heart good to see them. They will live and lay well for a couple of years sometimes but they never really recover the vigour and health of free-range-reared hens.

The trouble with the modern industrial hen (the 'hybrid') is that she does not go broody. Broodiness has been bred out of her, not being required by the agri-businessman. So if you wish to rear your own chicks naturally you will have to get some old-fashioned hens from somewhere. Light Sussex are a very good breed, for eggs, meat and rearing chicks, but they lay white eggs. The eggs are none the worse for being white but don't look so nice. Rhode Island Red is another fine breed, and lays brown eggs. The best thing you can get is the good-old backyard mongrel, result of a varied ancestry. If you want very brown eggs shove in a Cuckoo-Marran cockerel. He will father a brown-egg-laying brood, but they are not very prolific. My advice is stay away from the flighty highly-specialized egg-laying breeds like the modern hybrids and even the old White Leghorns. They will lay more eggs per year if highly fed and highly looked after, but they won't convert natural food so well, are no good for meat, and not so hardy. Also they are rotten mothers.

*Geese.* 'The full grown goose', Cobbett tells us, 'has solidity in it.' A pen of geese, say three geese and a gander, or two geese and a gander, or for that matter a gander and a goose, will run happily about the fields, and live on grass with just a handful of grain thrown to them every night to lure them home to shut them in from the foxes. They don't *need* any grain. When they begin to lay, say in February or March, if you are lucky enough to have broody hens then, or can beg, borrow or steal broody hens from a neighbour, you can steal the goose eggs from the geese and put them under the broody hens. You will have to splash the eggs with water every day, because a hen does not know about this part of a goose mother's duties. The hens will bring the young geese into the world, and look after them when they get there as well as the geese will. Also, by taking the eggs away from the geese you encourage your geese to lay more eggs. When you think that you are unlikely to get more than one more clutch of eggs out of your goose anyway—let her sit on a clutch (maybe fourteen. A hen will sit on six). But you must protect them from rats and foxes. Rats will pull goose eggs, or young geese, right out from under the feathers of the goose mother. A fox will go miles to get a sitting goose.

When you have your baby geese, waddling along behind their foster mother the hen, or their real mother the goose, feed them well at first on some meal and protein, but when they are teen-age geese they will begin to eat grass and they will live quite well on grass, and grow all summer. No goose should be eaten before Michaelmas, but it is then justifiable to celebrate with a Michaelmas goose. Straight off grass he will be 'green', he will not have 'solidity' in him. He won't be fat. Let the others go on running out on grass, with no more than the merest handful of corn to lure them in at night, until three weeks before you want to kill them. Some people say two weeks, or even ten days, but three weeks is quite enough. Then you must pen them and give them as much barley as they can eat. If you are going to kill them, or sell them, for Christmas don't forget they have got to hang for at least a week. Geese are very easy things to keep, they never get ill, and if you don't worry about setting their eggs under hens they are very good at hatching them out themselves, only you won't get so many geese. But after all, if a family eats half a dozen geese in a year it eats a lot of geese, and that is only half a clutch, so you don't *need* many geese unless you want to sell them.

*Ducks.* Ducks are not very good mothers, in the domesticated state, in fact I can't think of worse. They will drag their poor little chicks through the rough and the wet, lead them down to a muddy ditch, and before you know where you are they are all dead. Hens hatch ducks eggs out much better than ducks do, but if the ducks do do it then you must keep the ducks in coops, those old-fashioned hen coops where bars in front keep the mother inside while the babies can get out and run about. If you hatch ducks out under hens you must not let the ducklings go near the water: they lack the oil in their feathers that a mother duck would have given them and catch cold. Young ducks, in fact, should not be let go near water at all, until they become teen-age. They need plenty of clean water to drink of course, as indeed every living thing does. Feed them much as you would chickens.

When you want to eat your surplus cockerels, or ducks for that matter, it is a good idea to give them ten days fattening on barley meal mash before you kill them. Mix the mash with skimmed milk if you have it. If you don't bother to do this they also taste very good.

*Turkeys.* Turkeys thrive very well in the absence of hens, but if they run with hens you have got to medicinate their water or food with some stuff that protects them from blackhead, which they catch from the hens. They are tenderer as to climate than other poultry, and need shelter in bad weather. They eat what hens eat, but more of it.

## SHEEP

Now we come to sheep, and must hope that these animals will not object to being thrown in with a lot of cackling poultry.

Sheep are a very good thing to keep, for the self-supporter. For a sheep is of a size—a fat lamb is anyway—that makes it possible to eat him, in the winter at any rate, before the meat goes bad. If you can share your sheep between, say, four families, it means that each family gets one very good joint, either a leg or a shoulder, and a share of the ribs. Sheep live and fatten on grass. Don't even make demands on your hay unless the ground is covered with snow (and even then they won't eat hay unless they have previously learnt to); they are thus cheap to keep. Ewes only have one or two lambs at a time though, unlike sows which have a dozen or more, so their rate of increase is not high.

A self-supporting family might well keep half a dozen ewes, and consume all or most of their progeny throughout the year. The one slight complication here is—what about the ram? Does it really pay to keep a ram to serve only six sheep? An answer might be to ask a neighbouring farmer if you could borrow his ram for a few days. In a community, of course, this problem is much more easily solved as are so many other problems. If four families keep six sheep each it is quite justifiable to keep a ram for them all. If the people have any sense they will keep their respective sheep in one flock, which one person looks after. If grass is not short with you, well keep a ram by all means, even if he is underemployed. At least he will give you wool.

If you want a small sheep, and a small sheep is certainly best for the single-handed self-supporter, then I would suggest the Southdown as your best breed. She is not very prolific, which means less bother at lambing but fewer lambs, the mutton is very good and her conformation as a mutton animal unsurpassed; she is quiet and docile. If you live in the mountains, or on very rough ground, the Welsh Mountain is another small breed and has unsurpassed mutton. But you will have to fence well because he is as wild as a stag. If he can't get under he will get over, and he is quite unsuitable for folding, which we shall discuss later. If you want a big sheep, and are on good land, the Suffolk or a Suffolk cross are fine. But the advice

I would be inclined to give would be—choose the breed that is native to the country you live in. We had Suffolks while in Suffolk and Welsh in Wales but we crossed the Welsh with a Suffolk ram.

As to the husbandry of sheep, if you are not doing it commercially there is really very little to be said about it at all. Sheep eat grass. They will fatten on good grass in a summer time if they are not infected with internal parasites. Sheep men say the biggest enemy of a sheep is another sheep. The meaning of this is that sheep cannot stand overstocking. Very good pasture may carry three ewes with their lambs per acre, less good two ewes and their lambs. You might average one and a half lambs per ewe. But they will do far better if you rotate them around the farm: put them on, say, a quarter of your grass acreage and keep them there until they have nibbled the grass right down, then move them on to the next quarter. In this way let them *follow* the cows—sheep will graze very advantageously after cows have had all they can get: cows will starve after sheep.

The obvious plan is to lamb in the spring so that the lambs grow up on clean spring grass, have the summer growing season to fatten on, and are killed in the autumn and winter, so in the late winter 'hungry gap' you only have your small stock of ewes to feed. If your acreage is too small to winter your stock of ewes you can keep them indoors, at or least allow them to come indoors part of the time. You then must feed them on hay. And perhaps give them some oats, or other corn. Watch them carefully to see what sort of condition they are in.

If you have your own ram you can leave him with the ewes all the year, and leave their lambing date to them and him. If you borrow a ram try to do it so as to cause your ewes to lamb early but not too early: say about March. So put the ram in about the end of September and if you can keep him in for about six weeks. If you like put some reddle on his chest so that he marks the ewes as he serves them: then you know that they have been served and can even work out the date that they should lamb.

Folding sheep in the winter on arable land is a possibility, particularly in dry climates and on light land. Grow swedes, or mangolds (swedes are best), rape or kale. We never have done it but it 'does' the land, as farmers say, i.e., is good for it, gets the sheep off pasture giving the worms time to die out there, and rests the grass. Sheep need hay while folded thus on roots, and if you want to fatten them feed them corn too. Crushed oats and kibbled beans are very good. Give them as much as they will clear up quickly and no more (maybe a pound a day). But if you are just out for simplicity, and your own good mutton when you feel like it, I would suggest just leave them out to grass.

When they lamb there should be no problems, but if there are they will probably be the same sort of problems that we discussed at length when dealing with the cow. The same rules apply. If a ewe has a dead lamb and another has twins, it is advantageous to foist one of the twins on to the bereaved mother. Put the bereaved one in a small pen (four hurdles tied together) or a shed, rub the live lamb all over with the body of the dead lamb, and try lamb and foster mother together. If she knocks him for six take him out, skin the dead lamb and put the skin on the live lamb like a jersey. This nearly always works. After a day or two remove the skin and the adoption is permanent. You can then let them both out. If a lamb is very weakly, feed it cow's milk with a little glucose or honey mixed with it, warmed to blood heat. Many smallholders rear orphan lambs on bottles: Sally does nearly every year. I am against it but the children love it. And it is one way of getting cheap mutton *if*—and here lies the rub—you have the heart to kill them after you have brought them up as their mother. You must feed them very often for the first week or two, getting it down to say three times a day after a fortnight, twice a day after a month. It is an awful labour; they never do as well as natural sheep, they are an incredible nuisance, will follow you round baa'ing and bleating and trying to knock you over, will never, or hardly ever, join a proper flock of sheep, and if they don't get into your garden sooner or later and absolutely wreck it, then it is a miracle. They are murderous to fruit trees.

You do not shear your lambs their first summer, but the ewes, or any sheep left over from the previous year, you must shear in May, June or July. In Pembrokeshire we do it in June, to get it over with before the hay-making season. Shearing cannot be taught by a book and I am not going to attempt to do it. You must watch a skilled man and get him to teach you. You can sell the wool, but Sally always keeps a fleece or two back to spin on her hand-spinning wheel to use for knitting. After the shearing you must, if you live below seven or eight hundred feet, either dip your sheep or spray them against fly. Sheep fly are revolting green blow flies which lay their eggs on the dirty parts of sheep whereupon maggots hatch out and literally eat the sheep alive. If you have a few sheep only you might guard against this evil by constant vigilance. You should always keep sheep clean—when you see dung clinging to the backsides of sheep you should *clat* them—that is cut the dunged wool off with the sheep shears. If you see a sheep constantly twitching her tail catch her and examine for maggots. If you find these wash them off with dip or strong disinfectant. But I like dipping, because then you do not have to worry about 'fly strike' at all. Also it kills keds, another very nasty parasite of sheep. We always buy a proprietory dip, but if you object to unknown chemicals you can make one up with 2½ lbs. white arsenic, 2½ lbs. washing soda, 8 lbs. flowers of sulphur, 10 lbs. soft soap and 100 gallons of water. Sulphur alone is a preventive against fly, although it won't kill keds. Maybe you had better just go along to the chemist. We have a sheep dip, but spraying is equally good, or, in days gone by, we have used a tin bath.

You can kill your first lamb at three months old. Lambs are generally considered fit for sale at about 70 to 75 lbs. live weight. Personally I like mutton, and I think that a three-year-old wether (castrated ram), well fatted and well hung, is the best meat in the world. If you are going to kill your lambs before their first Christmas, or even soon after, you need not castrate them. If you are going to keep them on much longer then you should castrate, and you can do this very simply with a knife, a Burdizzo, or the new rubber rings. The latter require no skill and don't seem to cause the lamb much annoyance. You can then keep your wethers on for two or three years, if you can spare the grass. You can fatten them, for from two to four months, on such things as swedes, hay, crushed oats or maize or whatever corn you can get; and a small proportion of barley meal perhaps but not too much: it is heating for the sheep. Beans too are good but not more than a quarter of a pound per sheep per day.

## GOATS

Goats are creatures that I would never keep if I could possibly keep cows. Their milk is as good as cows' milk, as goat keepers will never tire of telling you, and is in fact better for invalids. (But if you are a self-supporter you will not be an invalid.) They can give up to two gallons a day, but the idea that they will do this on sticks and stones is an illusion. They want pretty high feeding, on expensive concentrates, to give very much milk at all. They will not eat much grass but do very well on wild brushwood and herbage. If you have some acres of rough hillside, or heath, goats might be your answer. They tether very well, on roadsides and the like. But they do not like rain, or too much cold. They are not hardy animals. They should be housed at night. Killed, they are edible but stringy. Hardly any fence will contain them and they will ruin your young fruit trees sooner or later—no matter what you do to stop them. I like goats one way only—and that is in curry.

## RABBIT

Rabbits are an obvious source of meat for the self-supporter, and their skins are fine to cure and make hats or waistcoats out of. It is said that three does and a buck will give you a rabbit to eat every three days of the year; but I think if I tried to eat a rabbit every three days of the year I should get fed up with them. We have made several attempts to keep them, but the general trouble, smell and mess has generally made us give up in the end. If you had good hutches, out of the rain, easily kept clean, and the time and patience to collect endless green stuff, they might be a source of cheap meat. They need some concentrate too though, oats or bran or the like. And keep the buck away from the does when they are kidding.

## PIGEONS

A pigeon loft is an obvious source of meat, and they say that the pigeons will feed off your neighbours' crops and not yours, but I have never kept them. There is a magnificent medieval pigeon tower at Dunster in Somerset, the round wall of which is perforated with hundreds of pigeon holes, and with a revolving ladder inside which enables the pigeon keeper to climb up and help himself to any pigeon he chooses. The adults should never be eaten, for pigeons pair for life, but each pair lays a pair of eggs every six weeks right through the year, fattens the resulting squabs up to one pound in weight each and then lays two more eggs. So if the squabs are harvested just before the new eggs are laid a constant supply of meat can be obtained. The adults live and lay for seven years. Corneaux and Mondain are the best food breeds.

# 9
## Meat

*The running to the butcher's daily is a ridiculous thing.*
WILLIAM COBBETT: Cottage Economy

And a very expensive thing as well.

### BEEF

We send an ox a year to the slaughterhouse. The slaughterhouse charges about three pounds to kill it but they pay us three pounds for the skin so this doesn't cost us anything, but there is the carriage in there and the fetching of the meat back.

We could kill the meat here of course. I have killed several bullocks in Africa and shot and cut up many a wild buffalo which is almost exactly the same thing. But to kill an ox you need a clean airy building which is high enough to hang him up in, and the means for hauling him up. After all, a very big ox *can* weigh a ton. I know a farmer who gets the butcher to come and kill his bullocks for him, in his hay barn, and he hoists the carcase up with the fore-end loader of his tractor.

You can only consider killing an ox in the winter of course (in Africa the meat had to feed thirty or forty people so it didn't have to keep). And really the individual family can only consider killing, or having killed, an ox if there is a deep freeze. A family without one might conceivably cope with one quarter of an ox, so if there were four families in some sort of community, or at least in liaison with each other, and no deep freeze, an ox might be killed between them occasionally, but they would then have to salt a lot. Salt beef is all very well but, like the sailors of old, one can have too much of it.

MEAT

We kill our ox when he is too young to die. The reason for this is that if he were, say, a three-year-old ox he would be too big to go in our deep freeze. It would be far better if we had a neighbour who also wanted to kill an ox every year. We could then take alternate years to kill our ox, and let him grow to three years at least and four years preferably and fat him as a bullock should be fattened. The sort of two-year-old or eighteen-month-old 'beef' that is sold nowadays is not proper beef at all. If you ever do get a roasting joint from a well fatted four-year-old animal, hung until it is a deep red colour and has a proper beefy smell to it, and not over roasted, you will see what I mean.

I used to have a fairly rough and ready way of killing, skinning and cutting up a beast, but a butcher friend of mine has given me the following advice:

Shoot or humane-kill the animal in the brain.

Stick just in front of the breast bone (sternum). Cut just deeply enough to sever the main blood vessels and let the animal bleed—do not stick too deep. With the shot animal lying on the ground, stand near its throat with your back to it, push its head up with one leg and its forelegs down with the other, and cut just in front of the brisket. Cut in carefully and you will find the you have severed the main blood vessels.

Whatever you do don't cut into the chest cavity. The animal cannot kick you in its nervous port-mortem kickings because you are standing too near to it. (Catch the blood either for black puddings, or to mix with the pigs' mash, or to activate the compost heap.)

Chop off the horns and skin the head.

Cut the throat across the larynx; tie off the weasand (wind pipe) and cut through it and go on cutting to the occipital joint (the first vertebra) and cut the head right off.

Cut through the tarsals and carpals (the knee joints). With a little practice you can find them and cut through without having to use a saw or a chopper. Open up the gam cords ready for the gamble (see Chapter 6).

Cut the skin right along the belly line without cutting into the abdominal wall. Skin the neck and the brisket and pull most of the hide off the belly but don't yet skin the fore shanks.

Insert the point of the knife gently through the abdominal wall just behind the brisket, shove your hand behind the knife so as to protect the innards from the knife, and cut right along centre line of belly to the cod fat (around the penis).

Remove the caul fat (the membrane to which the guts are attached). Empty the bladder (*not* over the meat!), split the buttock so that the bung, or arse-hole, can fall out, and tie the latter off (that means tie it with a piece of string so nothing can come out of it).

Saw through the breast bone (sternum) from the neck backwards. If you don't do this now, with the beast lying on the ground, you'll never do it later, for the guts will hang down and prevent you from doing it, and the guts can't come out until you have done it.

Insert the gamble and hoist the beast half off the ground.

Get the skin off the hind quarters and off the tail.

Hoist right up and the innards will fall right out.

Remove the liver carefully. Excise the gall bladder from it.

Cut the diaphragm away.

Haul out pluck (heart and lungs). Clean out chest cavity of odd bits and pieces.

Finish flaying. Haul the hide right off.

Split the carcase in two. (I would do this next day, but my friend didn't say so.)

Trim out all blood vessels, etc. Wipe it all down inside with a clean warm moist cloth.

You should treat the intestines as I recommended for pig's small intestines and salt down for big sausage casings (see Chapter 6).

There are four stomachs:

1. The *rumen*, or paunch, which is enormous. Open and clean it in a running brook, take it home, scald it with boiling water, scrape inside, put in brine for a few days. When you want it boil it and cool it in clean brine. Cut it up and cook it

as you desire. Tripe, well seasoned and piping hot, is a dish very much too good for a king.

2. The *reticulum*, or honeycomb stomach. Do as above, and it is fine for Tripe Normandy, but this is not a cookery book.

3. The *omasum* or 'Bible-bag'. Good only for the pigs.

4. The *abomasum* or reed. Where, in a young calf, the rennet comes from. Open and wash and it is good for tripe. Or the dogs?

The hooves should be scalded, when you can pull the hard hooves off leaving 'cow heels'. These make 'calves-foot jelly', or are marvellous in brawn.

The *suet*, which is the dry crumbly fat inside the belly, should be kept for puddings, mincemeat, etc. All ordinary fat surplus to requirements as part of a joint can be rendered down for dripping.

Now we have the weighty job of jointing our beef. Here I would strongly advise you to get a butcher to help you, at least the first time that you cut up a steer. Get him to do it slowly, and *label*, whatever you do, the joints that he cuts out of it. I am not going to describe the indescribable: that is how to joint a side of beef. It cannot be conveyed in words. It cannot be conveyed in pictures either, for you are trying to depict a three-dimensional matter of great complexity on a two-dimensional piece of paper. See the drawing, however, and here—very important—is a list of what the various cuts should be used for:

| | |
|---|---|
| Roasting joints: | topside |
| | sirloin |
| | ribs |
| | 'leg of mutton' |
| Steak meat: | rump |
| | fillet |
| Stewing meat: | shin and fore shin |
| | neck |
| | thin flank |
| Pickling meat: | silverside |

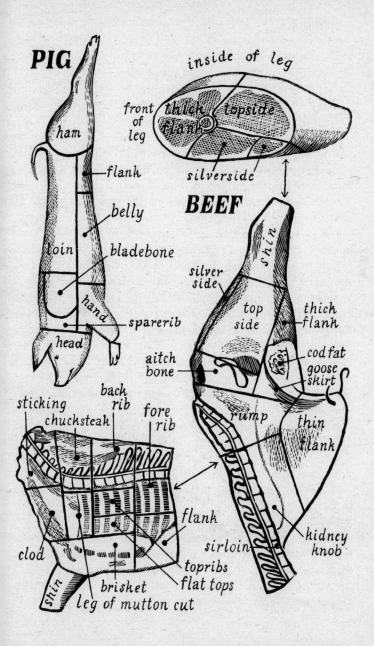

**PIG**

ham

flank

belly

loin

bladebone

hand

sparerib

head

inside of leg

front
of
leg

thick
flank

topside

silverside

**BEEF**

shin

silver
side

top
side

thick
flank

aitch
bone

cod fat
goose
skirt

rump

thin
flank

sticking

chucksteak

back
rib

fore
rib

clod

shin

brisket

leg of mutton cut

flank

topribs

flat tops

sirloin

kidney
knob

| | |
|---|---|
| Salting meat: | brisket |
| Sausage meat: | shin and fore shin |
| | neck |
| | thin flank |
| | brisket |
| Dog meat: | The stuck (the bit the knife went into) |

Any of the stewing bits will make soup. While on the subject of soup, the deep freeze comes to the aid of the would-be disciples of Mrs Beeton today. There is nothing in the world so nourishing as good 'beef stock'. In the small household of today we cannot have a stock pot constantly simmering over the fire. But we can boil up gallons of good stock all at once and freeze it. Simply boil it up for a long time, bones and all (bones especially), and all odd bits, cow heels too. Pour it off the bones and let cool. Take off fat. Reduce it some more if you like and freeze it into cubes in your ice-cube moulds, or pour into cartons, leaving $\frac{1}{2}''$ space at the top of the carton otherwise the stuff will expand over it. If you have a few dozen of these frozen blocks of beef stock in your freezer you can make the most magnificent soup whenever you want to, by simply throwing a block into the pot together with whatever vegetables or whatever you are making soup out of. Pour into polythene bag and put that in a square carton to shape it first. Stock is one thing that does not deteriorate in the slightest in the deep freeze, provided you get all the fat off it first. It does not want 'thawing'—just throw the ice straight into the pot. Try one day cooking some soup like this and at the same time heating up some tinned or packeted soup, to compare them.

But back to our joints. There is method in it all: it is not just superstition. Steaks must be cut across the grain of tender muscle. Muscle that does a lot of work, like the silverside, is tough. Silverside is on the outside of the leg and takes a lot of stresses while the beast is walking about: therefore it is tough and gristly and not too good for roasting, but it is prime beef just the same. It just happens to be very good for pickling. To pickle it prick it over with a needle, rub it with saltpetre and brown sugar and let it stand for 24 hours. Then put it in the brine tub for 8 to 10 days.

*The brine tub.* Brine should be clean water and salt boiled and allowed to cool. The concentration of salt should be such that a potato should float in it. If the potato sinks you haven't got enough salt. Any meat will keep indefinitely in brine: it was brined beef that took Drake round the world. The brine tub should have a loose round board under the meat, tradition-ally with holes bored through it, and another such board on top of the meat with a stone on it to keep the meat down. Do *not* use a metal weight for this purpose ever. Dorothy Hartley in her great book (it will become a world classic in time and will be read long after Mrs B. has been forgotten) *Food in England* (Macdonald), is good on how to treat and cook salted meats.

If you must try to cut up your steer yourself, this is the order in which you should tackle it:

*Forequarter:* Cut off the brisket, then the ribs, then the 'leg of mutton'.

*Hindquarter:* Cut off thin flank; then sirloin, aitchbone, shank, thick flank; then separate the topside out; then the silverside. You have left the thick rump of flank. Cut the best of this for steaks and boil the rest.

Of course all beef is eatable (even the bit the harness rubbed against!) and if you hack at it in complete ignorance you will still get a great number of good meals. But you will be roasting what you ought to grill, and grilling what you ought to boil and all the rest of it. Your ox is a very valuable animal. You could sell him nowadays for well over a hundred pounds. Surely it is worth the expense of having a butcher attend to him, or sending him to the municipal slaughterhouse and then bribing one of the butchers there to cut him up properly for you? If you do this go to any trouble that it takes to label each joint, and when you put the joints in the deep freeze label them in such a manner that the labels do not come off and you can really read them. Otherwise you might as well be hacking into a frozen mammoth. Everything that goes into the deep freeze has to go in a closed polythene bag.

The stewing meat, and I should classify a lot of it as this if I were you, is far better cut up in small pieces *before* you put it in the deep freeze in polythene bags of a size suitable for making one good stew for you.

*Potting* is another way of preserving beef:

1. Lay it in salt for three days.
2. Wash the salt off.
3. Season with a pinch of saltpetre, herbs and spices.
4. Put some suet and butter on top of it.
5. Leave it in a slow oven all night.
6. Pour off the fat.
7. Cut the beef up small and put, hot, into a pot.
8. Press down tight and pour on top of it clear strained fat—very hot.
9. Cover with greaseproof paper when cold.

It will keep for a couple of months.

Fresh beef should be well hung before eating. Ten days in cold weather is not too much. The older the animal the longer the hanging—a fortnight for a four-year old, if you ever have one.

Veal should be eaten within three of four days of slaughter though. But veal should be left to the French. We cannot afford to waste potential beef animals in that wanton manner, except a few to get rennet out of.

*The tongue:* soak in boiled spiced cold brine (with the silver-side if you like). Leave it there for six days. Bake it in oven. Skin it. Pot it and cover with clarified butter and/or suet as for potted beef.

Our ox keeps us lavishly in beef for a year.


## MUTTON

We kill two or three sheep a year, and now that we have got the deep freeze it is a very easy business indeed. I shoot the sheep with the .22 (in Africa we used to stun him with the back of an axe), lay him on his left side and stick him just below and behind the ear. One should then break his neck by grasping his lower jaw with one's left hand, placing right hand over his poll and jerking upwards. I omit this part of the little ceremony because, with the .22 bullet, he is already as dead as mutton.

I then skin his legs and throat out, open his throat, tie off his weazand and then haul him up on the gamble.

Finishing skinning him (and as much as possible of this should be done with the fist—not with the knife. The hide should not be cut, nor should the meat, and large areas of fat and flesh should not be left sticking to the hide). I rip his belly from the brisket upwards, remove the caul, cut the bung loose and tie it off, remove the bladder and *hulk* the sheep— that is haul out his stomachs and guts. As you do so you must pull his food pipe through his diaphragm. Then split the breast bone, remove the pluck (liver, lights and heart), wipe him out inside with a clean warm wet cloth and put in a stick called a 'back set', which is to spread him open and let the air in. The large intestine can be used for sausage casings.

Hang him a week, but of course you can begin to eat bits and pieces before that—the liver of course the first day. In Africa I used to kill a sheep in the dry season, when the days were as hot as hell but the nights were freezing. I would hang the meat outside at night out of leopard reach, bring it in early in the morning and wrap it up in many sheets of newspaper. Like this I could keep it for a month.

While on the subject of Africa I must here mention *biltong*. *Biltong* is salted and dried strips of buck meat or beef and it is almost worshipped by South Africans. Living in the back-veld of South West Africa, as I used to do, *biltong* formed an impor- tant part of my diet. If I shot a gemsbok or a kudu I would turn a very large part of it into *biltong*. I have made it in Wales since then, in fact I made some last year, out of beef, and it has been perfectly successful. The only drawback is you need prime cuts really; *biltong* made from odd bits of scrag end is not really much good.

But this is the way you do it. Cut lean meat up into strips, say an inch square but the longer the better, along the grain, or fibre, of the meat. This is most important: do not cut it across the grain. Lay it in dry salt for six hours. Wash the salt off it and hang it—if in southern Africa in the dry season—in the shade but in the breeze—if in the British Isles in the chimney. I leave mine in the chimney, in light smoke, for say three days, take it down, hang it up in the kitchen, and it is perfect *biltong*. It is as hard as hickory. To eat it you just pare or shred little shavings off the end of it across the grain with your Joseph Roger 'Lambsfoot' knife (old back-velders will know what I mean), put it on bread and butter, and it is delicious.

*Rennet.* If you kill calves you can make your own rennet, or you can make it if you cadge a few calf stomachs off a butcher. The calves must have been young suckling calves. The fourth stomach is the one you want and it is known, to rennet-makers, as the *vell*. Take your vell, or more if you have them, clean them with a cloth but don't wash them. Sprinkle dry salt on them and leave for a day or two or until they are needed. Then cut them into strips, put in water which should have had salt added and been boiled and then cooled. If you have four vells you will want a gallon of this brine: if one vell a quarter of a gallon. Soak the strips in the brine for five days, squeezing the strips in the hands three times a day to get the rennet out. Strain the brine off carefully and that is your rennet. You will need eight times as much as this for a cheese recipe as you would need of bought rennet. Sally and I have never made it and I got this out of a book.

## POULTRY

To kill a chicken grab its legs in your left hand, put your right hand over the back of its head, bend the head upwards at the same time stretching its neck. It is a turning movement of the hand. You will feel the spine snap. If you do it too hard you will pull the head off which doesn't matter but it looks disgusting.

Start plucking immediately if you are going to dry pluck. Every second counts, for the feathers come out easily when the bird is warm but very uneasily when it is getting cold. Sit down, put the wings (which will go on flapping violently for a time) between your knees, and quickly pluck the feathers off the breast. You will soon learn how to pluck without tearing the skin—it's matter of experience, and Old Mother Common Sense. Then pluck the whole bird. Sally and I sit, in the winter, and do it in front of the fire and throw the feathers straight on the fire, but the true self-supporter will not do this. The feathers should be preserved for stuffing pillows. If you do this with them pile them in a very slow oven, or on a grid over the stove, for some hours to dry first. At the very least throw them on the compost heap, where they will help to activate the compost. We are just lazy, and comfort-loving.

Singe the bird and hang it up by its legs in the meat safe (away from the flies).

Next day take the plucked bird, cut round its knees and haul its legs off, lay it on its tummy on the bench, stick a knife right through the flesh on the back of its neck above the spine and move the knife towards the head, taking it right out before getting to the head. This leaves a flap of skin and flesh with which to cover the neck-hole when you stuff the bird.

Take a pair of secateurs and snip the spine as near to the body as you can get. As you have already broken the spine near the head the neck will now come out. Put it in the giblet bowl.

Cut off the head and put it in the pig bucket.

Insert your finger in the neck-hole and describe a circle with your finger breaking away all the ligaments or whatever they are by which the innards of the bird are anchored to the neck flesh. In other words insert your finger, bend it, and revolve the bird through 360 degrees. You will feel the ligaments breaking.

Carefully cut right round the arse-hole so as not to pierce

the rectum, and start extracting the guts. Remove the soft fat that clings to the intestines and drop the latter in the pig bucket. I always make a cut each side of the hole I have got after this to enlarge it so that I can get my whole hand in. Put your hand in, keeping the back of it hard up against the inside of the back of the bird, and haul out all the machinery. Cut off the gall bladder and keep the liver in the giblets. Take the gizzard and cut half round it with a knife—but only severing the first layer. Pull that layer off—leaving a yellow bag full of grit. Throw the grit bag away and keep the outside as a giblet. Giblet soup. Legs too.

Make sure you get the lungs out (they are tiny) and the crop. The latter is right up in the neck end. These go in the pig bucket.

Wipe the inside with a clean warm moist cloth. Truss your bird in any fancy way you have. If it is young, stuff it and roast it. If it is old, boil it.

Ducks serve the same. Ducks are prime to eat at exactly 10 weeks, no more, no less.

Geese and turkeys are too large and tough to break their necks as I have described for chickens. Hold your bird by its legs also holding its wing-tips in your hands so it can't flap. Lower its head towards the ground. It will automatically lift its head, making an angle of its neck. Get your wife to lay a broom-stick over its neck. Stand on the broom-stick with one foot each side of the bird's neck and pull the legs upwards. Suddenly you will feel the spine in the neck snap. Don't pull the head off.

Singeing is done to remove the fluff and quills. You can do it with a burning bit of paper, a gas jet, or a meths sponge.

Wet-plucking is a grisly business, but if you want to do it (it is quicker) scald the bird for 30 seconds at 125° F. (52°C.) or for 5 seconds at 180°F. (82°C.).

# 10

# Grass

*Earth's increase, foison plenty,*
*Barns and garners never empty.*

WILLIAM SHAKESPEARE : The Tempest

The crop that covers most of the human inhabited world is
grass. This means, in the British Isles, grass and clover: in
many other parts of the world grass and various edible bushes.
Humans cannot eat grass, and so they must get it at second
hand, through animals, in the form of meat, milk or eggs.

Grassland, in the British Isles at least, can be classified as
either permanent pasture or ley (temporary pasture). It can
be divided cornerways to this too: into grazing land and hay
land.

Some of the best grassland in the world is permanent
pasture, and it is a crime to plough it up. Some of the finest
fattening pastures in England, such as the Romney Marsh
and some of the Leicestershire fattening pastures, were ploughed
up during the Second World War, owing to stupid decisions
made by ignorant people, and have never yet recovered. Much
permanent pasture, though, is pretty rough, and not very
productive. It can be rendered more so by ploughing up and
re-seeding, or by treatment that does not involve ploughing
up. Very heavy and drastic harrowing does a lot of good;
you can drag it about until it looks as if most of the grass has
been destroyed and the grass will be the better for it. Dressing
with lime if it needs lime will often work wonders, as will slag
or other phosphorous dressing. Both lime and phosphate
encourage the clover at the expense of the grasses, and this is
generally all to the good. Good draining is, of course, a *sine
qua non*. Grass (when I use the word grass I mean grass and

clover) will give you far more yield if you graze it really hard all at one time, and then rest it completely, rather than if you keep nibbling at it all the time. This is because the individual plants put down much better root growth if they are not kept nibbled off all the time. It is always a good thing to *top* grass, when it needs it, either with a mower of some sort or a scythe. This cuts the flowering heads off that the animals have left and forces the grass to make leaf instead of going to seed, and also kills the thistles. The application of nitrogen encourages the grasses and suppresses the clovers. This is because the clovers make their own nitrogen out of the atmosphere, by means of the symbiotic bacteria which live in their root nodules. This gives them an unfair advantage over the grasses. If you apply soluble nitrogen you take away this unfair advantage, and the grasses will grow at the expense of the clover. If you want very high yields from grass you must put on nitrogen and sacrifice the clovers. Personally I would prefer to give adequate phosphates and lime, and potash if it needs it, and thus encourage the clovers and then I don't have to *pay* for my nitrogen: the clover makes it. It has been proved conclusively that the grass produced by heavy applications of nitrogen is not so nutritious as that grown otherwise, but of course if you are, say, selling hay what does that matter? If you are using the hay yourself though it is a very different story. Also nitrogen in the bag is expensive. And if ever there is a power shortage (nitrogen is fixed commercially from the air by the expenditure of electrical power) it will become more so. Heavy applications of farmyard manure do nothing but good. The manure rots down and disappears very quickly: actually the earthworms drag it down into the soil. But if it is cow manure don't graze the land with cows for a while—no animal likes grazing near its own droppings. Where cows have been grazing in a field for long you will find long green tufts of grass growing around, or after, their droppings. The cows will not touch these. Put horses in though, or sheep, and the tufts will very soon go. This is another excellent reason for mixed stocking and not mono-stocking.

It is as well if you can retain some permanent pasture in your holding, if you are going to keep any animals. I remember in the Karroo, in the Cape Province, my employer on a big sheep farm had ploughed up some *veld* (which was all sparsely growing Karroo bushes) and planted lucerne, which he irrigated. In these paddocks he put his pedigree rams. They began to sicken and some of them died. The vet told him to re-fence the paddocks, taking in some of the Karroo pasture. He did this and immediately the rams got better. Ley pasture can be extremely productive, but permanent pasture will have more of those minerals and vitamins that animals require. So keep some permanent pasture if you can possibly afford the land.

If you want to break up permanent pasture to make arable land, or to plough and re-seed, then take my advice and do it with pigs. Shove in your unringed pigs, fold them over the land in *small* patches and move them on when they've thoroughly rooted up the small patches; pull the land about behind them with a spring-tine harrow or a spring cultivator; broadcast your seed. Another way (which we have tried) is to plough the old pasture up rough and as you do it plough Jerusalem artichokes in. Do this in the winter or very early spring. The artichokes will grow and smother every living thing under them with their dense, jungle-like cover. They will, if there are any about, attract pheasants by the score. Never mind the pheasants—put the pigs in, in late summer, fold them over the field all autumn and winter, and the pigs will thrive and leave the land as clean as a whistle. In the spring you can do what you want with it.

Probably the most profitable use of a small piece of land would be to farm it on a rotation that included one year in four of a one-year ley. The famous Norfolk Four Course Rotation (wheat—roots—barley—one-year ley) is an example of this. With the great variety of crops that the self-supporter will tend to grow his rotations must be far more complicated. You might grow something like: wheat—roots or kale to be fed to stock, potatoes or any of a great variety of row crops that have to be hoed and thus lend themselves to the suppression of weeds, 'cleaning crops' they are called—then spring corn of some sort, barley, spring wheat or oats—and undersow this with your ley: a grass and clover mixture. If you have decided on a one-year ley this mixture will be chiefly Italian rye-grass and red clover. A typical seeds mixture for a one-year ley might be: 20 lbs. Italian rye, 8 lbs. red clover, 1 lb. alsike. Italian rye-grass gives an 'early bite', that is it comes up early in the year when everything is dying for grass—soon after the 'hungry gap'. In fact it shortens the latter and therefore it is very valuable. You broadcast this seeds mixture after you have either broadcast or drilled your spring corn (barley, oats or spring wheat or rye—you couldn't undersow maize of course). You then harrow the land and the seeds mixture will come up as an undercrop, with the corn as a nurse crop. When you cut the corn you will have a good stand of grass and clover. Graze it lightly the first autumn (the treading of the stock will help consolidate the plants), rest it throughout the winter, and rejoice in an 'early bite' in March or April. After having had a full summer's use out of it—for grazing or hay—plough it up in the autumn and sow your winter wheat in it. The winter corn will benefit by the high fertility that is put into the soil by the ploughing in of all that grass and clover, plus the droppings of the animals that have grazed on it. The 'root break', that comes after the winter corn, is the one that gets the heavy dressings of farmyard manure. If you can put up to twenty tons to the acre on the land before you sow the roots, or plant the spuds, so much the better. If you go on treating your land in this way, and really hoe your roots or cleaning crop, and really do it all well, your land will increase steadily in fertility, workability and freedom from perennial weeds. When you die you will leave something valuable behind you: land in good heart. There's an immortality that is worth having.

You can, though, improve on the Norfolk Four Course Rotation by the addition of a pig break. There are several possibilities here. You should anyway run pigs over your potato and root ground after you have lifted the crop to clean it up and get what you have left. Or you could fold pigs on the one-year ley in the autumn and winter instead of ploughing it up. The pigs will plough it up for you. But that means that you can't get winter wheat in it that year—you'll have to follow the pigs with a spring-sown crop, either roots or spring corn. There are endless variations that you can play. Remember though that roots (turnips, mangolds, fodder beet, sugar beet, potatoes, and cabbages, kale or rape by favour) are your cleaning crop. You must hoe them and hoe them and kill the weeds. The ley, whether one, two or three years old, is your putting-back-of-fertility crop. You are, with it, plough-ing in a lot of vegetable matter which all rots down to humus. The winter corn, probably wheat, is a 'cash crop' in that it draws a lot out of the land. So does the spring corn, but that acts as a nurse for your ley. The roots, too, are a feeding crop in that you ought to manure them heavily, to the benefit not only of them but of the crops that come after.

If you want to have a two- or three-year ley, or longer, then you will need a much more complicated seeds mixture, and this is a fairly typical one:

> 12 lbs. perennial rye-grass
> 8 lbs. Italian rye-grass
> 6 lbs. cocksfoot grass
> 2 lbs. red clover
> 2 lbs. late red clover
> 1 lb. alsike
> 1 lb. Dutch white clover.

But your agricultural adviser from the Ministry of Agri-culture will advise you on a suitable mixture for your district.

If you want to put down permanent pasture you could have something like this:

> 14 lbs. perennial rye-grass
> 8 lbs. cocksfoot
> 4 lbs. timothy
> 1 lb. rough-stalked meadow grass

4 lbs. late-flowering red clover

1 lb. wild white clover

—

= 32 lbs. per acre.

In the above the red clover is to give a good bulk of clover the first year. If you can bear to sacrifice this bulk in the first year I would leave it out. This will give the wild white a better chance, and it is the wild white that is going to give you your permanent clover component. On very good rich land I would omit the cocksfoot. It will grow too coarse and rampant, and is rather an unpalatable grass anyway. Cut the timothy out on dry soils, it only really comes into its own on wet land. On light land cut the rough-stalked meadow grass out: that again is a wet land crop, or on good strong loams or clays. Again don't hesitate to get expert advice about your particular locality. There's nothing to beat the advice of your farming neighbours.

Deep rooting herbs are often included in permanent grass mixtures. M.Mc G. Cooper suggests:

$1\frac{1}{2}$–2 lbs. chicory

$1\frac{1}{2}$–2 lbs. burnet

1 lb. ribgrass or plantain

1 lb. sheeps parsley.

Personally I should leave out the plantain. M. McG. Cooper's book *Grassland Farming* is, incidentally, a very good one.

To establish your pasture, broadcast the seed on a very good firm seedbed either in the spring alone, in the spring under a nurse crop (barley or oats or spring wheat) or in late summer. If spring-sown graze it lightly later in the first summer. If sown in the late summer graze it lightly in the late spring. Don't overgraze it the first summer.

*Hay.* The earlier you cut the hay the more nutritious it will be, but the smaller the tonnage of it. We cut ours in July after the sheep shearing. Good weather is absolutely all-important.

If it stays fine you may get all your hay under cover in a few days and it will be perfect.

Cutting can be done by scythe, horse mower or powered mower. A man is supposed to be able to cut an acre a day with a scythe. I have cut hay with a scythe, in South West Africa of all places, and very hard work it is too. You must keep the blade as sharp as a razor, and use a finer wetstone (or 'rubber') than that which you would use for corn. A horse-drawn mower needs two good horses. Pulling a mower is very hard work for horses. The French have experimented with a horse-drawn mower the blade of which is driven not by the ground wheels, but by a fractional horse-power petrol motor—like a chain saw motor. This is said to be wonderfully effective, and its consumption of fuel is almost negligible. I have not seen it, but believe such machines can be seen working at Anthony, near Paris. Power mowers can be reciprocating or rotary. This year our hay was late, badly laid and matted and we hired a neighbour with a rotary mower. It made a very good job.

The old-fashioned method (in which I was brought up) was to turn the swathes by hand either with a pitch fork or a wooden rake, according to taste. As you turn them over fluff them up. Nowadays you can get an astonishing variety of machines to do this for you. There were some good machines that were pulled by horses for doing this work. When the hay is dry rake it up into big windrows, either with the big wooden drag-rake or with a horse-rake. You can still occasionally pick a horse rake up fairly cheaply and they are good tools. Then, when you are sure it is dry enough, the old idea was to cock it. Pile it up into little mini-stacks higher than a man and dome-shaped. Let it dry in the cock until the green has really gone out of it. If it is still too moist, and heating inside the cock, well then you must break the cocks and spread it about a bit. If it comes on to rain you must rush out and cock it quickly. In the cock it won't take much harm. When it is quite dry you can cart it, and stack it. Either stack it in a barn or else thatch the stack with straw or rushes.

Even then your troubles are not over. If it is stacked out of doors you must cut it with a stack knife before you can feed it. And that's a job to make the sweat run down your face.

The modern way is to bale it. There are plenty of contractors who will do this work, but everybody wants them at once. The modern way is to throw the hay about hard as soon as it is cut—scatter it well. There is a great variety of machines to do this, all tractor-drawn. As soon as it is anything like dry (you keep turning it about with machines as often as you can) you get it into windrows again and bale it. If the baler is busy somewhere else that day and can't come—and it pours with rain that night—well you may lose half the value of your hay and you may lose it altogether. If you can bale it though, it is pretty safe. But as soon as you can get the bales under cover. You can then heave a mighty sigh of relief and turn to a well-earned gallon or two of home brewed beer.

If you start the winter with at least a ton of hay per head of large stock (cows and horses) and a few tons for any sheep you may have, you can feel fairly secure. A very good yield is two tons per acre: you may get less. You can bump up the yield of grass enormously by applications of nitrogenous fertilizer, if you have no ideological objections to this. Personally I have pecuniary ones, but I do it on a modest scale sometimes nevertheless.

# II

# Wheat and Bread

*Without bread, all is misery. The Scripture truly calls it the staff of life: and it may be called, too, the pledge of peace and happiness in the labourer's dwelling.*

WILLIAM COBBETT: Cottage Economy

In case anybody should read this book who just does not know what the cultivation of the land and the growing of crops are all about at all, I will here describe, in the simplest way that I can, what is involved in these operations. Before man comes on the scene land is probably either covered with forest or with grass. If covered with forest men can cut down the trees, burn them, scratch the ground between the stumps and sow seed. In the forested parts of the Tropics this is how much farming is done. It is easy to cultivate this land, because under the trees there was no covering of grass. The land, when the trees have gone, is bare, and there are none of the seeds of the weeds that make arable farming difficult. There is, too, a big supply of plant nutrients in the soil, enriched as the latter is by centuries of leaf-fall. After five or ten years, though, arable weeds begin to creep in, the humus is used up, the land becomes infertile, and the cultivators move on and clear another piece of forest. The piece they have left regenerates itself, trees grow again, and in twenty or thirty years the *chena* cultivators, as they are called in Ceylon as an example, can come back, cut and burn again, and enjoy another five or ten years of profitable farming. There is nothing wrong with this kind of husbandry at all provided there are not too many people and enough forest. When populations expand, though, it becomes impossible: the forest does not have time to regenerate itself.

But in temperate climates the cultivator is more likely to be confronted with grass. What then does he do? If he sprinkles the seed of whatever it is he wants to grow on top of the grass nothing will happen to it except that the birds will eat it. So that is obviously no good. Somehow he must get rid of the grass. Now, either he can skim it off (that is what the old 'breast plough' was for) and remove it and either burn it or let it rot. Or he can bury it. The former course takes much labour, but the latter operation can be done by machinery (i.e. a plough) motivated by animal power or engine. Also it has the advantage that it does not rob the land of nutrients and humus. So he ploughs it. If it is a very small piece of land he digs it, which has the same effect.

He leaves it long enough for the grass to rot. He then probably ploughs it again. He must now get the earth in a soft and workable enough state to be able to put his seed below the surface of the ground where the birds won't get it. So he drags the land about with pointed instruments, such as we call harrows or cultivators. He goes on doing this until the land is soft enough, and the 'tilth' fine enough (meaning that the bigger clods have been broken up) to make it possible to get his seed in. The smaller the seed the finer the tilth needed. To get his seed in he either scatters it over the surface of the ground and then drags harrows about over it, or hand rakes if it is a small piece of ground, or he drills the seed in. The drill is like a pipe with no back to it which is dragged through the loose soil while the seeds are dropped down the pipe. The pipe opens a furrow, or tiny trench, the seed falls in, and the earth closes in on the seed after the drill has gone past.

Now the seeds begin to grow, but there are sure to be weed seeds in the ground too and they begin to grow also. If the crop is sown very thickly (like wheat) it may grow fast enough to smother the young weeds, and that is all right. If it is not that sort of crop (but is what we call a 'row crop'—like turnips) then the husbandman must give his crop an unfair advantage over the weeds by cutting the weeds out with some implement. Normally this will be a hoe: either a hand hoe or a hoe pulled by a horse or tractor. The latter can only go between the rows of course: only the hand hoe can kill the weeds in the rows between the individual plants. If the weather is dry the weeds he has hoed out will lie on the ground and die. If it rains they will get their roots in again and go on growing. Then the husbandman must hoe them again. If the crop beats the weeds he will have a crop. If the weeds beat the crop he will have only weeds. There is only one crop I know that just does not want weeding at all, and that is the Jerusalem artichoke. This will grow—weeds or no weeds—and make such a dense jungle that it will smother every weed underneath it. Wheat and other corn is sown so thickly, and grows so fast, that it may beat annual weeds, but the land must be fairly clean of perennial weeds (chiefly spear, or couch, grass) otherwise you will not get very much of a crop.

When the crop is ripe it is harvested. The husbandman must now plough or dig the land up again, to bury the weeds that have grown (and there will be some), to make the land soft enough again to get his drill coulters into it, or the points of his harrow if he intends to broadcast his seed, and to aerate the soil, for this stimulates the aerobic bacteria which benignly break down the waste vegetable matter and turn it back into plant nutrients again. He will also cultivate or harrow. The cultivator is like a giant harrow; it has long teeth that go deep into the soil and take much more power to pull them than a harrow, which has a lot of little spikes sticking down out of a framework. A thorn bush will do, and I have used one.

The husbandman must wage constant war against weeds. When he does not have a crop on the land he attacks weeds by allowing the weeds to grow and—before they seed—ploughing them in or otherwise killing them. Then, if he has time, he will let another crop of weeds grow and treat them the same. If a field gets too 'foul', that is grows too many weeds, then he may 'bare fallow' it, that is leave it for a summer without growing a crop on it. During this summer he constantly lets a crop of weeds grow, then ploughs them in or drags them out with the cultivator, and then repeats the process. The modern husbandman cannot abandon land when it becomes too weedy and move on and plough up the wilderness. His husbandry must be a self-regenerating process.

Also the husbandman must put back nutrients into the soil. You cannot keep taking large quantities of nutrients out of a piece of land and put nothing back for ever. The land will get poorer and poorer and eventually become sterile. In a primitive economy what is taken out of the land is put back again. This happened in England until sewage started to be dumped into the sea. Now we make up what we lose by dumping sewage by importing potash and phosphates from mineral deposits in various parts of the world and extracting nitrogen from the air by electricity. It is perfectly easy to treat sewage in such a manner that it can be put back on the land again, and does not have to be dumped into the sea. A big capital investment is needed to do this, but the money is got back after not many years in the sale of fertilizer.

Every civilization that the world has so far seen has been founded on corn, by which I mean crops of the grass family. The Mesopotamian and Indus Valley civilizations, the Egyptian civilization, the North China civilization, were founded on wheat. The south Indian, Sinhalese, Bengali and South Chinese and Indonesian civilizations were founded on rice. As Europe, belatedly, was occupied by civilized people they brought wheat with them. Classical Greek civilization was founded on wheat until the Greeks ruined their topsoil, whereupon they had to grow subsoil crops like the vine and the olive, and become a trading and ship-building nation and get their wheat from other places. The Roman Empire was founded on wheat. When the Romans too, ruined their topsoil, and turned the wheatlands of North Africa into a desert, their civilization collapsed in ruins. It is hard to think of any other food that would give sufficient security from famine, and energy, to a people to allow them to develop that fragile thing, a civilization, excepting one of the *graminae*. True, potatoes have been the foundation of rather inferior civilizations in South America, but I don't think the Parthenon could ever have risen up from a diet of spuds.

So we will begin with wheat. Before you begin growing wheat remember what has to be done to it. It must be harvested, dried, threshed, winnowed, cleaned, ground, and baked before you can eat it. You can do all these things by hand, but they can be done very much less laboriously by machine. Maybe you would be advised to trade some other product that you can produce more easily with the rest of the world for flour? To buy bread from the bakers is absolute nonsense: you are paying through the nose for something you can quite easily make yourself (just don't believe the people who tell you it's as cheap to buy bread as to bake it—they just don't know what they are talking about). But you can easily buy flour and bake your own bread. Better still, far better in fact in every way, is to buy your wheat, straight from a farmer if you can get it, store it in ordinary gunny bags, turning the bags every so often and keeping them on wood—not on cold concrete, but in a nice dry place—and grind your own flour in the sort of small mill that we shall discuss later.

But we have grown our own wheat on a garden scale, quite successfully, threshed the corn by bashing it on the back of a chair, winnowed it by tossing it up in the wind, and ground it, God help us, in a coffee grinder. And it has made the most excellent bread: no better than other good bread made from English or Welsh wheat but not a whit worse. For communities of any size it would be most sensible and economical to grow your own bread wheat. We will discuss the possible ways of harvesting, etc., when we come to them.

A word first of all about the often misunderstood business of 'strong' wheat and 'weak' wheat, or 'hard' and 'soft', and the widely held superstition that wheat grown in the British Isles is 'weak' or 'soft' and therefore incapable of being turned into good bread. Well, the battles of Agincourt and Crecy were won by men reared up on bread made from English wheat, whether it was 'soft' or 'hard', and 'hard' wheat was never heard of in the British Isles, one supposes, until the opening up of North America as a wheat-exporting country in the nineteenth century. The fact is that commercial bakers prefer 'hard' wheat because it yields the largest number of loaves per sack of flour. For that reason and for that reason only. And the reason why 'hard' wheat yields more loaves per sack is that the more tenuous gluten of hard wheat is capable of withstanding greater pressure of gas (bread is 'leavened' by carbonic acid gas produced by the yeast organism) and therefore the bread contains larger *holes*; also flour made from hard wheat can absorb more *water*. Bread made from soft wheat may have 40 per cent of its weight in water; bread made from hard wheat up to 75 per cent. Water and gas cost the baker very little, if indeed anything at all, and so if he can sell water and gas for the same price as flour (which costs him quite a lot) he is on to a good thing. Therefore bakers shy away from English wheat. Now Sally has baked our bread for the last eighteen years always using English wheat, and I'll warrant that there is no other bread in the world better than it. She uses whole meal because we happen to like whole meal (not because we have any dietetic theories about it—although it may not be a coincidence that when our family of six goes to the dentist on its annual visit—there is *never* anything for the dentist to do) but when we compare her whole meal loaves with any bought whole meal loaves we can get hers are always superior. But her loaves are closer textured than bought loaves, because the flour that she uses being of 'soft' English wheat, the dough will not retain so much gas in it. In other words, we don't have to eat so much hole. Also her bread contains less water per pound of loaf. One requires far less of bread made from soft wheat than one does of bread made from hard wheat: the former is more 'filling' and certainly far more nutritious measured pound for pound—simply because there is nothing very nutritious about carbon dioxide and water. The miller also can make more money out of foreign hard wheat than he can out of home-grown soft, simply because with modern methods of milling separation of the endosperm from the rest of the grain is easier with hard wheat than it is with soft. With whole meal milling this does not matter, but for the production of white flour it does. The baker and the miller can both make more money if they use imported hard wheats and not home-grown soft ones. But for the self-supporter there is no advantage in using hard wheat. He is not out to make money out of anybody. I can't compare bread made from soft wheat with bread made from hard because we never have made any from hard wheat flour and really you can't call the wrapped pap one buys from the shops bread at all. But we will discuss the flour and bread aspects of wheat when we get to them. For the moment we will discuss the growing of the stuff.

*Varieties*. There is such a bewildering selection of varieties nowadays that one could fill a whole book with them. This is because the growing of wheat by monoculture has resulted in a large selection of virulent diseases, fungoid and bacterial and virus, and plant breeders are ever trying to keep ahead of the evolution of the disease organism by breeding resistant strains of wheat. So far they have more or less succeeded. Hardly a year goes by without the announcement that some new strain of smut-resistant, or rust-resistant, or other disease-resistant, wheat has come on the market. But then in a few years the farming press records sadly that the resistance of this particular strain seems to have vanished. What has happened, of course, is that the disease organisms have evolved too; they also know as much as the scientists about natural and artificial selection—maybe a bit more. Both experts and farmers are becoming more and more concerned about the disease problem in white straw crops. But the homesteader need not concern himself about such problems. We have grown wheat, oats or barley for several years now and have never had any hint of any disease. This is because we never grow white straw where white straw has been the year before, and our soil is healthy and organically alive. So, in selecting a wheat variety, I would plump for a wheat with a good strong straw (one that does not get blown down too easily) and a good fat grain, and leave disease resistance to people who get disease. If you want a long straw for thatching, or for making corn dollies, or for any other purpose, then get a long-strawed wheat, such as Marris Widgeon or Flamingo. If you do not have your own ideas on which variety of wheat to plant then ask your neighbours, or the local N.A.A.S. officer. If you can get hold of one of the old breeds of wheat like Square Head's Master, or Little Joss, Victor or Yeoman, Rivet or Japhet, do so. Yeoman, by the way, used to be the 'hardest' or 'strongest' of the English wheats, so if you feel you must have a hard wheat get that. All these strains of wheat have been retained for breeding purposes, and places such as Rothampstead will certainly have them, but whether they will sell them or not I do not know. Last year we planted Attlee and it was very good.

*Soil.* Wheat will not grow on light, poor soil. If your land is light you must manure it and 'do' it well, maybe for some years, before it will grow good wheat. If your land is heavy and strong you will need a strong-strawed variety, or it will 'lodge', that is fall down, owing to the weight of the crop.

*Winter or Spring Wheat.* Another thing you must decide is whether to sow winter or spring wheat. Winter wheat should be sown, in England or Wales, in September or October (copy your neighbours). It grows a little before the winter sets in and then remains dormant until the spring. It then gets off to a head start, grows a heavier crop than spring wheat and can be harvested earlier. Spring wheat is sown in late February or March. It does not give such a heavy crop as winter wheat, but in very cold wintered countries winter wheat will not survive. In Russia and North America spring-sown wheat is almost universal.

Winter wheat can come nicely after potatoes. After the potatoes have been ploughed out the land has only to be cultivated a few times to make a seed bed for wheat. Wheat does not need too fine a seed bed. Potatoes are always manured heavily, and this is good preparation for a succeeding wheat crop. If wheat comes after 'seeds', meaning a grass and clover ley, you can just plough the ley and broadcast the wheat on the ploughed land and then harrow it in.

*Sowing.* Sowing can be done by drilling or broadcasting. Broadcasting is the oldest method, very Biblical. It is one of the most satisfying occupations in the world. You split a sack down, tie two corners of it to make a kind of bag-sling, hang it over one shoulder, fill it with wheat, and walk down the field scattering it. Some people use both hands, I prefer one. Winter wheat should be broadcast at the rate of about three bushels an acre, spring wheat perhaps four. Winter wheat *tillers* more—that is one seed branches out into numerous plants, therefore you don't need so much seed. As to how to broadcast, so long as you are covering the ground evenly with seed, leaving no 'holidays' (bare patches), nor clumps, and making your three or four bushels *more or less* stretch to an acre, you are doing all right. The only way to learn is to use the common sense that God has given you. If there are no parallel lines, like furrows, along the field that you can use as guidelines put a white wand at each end of each stretch that you sow (or a white rag on a bush) and walk straight for that.

With a drill you need less seed, perhaps a bushel less an acre. It is noteworthy that where we live in Wales the farmers, who all tried seed drills, have mostly gone back to hand broadcasting of oats and barley. They don't grow wheat nowadays, although they used to. Whether you drill or broadcast it is a good plan to harrow afterwards: you must in the case of broadcasting or the birds will get all your seed. Then all you have to do is to wait for the crop to get ripe and reap it, although it helps to run a roller over it in the spring and maybe give it a cwt. an acre of nitrogenous fertilizer. If wireworm are a trouble rolling helps to restrict their nefarious movements. If you run hens over your land after you have ploughed it you won't have many wireworm; unringed pigs are also doughty wireworm slayers.

*Harvesting.* Cut the wheat as late as you can before it begins to shed—that is knock out when you cut it. You can cut it with a sickle, a scythe, a grass mower, a binder, or a combine.

The sickle is laborious beyond words. The scythe in the hands of a good man should cut an acre a day, but it will take two other people coming behind the scythe to bind the sheaves. Traditionally this work was done by women and children: the use of the scythe is a man's job if there ever was one.

*Mowing*, as cutting with the scythe is called, is an arduous but delightful job. The blade should frequently be wetted with a rough stone (grass needs a very fine-grained stone), and the throat of the mower should frequently be wetted with not-too-strong home brewed ale.

If you cut with a grass mower, either horse drawn or tractor drawn, you will have to go behind and tie the sheaves. A sheaf is a bundle of straw, grain all at one end, that you can comfortably hug, tied either with a tie of straw, or a piece of twine. The knot for tying with its own straw is made thus: take a handful of straw from the bundle, pass it round the sheaf, twist the ends together and tuck them under the tie itself.

The binder does this job for you. But do not expect two horses to pull a binder for long. It takes three big horses to pull a fair-sized binder and it is killing work. An acre of land will give you at least a ton (may give you two) of wheat. Do you need more than that? If you don't, cannot you spare a day or two to cut it with a scythe? A binder is a huge great cumbersome machine to cut an acre or two of corn a year with. Like shooting a gnat with an elephant rifle. The combine is out of the question unless you hire one. It then does your cutting, threshing and winnowing in one. *But* you have to dry the corn, and we will deal with that later.

Assuming you use any other method except a combine—you will be faced with a field-full of corn sheaves. As soon as you can, put them up into *stooks* or *shocks*—or *traives*—the name depending upon what part of the country you live in. You do this by picking up two sheaves, banging the butts of the sheaves hard into the ground to settle them, and rubbing their heads together. Thus they stand up. Put two more alongside them—then more until you have six or eight sheaves

—making a sort of shed. Now if it rains they will get wet—but they will get dry again. If it blows a gale they will fall over and you will have to put them up again. Now if you live in a dryish area you can leave the corn in the stook for say three weeks. Then cart it and stack it in ricks, but see the chapter on barley for 'mows'. For small fields a circular rick is best. Mark out a circle on the ground, lay a platform of brushwood (*not* old sheets of corrugated iron), build a base of sheaves with the butts of the outer ring of sheaves outwards, and build layer after layer, like this, keeping the rick level—not hollow in the middle by God—the outer lot of sheaves always sloping down outwards so as to cast the rain that blows into them, the walls leaning slightly outwards until you get to the eaves, then pull the layers in until, after a steeply-pitched roof, you come to a point.

Thatch this with long threshed straw, or reeds if you can get them. If you use threshed straw you must chuck a pile of straw onto the ground and wet it well. Then you *pull* it—drag handfuls out from the bottom. In its wet condition the handfuls will come out straight. Lay the handfuls in bundles. Get the bundles up to the eaves of your rick, lay them flat (say two inches thick), and pin them down with twine held down with 'brortches', which are sharpened sticks hammered in to the rick with a mallet. When you have done one complete circle do another, half on top of it but higher up. Go on like this until you get to the top. Then make a sort of cone of straw and tie its neck tight up above, and if you have the imagination and skill to fashion a corn dolly to go right at the top, and add a final flourish to the job, you will have something to be proud of.

*Drying.* The corn inside this rick will go on drying out, maturing and improving, until you run out of last year's wheat and start threshing it. Wheat thus dries and matures naturally, and is better than combined and artificial dried wheat. There is one way you can get your wheat threshed without threshing it. That is throw it to the chickens. They will eat the grain and use the straw for litter.

However, if you have had it combined you will have to dry it, or to store it in an hermetically sealed container. If conditions were fine when it was cut it may be enough to leave it out of doors in the sun and wind in gunny bags for a few weeks, turning the gunny bags once a day. The bags must stand on boards or corrugated iron; not on the ground. Then take the bags into your barn and store them, *not* touching each other, and turn them every three or four days. It is hard work. Or you can have the grain mechanically dried by a man who owns a grain dryer. He will charge you for it and you will have all the bother of getting the wheat to him and getting it back again. Or do what our Neolithic ancestors did and keep the grain hermetically sealed. They used to do this by digging pits in chalk or well-drained soil, lining the pits with basket work, putting the grain in and sealing the top carefully with clay. The fact is, hermetically sealed grain generates carbon dioxide which inhibits the growth of moulds and other organisms which would otherwise ruin damp grain. This principle, after having been lost for four thousand years, has been rediscovered in the last ten, and those tall, rather beautiful, metal grain silos rising up near farmsteads mostly contain undried grain, straight from the combine harvester, and are hermetically sealed to prevent deterioration. This grain so far has been used only for animal food: I am not aware that 'moist-stored' wheat has yet been milled for human consumption, but our Neolithic ancestors did it. The Romans built elaborate under-floor flues in which they burnt wood for the drying of wheat.

The Sinhalese get over the grain drying problem very aesthetically by building the most beautiful baskets of *cadjan*, or woven coconut fronds, some of them as big as houses, and supported on stilts. The paddy (which is the correct name for unhulled rice) is stored in these, and the movement of air through it dries it out. Some African tribes (notably the Kikuyu) store maize and millet by the same method.

But nothing can beat, in the climate of the British Isles, the good old method of ricking the corn, in the straw, thatching it, and then threshing it out in the winter after it has naturally dried. If you have, by the way, a Dutch barn or something like that, by all means build your rick in its shelter and you don't have to go to all the trouble of thatching it. The Dutch have a marvellous method. They put four tall poles up, sling a light roof inside them on four ropes which pass over four pulleys at the tops of the four poles, haul the roof up to the top while they build their rick underneath it, then lower the roof down to fit comfortably over the rick. When they want to start threshing they simply haul the roof up again and chuck the loose sheaves down. They use this system mostly for hay, for which it is perfect, for it does away with the laborious use of the stack-knife, but it works with grain too.

*Threshing.* First we have got to thresh the grain. You can take the sheaves and bang the heads of corn over the edge of a barrel or the back of a chair (or a 'threshing horse' made for the purpose with several parallel horizontal bars). The grain will fly all over the place and so you must have an unencumbered floor. This method is still much practised on the west coast of Ireland. Or you can pile the straw higgledy-piggledy in a big heap on the floor and wallop it with a flail. Or you can lay the straw on a clean, hard floor and drive animals over it as the Sinhalese do with their rice and the Spaniards their wheat. Or you can get a threshing machine. The latter has the advantage that it will winnow it too. (To winnow is to blow the lighter chaff out of the grain.) There used to be plenty of little barn threshing machines—every farm had one, often driven by a water wheel, or a horse walking around in a circle pulling a bar. If you could get one of these you would be well away. But the bashing over a chair method is quite satisfactory for small quantities (say up to a ton) and is quite fun.

*Winnowing.* If you spread a tarpaulin on the ground on a windy day, and pour your threshed grain and chaff on to it from a height, the wind will winnow your grain—that is the chaff will blow away and leave the clean wheat. There is nothing difficult about this at all. The chaff is good, mixed with oats, for your horse. You can sometimes pick up a winnowing machine from a farm sale: it is a good buy.

*Milling.* This used to be done by rubbing two stones together. The quern was a refinement of this—two round stones, one on top of the other, the top one revolved by woman-power. Then came the big stone mill which is in use in many places today: once driven by slave-power (that is what Samson was doing when he was 'eyeless in Gaza among slaves'), then horses or other animals, then wind or water, then steam, now diesel. Stone milling is a highly skilled profession, and far out of the scope of this book. If you can get a stone mill, and know how to dress the stones when they need it, or can find somebody who does know, you are lucky.

Otherwise there is the steel plate mill which is to be found on every farm, which has two steel plates, one of which revolves against the other, and this is fine for grist (that is meal for animal feeding) but murders wheat rather than mills it. And there is the modern small electrically-driven mill or coffee grinder. This is what you will probably come down to in the end, and it is perfectly satisfactory. The large Kenwood with coffee-grinder attachment is O.K.

Industrial milling today is a very complicated process. Before the eighteenth century wheat was stone ground and often passed through a sieve to get the coarsest of the husk out. This · resulted in good whole meal bread. Just before 1700 an Austrian invented 'high milling' which consisted of grinding the flour very fine and passing it through fine cloths. This resulted in white flour, because only the endosperm, or starch of the grain, was fine enough to pass through the cloths. Most of the later windmills in England had things called *bolters* towards the end of the wind era. These did this job of passing the flour through a 'bolter cloth'.

Nowadays the whole process is complicated in the extreme. The wheat goes through a *cockle cylinder* which gets out small weed seeds, a *barley cylinder* which gets out large ones, a *scourer* which is a cylinder lined with emery, a *washer* which is what it says it is (the wheat floats while the rubbish sinks), *whizzers* which centrifuge the wheat to dry it, the *dry brusher*, and then the main thing—the *break roller*. This splits the grain and sets the endosperm free. The little bits of endosperm are then called *semolina*. Then come the *grinding rollers*, or reduction rollers which grind the semolina into fine white flour. The flour then goes through silk screens and the germ is all got out. (Hovis process this germ separately and then return it to the flour.) But for white flour it is left out. As little as 20 per cent of the whole meal may be extracted as flour in the case of 'patent flour', but 'straight run' flour is about 70 per cent of the grain. The rest goes for animal food. Lucky animals, because they get the best of it. The flour then has various additives put to it: chlorine dioxide to bleach it to an even whiter-than-white whiteness so beloved by the working class housewife (who is *still* reacting from the time when the upper class could afford white bread and the working classes could not), ammonium persulphate, potassium bromide which causes the dough to retain more carbon dioxide and therefore make a bigger loaf for less flour, glyceryl mono-stearate or polyoxy ethelene stearate which are anti-staling agents— in other words they make the stuff keep longer, and sometimes Epsom salts or Glauber salts. Ground chalk is often added to it: in fact in England the law is that some calcium must be added to it to take the place of the calcium so laboriously milled out of it, and certain vitamins are added too.

Some grain is milled as *whole meal* and that is exactly what it says. Nothing is added to it and nothing is taken away. This can be finely or coarsely ground according to taste. Other grain is milled as *wheat meal*. This has the bran removed. What you will get, if you mill your grain yourself, will be *whole meal*.

*Baking.* As for baking, nothing, in cooking, is easier except possibly boiling an egg. But it is very easy to go wrong in the latter operation. I am a terrible cook, but I never had the

slightest difficulty in baking perfect bread, and nor need anybody else who is fit to live outside an institution.

To bake bread do this last thing at night:

To make six medium loaves take four and a half pints of water about blood heat (don't mess about with thermometers); put in a mixing bowl, chuck in two ounces of salt and two ounces of sugar and a tablespoonful of yeast. When the yeast has dissolved pour in enough flour to make a fine sticky mush— such as you might feed to the pigs. Stir it well; make sure that every bit of flour is wetted. You must not have too much dough in the bowl or it will overflow when it rises.

Stand it in a warm place, out of draughts, and go to bed. The above operation takes about five minutes. If you have a stove that keeps in a'nights stand it near that.

In the morning stagger out of bed, go downstairs, dump some dry flour on a table (I am not going to use such culinary terms as a 'clean table' in this book—I shall leave that much to the common sense of my readers), dump the dough—which by now will have risen until it is overflowing the bowl—on to the flour, sprinkle dry flour on top of it and then comes the process of *kneading*, which takes a little practice. The aim is to make a moderately stiff dough, dry on the outside. At first when you begin to knead the dough will stick messily to your hands. Don't, whatever you do, wash it off with water. 'Wash' it off with *more dry flour*. Fling dry flour on top of the mass. Wherever it is wet—fling on dry flour. Push the mass away from you with the palms of your hands, and then pull it together again. Whenever it sticks to your hands 'wash' your hands again with dry flour and wash the table too. Soon it will stop sticking, and turn into a most satisfying lump of floury substance, delightful to roll about. Roll it about to your heart's content and then put a dollop in each baking tin. Only fill the tins three quarters full. There will be some left over; make little rolls of that and put them on an iron oven-plate. Make pretty scores on the tops of your loaves in the tins. Balance the tins on the cool side of the stove and cover with a cloth and leave to rise ('prove') yet again. Bread rises twice.

Leave the rolls to rise too. When the rolls have risen pop them in the very hot oven. In ten minutes they will probably be done, and you will have splendid hot whole meal rolls for breakfast. After breakfast take the bread tins *gently*—and here is the whole skill of the thing—to jog them is to make them collapse and you'll get heavy bread. *Do not jog them!* Place them gently in the oven. After half an hour look at them, and if you wish to, *gently* change them round—the top ones to the bottom. In three quarters of an hour, if the oven is hot, they should be done. If the oven isn't hot you shouldn't be making bread. You can test them by tapping their undersides (if done they will sound hollow). Balance them on top of their tins to air well as they cool. You probably don't spend more than half an hour of the morning actually working with the bread: while you are waiting for things to happen you can be doing other things. If your flour is good, and fresh, the above method makes, quite simply, the best bread in the world: as superior to wrapped factory pap as good butter is to cheap margarine.

Below is a comparison of the food values of white flour and whole meal flour:

| | Pro-tein | Fat | Carbo-hydrate | Calcium | Iron | Vit. B1 | Ribo-flavin | nicotinic acid |
|---|---|---|---|---|---|---|---|---|
| White flour: | 2·3 | 0·2 | 15·6 | 4 | 0·2 | 0·01 | 0·01 | 0·2 |
| Whole meal flour: | 3·1 | 0·6 | 11·2 | 7 | 0·7 | 0·09 | 0·05 | 0·6 |

The wrapped-pap factory lobby always trots out the hoary old folk tale that the *phytin* which whole meal has and white flour hasn't inhibits the absorption of calcium in the human. What they forget to add is that four hours of fermentation in the dough lowers the phytin (phytic acid) content by 75 per cent which renders it practically harmless in this respect, also that habitual whole meal eaters develop an enzyme named *phytase* in their bodies which destroys any phytin that they do ingest. You have only to look at the teeth of any whole meal-bread-fed family to realize that they get enough calcium.

If the bread-maker wishes to be scientific he might know that the dough fermentation should be at about 80°F. (27°C.) and the temperature of his oven should be from 200° to 240°C. At 60°C. all yeast is killed. But you won't make any better bread because you know this.

If you are a North Indian you will probably prefer *chapatis*, or unleavened bread. These are made by mixing a very stiff dough of whole meal flour and water, with (common sense will prompt?) a pinch of salt; divide it into egg-shaped lumps, roll it out very thin (Indian cooks do it by clapping it between the palms—hence that persistent clapping noise that emanates from North Indian kitchens) and bake it on a very hot plate for not many seconds. Turn it over. (If you then throw it *on the fire* for a second it will inflate like a balloon.) The hub-cap of an American automobile placed over the fire makes a splendid hot plate, which is why so few American automobiles in North India have any hub-caps on them.

There are other things you can do with wheat. Soak it overnight then put it in the slow oven for three days. It jellifies and makes an ideal breakfast food, and when you eat it you don't have the feeling that you are helping to pay for somebody's vast advertising campaign.

*Yeast.* A word about that marvellous substance: yeast.

Yeast is a living organism, which will live and multiply at from 48°F. to 95°F. It eats sugar and excretes carbon dioxide and alcohol. There are three main species: *Saccharomyces cerevisiae*: for beer and bread; *Sacchanomyces ellipsoideus*: for wine; *Saccharomyces pasteurianus*: for cider.

The grape wine and cider yeasts are always present on the skins of their respective fruits, so don't need to be added. Beer yeast should come from the *top* of the previous brew, not the bottom, for it is an aerobic yeast. Bread yeast can come from the bottom. We ferment our beer and bread with the same yeast, the beer mash tub providing enough for both—and many pounds to spare.

A recipe for making your *own* dried yeast:

3 oz. hops
3½ lbs. rye flour
7 lbs. corn or barley meal
1 gallon water.

Rub the hops and boil them in the water for half an hour. Strain. Stir in rye flour, then corn or barley meal. Knead and roll out very thin. Cut into circles with a tumbler and leave to dry hard in the sun. Wild yeast will infect the biscuits. To use it, crumble a biscuit and soak in warm water with sugar and salt in it and next day use as yeast. I have never done this but I have made 'sour dough' bread. Here you make your dough, make a hole in the top and put in a mixture of warm water, sugar and salt; leave in the warm for a day. If you are lucky it will ferment and you mix it up and make your dough. In South West Africa we made a lot of bread like this and it generally used to work. We also baked in a termite hill. You knocked a hole in the side of the hill, made sure that there was a chimney coming out at the top (the termites had already ensured that there was one almost all the way), built a hot fire in your new oven and kept it going for an hour or two until the termite hill was very hot indeed, drew the ashes and shoved in your bread and bunged the entrace and the chimney up. In an hour the bread was perfectly cooked, and so was anything else you liked to put in there.

The termites didn't like it at all.

*It is labour, but what is exercise other than labour?*
*Let a young woman bake a bushel once a week and she*
*will do very well without phials and gallipots.*

WILLIAM COBBETT: Cottage Economy

# 12

# Barley, Beer

*I view the tea drinking as a destroyer of health, an enfeebler of the frame, an engenderer of effeminacy and laziness, a debaucher of youth and maker of misery for old age.*

WILLIAM COBBETT : Cottage Economy

And nowadays we get people worrying themselves about a little pot. But whether we agree with Cobbett about the evils of tea or not (he thought the clatter of the tea tackle was the short road to the brothel and the gallows!) we must agree with him as to the wholesomeness of good beer brewed from good malt, made from good barley, flavoured with good hops, and fermented with good yeast. What could be more 'natural' than that?

## BARLEY

And so to grow the good barley—the basis of it all.

Barley is traditionally grown after the root break, and in the days of High Farming after roots had been fed off to folded sheep, and the latter had trodden the ground and enriched it with their manure. On the light lands of Norfolk the effect of sheep used thus was termed the 'Golden Hoof'. The very finest malting barley, however, is that grown after another white straw crop, when the ground is not too rich in nitrogen, and the barley therefore richer in starch and not so rich in protein, for it is the starch content that makes the beer. Barley will grow well on much lighter land than wheat demands, and in wetter climates. It is much faster growing than wheat and I have seen barley sown in May in England give a good crop. You can, in England, grow winter barley in the same way as

149

winter wheat; but most barley is spring-sown: usually in February or March. The preparation of the land is much the same as for wheat, except that the tilth should be much finer and the last ploughing not too deep: four inches is enough. If you drill it you need two to three bushels to the acre (one to one-and-a-half hundredweight); if you broadcast it about a bushel more. Very often you will probably undersow the barley with 'seeds' (grass and clover seed) for a subsequent ley (see Chapter Seven). After sowing it must be harrowed of course, and rolling helps. If the land is very rich in nitrogen a dressing of phosphate and potash will counterbalance this, make for earlier ripening, and give a better 'malting sample'. If the land is poor add to this a hundredweight to the acre of nitrogen, if you can afford it and have no ideological objections. But the organic farmer will say to this: well, the land shouldn't be poor.

Harvesting can be just the same as for wheat in every respect. For a malting sample do not harvest until the grain is dead ripe—the ears all falling over. The traditional way to harvest fine barley was to cut it with a scythe and not tie it, but 'make' it like hay. That is rake it up into swathes, turn it by rake or pitchfork until both straw and grain are bone dry, then cock it like hay, cart it to the stack and stack it, and thresh it out in the winter when there is nothing else to do. I think for the smallholder this is a very good way of harvesting barley.

A word here about the 'barley mow'. There is many a pub up and down the land of England of that name, and very often the landlord, even, does not know what it means. In the wetter parts of the country today, and at one time all over the country, much corn was put into 'mows' after it had stood for a week or two drying in the stook. We harvest our barley and oats in this manner in Pembrokeshire now. As soon as you get a dry spell, after the corn has been stooked for long enough to turn the grass that clings to the roots of the sheaves into hay, you stack the sheaves in the field in little stacks which are known as 'mows'. You do it like this: make a circle of sheaves standing upright and leaning against each other. The diameter of the circle should be fixed by the length of the sheaves, but after you have made one mow you will see how big the circle should be. If the sheaves have been tied by a binder it takes about fifty of the little sheaves to make the circle. For stability the outer rings of the circle should lean inwards (of course). On top, in the middle, lay a ring of sheaves ears together in the middle and butts outward. Secure each sheaf to the next by grabbing a handful of its straw and stuffing it under the string, or band, of its neighbour. You are left with a ring of sheaves each one tied securely to the next. Place another ring on top of this one, but bigger, also secured in the same way. Work, in fact, in a spiral. Arrange it so that the outer sheaves are lying on a steep slant—because the middle of the heap is much higher than the outside. The reason for this is of course to shed the rain. Then continue your spiral upwards, reducing your dia-meter until you come to a point. This point will consist of say five sheaves with their ears blowing up in the air. The whole mass will be tied together sheaf to sheaf and completely rain-proof, and yet the wind can get through it. When you have got your corn in the mow you can heave a long sigh of relief, because you need have no further anxiety about it. You can leave it there nearly until Christmas if you want to, but probably before the terrible gales of January and February set in you should have carted it away to the rick or the barn. The mow is very weatherproof but not quite gale-proof as the proper corn-rick is.

Threshing, winnowing and all the rest of it are the same as for wheat. For feeding, barley can be ground, in which case it is unsurpassed pig food, or cattle-fattening food. It should not be fed to horses as it is too 'heating', and fed only in moderation to sheep. If you haven't got a mill it is just as good to *soak* your barley: dump it in water for at least twenty-four hours. It then makes a most excellent stock feed: quite as good as barley meal.

## BEER

Barley meal can be baked into bread, and in fact used to be extensively in the western parts of Britain where barley is easier to grow than wheat. Never having tasted it I cannot comment on it, but folk-lore gives it a pretty bad name:

> *I'll eat no more of your barley bread*
> *Nor drink no more of your water,*
> *I'll sleep no more in your flea-ridden bed*
> *Nor court your pudding-faced daughter!*

sang the 'living-in' farm hand to his parsimonious master. Mixed with wheat flour it is said to be not so bad. The fact is that the barley grain differs from the grain of the wheat in that the protein of barley is soluble in water while that of wheat (gluten) is not. It is the insoluble gluten of wheat that makes the dough 'rise': in other words entraps the carbon dioxide given off by the yeast.

But barley has, thank God, one noble use to which it can be put, and that is the making of beer.

*Malting.* Alcohol is made by permitting the yeast organism to feed upon sugar, whereupon it excretes carbon dioxide and alcohol. The yeast needs more than just sugar for its life, just as we, we are told, cannot live by bread alone. Now the grain of the barley is mostly starch, but before the barley can grow this starch must be turned by chemicals called enzymes into sugar. The malster and brewer take the starch of barley, turn it into sugar, and then 'ferment' this sugar (as eating it with yeast is called) into alcohol. The way the malster turns the starch into sugar is simply by encouraging the grain to *grow*. This he does by keeping it wet and warm. When it has grown to the optimum stage, i.e. when the enzymes have already converted most of the starch into sugar and are ready to convert the rest but before the sugar has been turned into plant tissue, he stops the process of growing by roasting the grain. He then has a grain that looks very like an ordinary grain of barley but which is in fact composed more of sugar (maltose, which is a particular form of sugar) than of starch. This grain is called malt. He cracks the malt, so as to make the sugar available.

In practice what you do is dump your barley into warm

water and soak it for four days. Drain the water off and keep
the wet grain on a floor at between 63°F. to 86°F. (17°C. to
30°C.), turning it from time to time to keep it at the right
temperature. Turning cools it. Keep it moist, occasionally
sprinkling it with warm water. After about ten days of this the
*acrospire*, as the shoot of the grain is called (the shoot which
intends to grow up into the air—not the root), should be about
two thirds of the length of the grain. The acrospire grows under
the skin of the grain, but you can see it easily. When this has
happened you must 'kill' the malt, and commercially this is
done in a kiln. With small quantities you can more easily do it
in the oven. If you want to brew a lager or fairly pale ale
keep the temperature of your oven down to under 120°F.
(about 50°C.). When the grain is quite dry, and brittle between
the teeth, raise the temperature a little for a quarter of an
hour but to no more than 140°F. (60°C.) whatever you do or you
will 'kill' not only the malt but also the subtle enzymes within
it which are going to go on converting more of your starch into
sugar. If you want to brew a dark beer you can roast the malt
until it is brown, but I would advise against this. If you must
have a dark beer burn a bit of sugar and put it in your beer:
it will do no harm if it does no good.

If you are malting more than a bushel or two the oven will
be too laborious, and you will need to make a kiln. This can
be quite simply a perforated iron plate (the perforations being
too small to let the grain drop through) placed over a fire. A
coke fire is the best, and the malt must be turned continuously
with a shovel while it is being kilned. Great care is needed to
dry it properly without overheating it, and there is nothing,
for this, to take the place of Old Mother Common Sense. You
must keep looking at the grain, and biting an occasional one,
and decide for yourself when the grain has that brittleness of
complete dryness, and wholeness roasted malty smell of good
malt, and then stop. Of course if you didn't 'kill' the malt it
would go on growing and waste all its sweetness in growth and
be no good at all. Above all—kiln *gently*. Never get it too hot:
never above 140°F.

In a commercial maltings (which the malting activity of a large community will more closely resemble) this is the sequence:

1. Steep the barley for 60 hours or more: up to four days.
2. Drain and put on the malting floor in a 'couch'. This is a high steep-sided heap.
3. Leave for 12 hours if it heats quickly—48 if it heats slowly. The grain should heat to a pleasantly warm temperature when you shove your hand in.
4. As soon as the barley has 'chitted' (that means when the root has just burst out of the skin) *break* the couch. That is shovel the barley out into a flat layer about five inches deep.
5. Now comes the *flooring*. You must watch the barley continually to see that it keeps warm enough but does not get too hot. It heats spontaneously. When it gets too cold pile it up in a thicker layer. When too hot spread it out thinner. Use a wooden shovel and wooden rakes, and work barefoot among it so as not to crack the grains. 'Freshen' occasionally by sprinkling with water. The temperature must stay between 60° and 62°F. (about 16°C.).
6. After about ten days (i.e. when the acrospire is two thirds the length of the grain) *couch* it again for twelve hours, and hope to get it up to 68°F. (20°C.). The rise in temperature is, of course, spontaneous.

You now have 'green malt'.

7. *Kiln* the green malt as described above: not above 140°F.

You store your malt in the whole-grain form, but before you use it you must *crack* it. This you can do with any mechanical device from a rolling pin to a cracking mill. A coffee grinder will do. Do not grind it to powder though—just crack it.

*Making your beer.* This is the principle of the operation:

Put your malt into a tun, mash-tub, or kive or whatever they call it down your way—a big open-topped barrel (many poor people nowadays have to make do with plastic dust-bins) and mix it into a mash with water that has been boiled and cooled to about 150° to 155°F. (66° to 68°C.). Old people say you can tell the temperature by looking into your copper—and when the water has cooled enough so that you can see your face reflected in the water it will do (but I prefer a thermometer). Mix it up into a thick mash, such as you might feed to the pigs. Cover it over and leave it all night. In the morning run the liquor (called *wort* in England; *spree* in Wales) out of the bottom of the kive, at the same time *sparging*—that is sprinkling more boiling water on top of the drying mash. This sparging water can be boiling—it doesn't matter now. Before it *did* matter—boiling water would have killed the enzymes—that's why you had to be able to see your face in it. Now the enzymes have done their work.

When you have as much wort as you think you ought to have from the quantity you used of malt (we will deal with this later) stop sparging and let the mash drain dry.

Put your wort back in the copper and boil it together with as much hops as you think you need wrapped up in a cloth. You should strain the wort into the copper through a muslin, for any bits that get in will stick to the bottom of the copper and be hell to get off, besides tainting the beer. If you wish to add sugar to give extra strength (cheating really) now is the time to do it. Boil for an hour.

Put the wort back into your kive (or another vessel if you have one) for fermentation. Now the faster it cools the better. In the old days people used to run it into large shallow pans to cool it quickly. Modern breweries use refrigeration. We just let it cool by itself, which is all right in the winter but I think a bit risky in the summer. It is during this cooling process that the wort may be attacked by enemy organisms which will beat your yeast and turn it nasty. I am making, this very day, a copper 'worm': a spiral of copper tubing which I intend to lower into my wort and run cold water through it, like the 'in-churn coolers' dairy farmers used to use. But, up to now, we have been brewing for six years and have only had one bad brew. But still, one is too many: it must be cooled quickly.

While the wort is cooling you should be breeding your yeast.

You do this by taking some of the hot wort (a jug-full), cooling it very quickly by standing it in cold water, dropping in a handful of yeast, and letting it stand in the warm. By the time the main body of wort has cooled to 60°F. (or about blood heat—we use common sense not thermometers) dump your jug-full of breeding yeast in it.

To simplify these instructions I will describe exactly what we do to make from eight to ten gallons of beer.

1. In the evening, before we go to bed, we boil ten gallons of water in a ten-gallon electric copper. We used to use an old-fashioned copper heated with a stick fire and it was a darned sight quicker. Now we haven't got one, or we would use it again.

2. While the water is boiling I make a strainer for the kive. Our kive is a big open-topped tub with a hole in the side near the bottom in which fits a cock. A cock in this context is a wooden tap, or spigot. Obviously there has to be a strainer to let the wort run out of the cock without letting the mash get in and bung it up. The way we make the strainer is this. We cut a bunch of gorse, tie a string round it, put it inside the kive, poke the loose end of the string through the cock-hole and—holding the string tight outside—drive the cock in with a mallet. The pressure of the cock then holds the string tight—and the bundle of gorse against the inner end of the cock. As this straining is very important I often put a layer of gorse all over the bottom of the kive and lay a muslin over this also.

A better way of doing this straining is not to have a cock at all, but drill a hole in the middle of the bottom of your kive. Push a long stick down from the top so that the end of it goes in this hole and bungs it up. Now, if you pull the ash stick out you will open the hole. But push the ash stick in, put a layer of gorse around it on the bottom of the kive, put a layer of clean straw on top of the gorse, and lower a big flat stone with a hole in the middle over the ash stick so that it rests on the straw, and compresses it, and turns it into a first-class strainer.

3. We let the water boil, and then let it cool until it is

150°F., or until we can see our face reflected in the water in the copper. We then mix the water and *one bushel* of cracked malt into the kive, making sure that the malt is thoroughly wet right through.

4. We go to bed.

5. We get up and start draining the *wort* as the liquid is now called into buckets (traditionally the vessel that you drain into should be wood and is called an *underbuck*). In our case we open the cock to do this; in the case of the ash stick users they loosen the ash stick—and of course the kive is held up on something so they can get their underbuck underneath it.

6. While this is happening we pour kettle after kettle of boiling water on top of the malt (this is what is called *sparging*). We go on doing this until ten gallons of wort have drained out. The original ten gallons of water we put in has been reduced somewhat by natural causes.

7. We put the ten gallons of wort in the copper again, put a pound of hops in a pillow-case, and boil for an hour. If we wish to cheat and use sugar we stir it in at this juncture—either six pounds of sugar or, as we always do nowadays, half a 14 lb. tin of malt extract, which is simply maltose, or sugar of malt. Last time I used a whole tin of malt extract and made 20 gallons of beer with a bushel and a quarter of malt and the extract.

8. We transfer the boiling wort back to the kive which by now we have cleaned out. Now what we ought to do is to have another fermenting vat (a plastic dustbin would do) and put it in this, and then we would be able to make 'small beer' of the mash in the kive. Not having a spare kive however we just have to throw the mash out and wash the kive and use it again.

9. We take a jug-full of the wort and cool it by standing it in cold water.

10. When it is blood heat we plop some yeast into it—generally yeast which we have borrowed from a neighbour who brewed beer recently. Some neighbour will send a child to us for yeast in due course, for his beer, and thus the neighbourhood is knit together in a friendly mesh of yeast-borrowing, and the strain of living yeast with which we brew our beer may go

back, in ancestry, to the brewers of Caractacus—who knows?

11. When the main body of wort has cooled to blood heat we pour the jug of foaming yeasted wort into it—with a prayer. We cover it well with blankets to keep vinegar flies out. The generation of carbon dioxide inside the kive now is such that, so long as we keep the blankets over it, no vinegar fly could live.

12. Now all we have to do is to keep our hands off it. And here I might say that in our part of Pembrokeshire—the 'Home Brew Belt'—we farmers cannot keep our hands off it for very long. I have known us be at it like dogs before the yeast has been in twelve hours. This practice is, of course, barbarous, and the stuff is far better left alone. It does not, however, as the uninitiated always suppose it does, make you ill.

We skim the floating yeast off after three days. If you leave it another day it will sink, which is bad. It is this floating yeast which our neighbours will send for to make their beer in due course. Kept cool (many people around here keep it in a screw-topped bottle in a stream) it will keep for a month or more.

After eight days we rack the beer (pour it) into a nine-gallon barrel, and if we can keep it bunged up for a month or two it is absolutely superb. If we get eight gallons from a bushel of malt it is very strong indeed. Twelve gallons, which many people make, is strong enough. The stronger it is the better it will keep: eight-gallon-to-a-bushel beer would keep for a year easily. It should not be golloped down by the pint like pub beer —it is far too good for that. To people not used to it it is dangerous: in spite of all warnings they are inclined to drink too much. For such people—water it, they won't know the difference. Water it for the harvest field too, or you won't get much harvesting done.

*Small Beer*. Now to make small beer (which we have never done but will do) you pour say another ten gallons of boiling water (yes—you don't have to wait this time until you can see your face in it) on to the mash after you have taken your first lot of wort out of it, let it stand until you have finished boiling your first lot of wort, then run it off and boil it in the copper like the first wort with hops, put it back into the cleaned-out kive and ferment it with yeast in the usual way. It is said to be an excellent nourishing and slightly alcoholic drink (about the strength of pub beer), but, like pub beer, it won't keep long. It is good for the harvest field.

The mash, after you have used it, is very good stock food, and you can feed it to any animals you feel particularly kindly disposed towards.

*Vinegar.* This is beer, cider or wine which has been exposed to air. It is attacked by *Aceto bacter*, an organism which converts alcohol into acetic acid, thus: $C_2H_5.OH + O_2 = CH_3.COOH + H_2O$.

The traditional way to make malt vinegar is to sprinkle beer on to the top of a big open funnel which is filled with birch twigs. The birch twigs have previously been impregnated with vinegar. The beer runs through the birch twigs and picks up the *Aceto bacter* in the presence of air and turns to vinegar. Strong vinegar contains $6·2$ per cent acetic acid and for pickling it must not be less then 5 per cent. You will know if it doesn't because, exposed to the air, it will grow mould on it. It shouldn't. If beer or wine 'turns sour', turn it to good account by turning it into vinegar.

*Distilling.* If you fill your copper with beer, float a basin on the beer, cover the copper with a big shallow dish of either copper or stainless steel or some clean metal (*not* galvanised), allow cold water to pour into the dish and trickle away over the lip of it, and light a fire under your copper, you will make moonshine. The alcohol will evaporate before the water of the beer does, it will condense on the cold underside of the shallow dish, run down to the lowest point of the dish, and drip off to be caught by your floating basin. Distilling is illegal in the realms of Her Britannic Majesty without a licence, which is very difficult to obtain.

A word about *gas*. If you want your beer to be gassy, like pub beer, you must keep it in pressure-proof containers. Screw-topped cider bottles are the usual things for this purpose, and don't blame me if one of them blows up and kills somebody. Personally I don't like your windy liquids, and believe that the cult of making gassy beer is deleterious. Most of the horrible liquid termed 'home brewed beer' that one has been subjected to by one's city-dwelling friends is of this nature, and generally brewed, too, from 'malt extract' bought from the chemist. The makers, nurtured on the windy chemical liquid made by the giant brewing combines, cannot recognise beer as beer unless it is bubbling like soda-water, and so they mess about with their hydrometers, their dollops of sugar, their screw-topped bottles until they end up with an inferior imitation of bottled pub beer and it is horrible. Real *beer*, such as nurtured the Englishman and the Welshman in days of old, is a beautiful rich, slightly viscous, bitter, completely unwindy (yes—'flat') liquid, akin to the ambrosia of the Gods.

# 13

## Other Field Crops

*Behold, I have given you every herb bearing seed, which is
upon the face of all the earth, and every tree, in the which
is the fruit of a tree yielding seed; to you it shall be for meat.*

GOD: Genesis 1 : 29

### OATS

Oats is a most excellent corn for stock feeding, and grows very
well in a damp or cold climate. Thus in Scotland it grows
better than wheat and is there used as human food, which
prompted Dr Johnson to jibe at his Scottish friend Boswell
that they fed men in Scotland on what in England they only
fed to horses, to which Boswell replied: 'Yes. Better men—
better horses.' It will grow on wetter and more acid land than
either wheat or barley.

Oats is a fine grain crop to grow on the smallholding,
because not only can it be very easily crushed to feed to stock
or fed in the whole grain, but also it can be fed 'in the sheaf'.
This is the way we feed it, and a very good way it is too. We
cut it with a binder, harvest it in the usual way, and then throw
each cow, bullock or horse one sheaf a day each all through
the winter. The animals eat the straw and grain and the
whole lot (and would eat the string too if you left it on) and
they absolutely thrive on it. Thus we save ourselves the trouble
of threshing and winnowing and milling and all the rest of it,
for the cattle do it for us. Horses thrive on their oats given in
this form too, although horses on heavy work would need a
proportion of crushed oats as well.

Oats do very well after permanent pasture or a long ley,
for they will grow well on rotting vegetable matter. As they
are normally planted in the spring it means that you can go

on grazing the ley right up to December. Then you should plough the land to give the frost a chance to break it down and help make a seed bed. You can broadcast the seed straight on to the ploughed land, in March or early April, at the rate of four bushels (1½ cwt.) an acre, and harrow hard afterwards. If the land is heavy and cloddy go on harrowing half a dozen times until you have broken it up pretty fine. Harrow at first *along* the furrows—not across them. It's a good thing to roll oats after the shoots have come up above the ground, to press the roots in and give them a firmer hold. You don't have to though.

If you are going to feed it in the sheaf I suggest you harvest it early, when the straw is just beginning to yellow, because at this time the straw itself, which the cattle will eat, is highly nutritious. If it is the threshed grain you are after then you should cut it when the straw has gone completely yellow but *before* the grain is so ripe that it sheds easily when you pull it about. Oats need more drying than wheat or barley, and the old saying is that it should be 'churched' in the stook three times. That means that after it has been stooked it should see three Sundays in the stook before it is carted and put in the rick. But if you put it up in mows for a month or two you don't need to leave it in the stook (where it is more vulnerable to rain) for so long.

Oat straw, by the way, is by far the most nutritious of the straws in the British Isles, and good oat straw is better than indifferent hay. Wheat straw is very poor for feeding, although good for litter or for thatching. Barley straw is better for feeding than wheat straw and worse for thatching or litter.

## RYE

Rye is little grown in the British Isles, but will grow and makes good bread (if you like rye bread). In North America it appears to make good whisky—if you like rye whisky. What rye is superb for is planting in the autumn with the intention of feeding it off to your cattle very early in the spring (during the 'hungry-gap') as a green fodder crop. If you feed it off hard, behind an electric fence or with tethered cattle, it will give the cattle some green stuff just when they need it most, and if you spare it thereafter it will grow again for another 'bite', or even for a harvested grain crop in the autumn. The straw is good for thatching, and for making corn dollies.

## MAIZE

The other corn crop occasionally grown in Britain but very extensively grown in America and Africa is maize. Maize, planted just after the last frosts of the year on good, deeply cultivated, well-manured land will give you an enormous crop of green fodder for your cows just when you don't want it because there's plenty of grass. Actually this is a simplification, because there *is* a slackening off in the nutritive value of the grass in late July and August when you might want to feed the maize. But if you make silage then maize is an excellent crop. As a crop to ripen and harvest the grain of it is a doubtful starter in Britain, but has been grown for this successfully. As a vegetable we will deal with it later, under 'sweet corn'.

## POTATO

And so we come to the almighty *potato*. Anybody can grow potatoes. But to grow a good crop of clean potatoes your land must be in very good heart. You can put up to twenty tons of muck (farmyard manure) on an acre and plant the tubers straight into the muck in the furrows, and you must cultivate them properly and keep the weeds down. If you have a ridging plough, either a horse-drawn single-furrow one or a tractor-drawn three-furrow one, draw out your furrows, chuck as much muck as you can get hold of in the bottom of the furrows (in the old horse days in England the furrows were of such a width that the wheels of the dung-cart would comfortably run in them and thus not break down the ridges, and the muck was scraped straight out of the back of the dung cart into the furrows with a *croom*, which is like a long, strong, four-tined rake), then sow your seed potatoes (really tubers—you sow the actual potato itself of course) on top of the muck, then *split* the ridges into the furrows with your ridging plough again. As weeds grow run your ridging plough through again sometimes. At least once, before the potatoes get too big, hand-hoe by pulling the ridges in which the potatoes are down into the furrows (without actually disturbing the growing potato plants). Then, a few days after, ridge them up again with the plough. When the potato plants get really big and meet each other then they will suppress the weeds to some extent themselves. But weeds grow like mad in the well-manured potato field, and if you don't look out you'll have a huge crop of weeds, a miserable one of potatoes, and a legacy of foul land for the next year.

If you haven't got a ridging plough you can simply plough your potatoes in with an ordinary plough, planting them in one furrow and then missing one furrow in the case of earlies and two furrows in the case of main crop and then planting another furrow.

On a garden scale you can either grow potatoes on the flat or in ridges, doing your work with the spade. Or we have a tool called a potato planter, common in Kent and Surrey, which is like a strange pair of tongs which you push into loose soil, drop a tuber into it, and open the tongs thus leaving the potato under the soil. The land has to be deeply dug or ploughed and well-worked for this.

Plant main crop potatoes in rows about 26 inches apart and about 20 inches in the rows. Earlies can be in rows 22 inches apart. As for your seed, you can use your own seed once at least (that is use your own small potatoes—'chats'— for seed next year), and twice perhaps. After that, if you go on using your own seed, your yields will fall off. So you will have to buy seed. The reason for this is that seed, to be good, must be grown either north enough, or high enough, to be out of the reach of the aphids which cause certain virus diseases. If you had a patch of land over 800 feet in the south of England or Wales, you could indeed grow your own seed on it. But most people must buy their seed, at least every three years. In Britain it mostly comes from high land in Scotland; in India from Himachayal Pradesh. As for strain, everybody eventually develops their own preference. At first use what your neighbours use. Potatoes are a potash-hungry crop. Seaweed is the best manure for them—better than muck.

There is one disease that you will have to guard against, and that is *blight*—the disease that killed five million Irish people. In dry areas you may escape blight—in dry seasons. In wet areas you will never escape it. To guard against it you must spray, either with a modern anti-blight chemical or with old-fashioned 'Bordeaux mixture', which is made like this:

Dissolve 4 lbs. copper sulphate in 35 gallons of water in a wooden barrel (or plastic dustbins). Then take 2 lbs. freshly burned quicklime and slowly slake it with water and make it into 5 gallons of 'cream'. Pour the 'cream' through a sieve into the copper sulphate solution slowly. Make sure that all your copper has been precipitated by putting a polished knife blade in the liquid. If it comes out coated with a thin film of copper you must add more lime. Then spray on your potato tops immediately: the stuff will not keep more than a few hours. Spray the foliage well, under the leaves as well as on top. From 120 to 160 gallons are needed for an acre. The first spraying might be in the middle of June in the south of Britain, in mid-July in the Midlands, in the last week of July in the north. Another spray should be given two or three weeks later. If you do this you will probably not get blight.

What happens if you—like most of us—do not spray? You will get blight. In a spell of warm, damp weather, when 'blight warnings' are given out over the wireless, small black spots will begin to form on your potato foliage. Gradually the whole of the tops of your potatoes will go black, and rot away. Now if you do not touch those potatoes for a month, the blight spores may not go down and infect the potatoes. Leave the tubers underground, undisturbed, and they may not be infected with blight. Lift them when you need them to eat, or at any rate not before the deepest frosts of the winter are imminent, when the ground will become too hard for you to lift them at all. Your tubers will then not have blight. *But* you will have a much smaller yield of tubers than you would have had if you had been a good farmer and sprayed and *not* had blight at all. Some strains of spuds are more blight-resistant than others, but all will get it.

Here in Wales we are inclined to leave our potatoes in the ground until we want them, digging them as we need them, until at least after Christmas. In Suffolk, where there was intense frost, we used to get them out in fine weather in October or November, leave them on the ground for a day or two to dry out, and then *clamp* them. Clamping consists in making a long pyramidal heap of them, covering them with straw or dry bracken about six inches thick, and covering the straw or bracken with earth, which you then tamp down with the back of the spade. You should leave little 'chimneys' of straw or bracken sticking up through the earth along the ridge to allow for ventilation, and little 'doors' of it down at ground level for the same reason. The straw will keep the frost out and the potatoes will keep well until you want them: *provided* the actual tubers themselves have not been infected with blight spores. If you leave the spuds a month after the haulms (tops) are completly rotted from blight, your potatoes should not rot in storage. The sight of a nice long clamp of spuds near your house is a satisfying one, and it makes you feel that you will probably survive the winter.

## TURNIPS, SWEDES, MANGOLDS, BEETS

*Turnips* and *Swedes* are *brassica* (like cabbages, mustard and curly kale), and biennials. The latter words means they live for two years making a big bulbous root the first year and producing flower and seed the second. We harvest them when they have made their swollen root the first year. *Mangolds* are like much larger turnips. They do not have the nutritive value of turnips but give much heavier crops. Agricultural chemists are apt to sneer at mangolds and say they are 'all water', but farmers reply 'maybe—but what water!' For mangolds, water or no, seem to produce a benefit in cattle that eat them out of all proportion to their chemical analysis. *Sugar beet* is smaller than mangold (mangolds may give up to forty tons an acre of crop in ideal conditions) and is used for sugar production. To make sugar yourself, chop the beet up as small as you can, boil the pulp, run the water off, and boil the water away, first mixing lime with it and passing carbon dioxide through the solution. Unrefined sugar will be left as crystals. *Fodder beet* looks just like sugar beet but is grown for stock feeding. It is a most excellent fodder crop for cattle, pigs, sheep or even horses. It is high in protein.

The cultivation of all these root crops is similar, and so I will deal with them all together.

1. Dung the land well in the autumn.

2. Plough deeply.

3. *Turnips:* make a very fine seed bed and sow in May, but I would not recommend turnips or swedes for the self-supporter if he can possibly get in one of the other roots. For mangolds, sugar beet or fodder beet sow in rows about 20 inches apart (maybe 22 for mangolds) pretty thinly. Sow in the last fortnight in April in England, May in Scotland.

4. Horse hoe after a fortnight if you have a horse hoe. If you haven't 'side hoe' with the hand hoe. That is hoe only between the rows.

5. When the beet are dear little things with just four leaves, then *single*, or 'chop out and single'. This is done with the hand hoe and is very skilled work. Cut all the little plants out except one about every 8 or 9 inches with sugar and fodder beet, 12 inches with mangolds.

6. Horse hoe again if you can in, say, a fortnight. If not, hand hoe.

7. 'Second hoe' again by hand when weeds begin to show again.

8. Horse hoe again if you can. The more you hoe the better,

for this is your 'cleaning crop', and your chance to get your land clean.

Harvest in September or October. Mangolds won't stand much frost at all, fodder beet little more. Harvest by pulling out of the ground, cutting the top off with a knife, throwing into a little pile, and covering with the tops against the frost. When you have done the whole field cart and clamp, just like potatoes. The beet will now keep the winter through and be a very valuable source of food for your cattle in the winter and 'hungry gap'. The hungry gap is at its worst in March and April. The grass hasn't begun to grow at that time, you have used up most of your hay, most of your roots, the animals are thin from the winter, it is a time when to be able to break into a big clamp of fodder beet or mangolds is very satisfying indeed. If you farm animals, farm all the year for the hungry gap and you won't go far wrong. I would recommend fodder beet more than anything.

## CARROTS

Carrots grow well on light land. They want deeply cultivated land, and it should not have too much muck put on it the same year. Sow in rows about a foot apart (4lbs. seed per acre), single when the plants come up to four to five inches between plants. Harvest and clamp like other roots. They are very high in feeding value, and will almost fatten pigs.

## BEANS AND PEAS

I am dealing now only with fodder crops: that is crops to feed to animals. Beans and peas are the only really high source of protein than you can grow yourself, but unfortunately very little development has taken place in the British Isles about them. The old field bean, horse bean or tick bean, is still grown as a field crop on some farms on strong heavy land, but it has many disadvantages. It is a martyr to chocolate-spot, a fungoid disease, it can be ruined by aphids (particularly spring-sown varieties can), can be mown down by frost, and is very easily choked by weeds. Sow winter beans by the second week of October at $2\frac{1}{2}$ bushels per acre (a bushel weighs 65 lbs.). If you can't drill them plough them in—drop them behind a plough. Spring beans sow in February at $3\frac{1}{2}$ bushels an acre, but I don't recommend them. Beans must have lime if on acid soil and like potash and phosphates but do not need nitrogen because they make their own. If you harrow the field in dry weather in March it does good—lets the air in and tears out weeds. If you can horse hoe or hand hoe or hand weed so much the better. The land will get foul whatever you do. Winter beans should be ready to harvest in August, spring beans (if the aphids have not eaten them) well into September. Cut with a binder, or by hand, stook like wheat, and you can leave the stooks in the field until all your other corn is in because beans don't mind the rain. Thresh how you like, but normally they are not threshed until spring because fresh beans are not good for stock. They mature in the rick.

But the whole question of fodder beans has been neglected in Britain because we are getting so much cheap protein from other sources—principally the sea. At the present rate of exploitation though the main fishing grounds will be sterile in ten or twenty years and the supply of fish meal will begin to dry up. Then we will be searching around frantically for a source of protein that we can grow ourselves, and beans will probably have to be the answer. The soya bean is one of the major sources of protein in the world today, but unfortunately it will not grow in cold climates. We grew the kind of bean that Heinz. use for their 'baked beans', in Suffolk, and it grew marvellously and we got good crops. We did not grow enough to feed much to stock but ate it ourselves. We tried it in Wales but had no success, but there is a small insect in ploughed-up grassland here which nips beans off at ground level for the first few years of ploughing. I suggest that every husbandman tries out every kind of bean he can lay his hands on to find the one which will crop best. Haricots and other beans of that nature must not be planted before the last frost, otherwise it will nip them off.

## LUCERNE

Lucerne, or Alfalfa, is a marvellous plant. It is like a clover except that it stands more upright, and pushes its roots down to incredible depths in the soil. It can be cut three or four times in a summer, and even in England up to 15 tons of fodder can be got from it, of the highest quality. It makes fine hay, fine silage, and is marvellous fed green. If it is ensiled it must be mixed with say grass or green rye or oats, as it is too rich by itself. In South Africa, where irrigation allows it to be grown on the deep rich soils of the Karroo, I have seen eight cuts a year taken off it. It is only really of use in England in the dryer areas, such as Suffolk (where we included it in our 'seeds' mixture for establishing permanent pasture). If sown by itself the land must be super clean (i.e. weed free) or the weeds will get the better of it in a year or two. Your seed merchant may recommend inoculating your soil with *B.radicicola*, the bacterium which grows at its roots and enables it to fix nitrogen. It enriches the soil enormously, and much of the near-desert land of Breckland was reclaimed and made fertile by lucerne. Sow it in August, after you have spent most of the summer cleaning the land.

## KALE AND CABBAGE

Kale and cabbage are great stock foods. They can be manured heavily with muck, and respond to large dressings of nitrogen if you want to give it to them. Cabbages and marrow stem kale should be used up first. Marrow stem kale is often grazed off the land behind an electric fence. If you cut the cabbages by hand leave the stalks and they will sprout again to provide a bite for sheep or cows later on. You can clamp really hard drum-head cabbage. Hungry-gap kale should be planted as well, for this will withstand the winter frosts and give you a bite of green stuff in the dreaded 'hungry gap' when you most need it. If it is milk you are feeding for, in any sort of animal, nothing is as good as fresh green fodder. Kale can be drilled and hoed, or broadcast on clean land and not hoed. It makes most weight drilled and hoed but it is more work.

# RAPE AND MUSTARD

Rape, which is a turnip that does not make a turnip if you see what I mean, is useful because you can sow it so late—right up to the end of summer. It is a 'catch crop'—can be grown after another crop has been taken off. It's good to feed off the land in the winter. Mustard does the same job. If I grow kale for folding off behind an electric fence I like to grow three rows of rape to every three rows of kale, so that the electric fence can go over the rape and not be shorted by the taller kale.

# 14

# Garden Crops

*The very idea of being fed, or a family, being fed, by daily supplies, has something in it perfectly tormenting.*

WILLIAM COBBETT : Cottage Economy

He meant, of course, supplies from the shops. And I am sure that if the 'average housewife' spent half the time that she spends in that silly occupation *shopping* cultivating a small garden at least she would never have to spend any of her housekeeping money on vegetables.

On a farm or smallholding, the garden should be for growing those vegetables and fruits that cannot be better grown on a field scale. Perennial vegetables, such as asparagus, globe artichokes, luxury crops such as celery, tomatoes, squash, melons, are obvious candidates for the garden rather than for the field. Also, you don't need much of most garden crops, and therefore it is useless growing them on a field scale. There are many smallholdings, of course, where only permanent grass is grown in the fields, and where the garden is the only arable land on the place. Then all must be grown in the garden.

The making of a garden from virgin soil is hard work, but the work can be eased in various ways. When Sally and I came to Pembrokeshire we found, next to our rather primitive and deserted house, a little circle of tumble-down stone 'hedge', as stone walls are called in this county, which had obviously once been a garden. In the middle of this was an outdoor lavatory, with a bucket in it, the ground was invisible under a very rank growth of long grass and weeds, and under the weeds was an enormous accumulation of rubbish. For many years, one would guess, the garden hadn't been 'farmed' (a way of saying looked after) and had simply been used as a rubbish dump. It was the only spot on the farm where cows and the ubiquitous Welsh sheep could not get.

Having removed the outdoor lavatory for firewood (we used the woods for a long time, and a spade of course) we put a pig-netting fence around the garden and put two sows in it. As the sows cleared the weeds and grass, which they did in a very few days, we realized the enormous *quantity* of rubbish. There must have been years of accumulation—and no matter how deep those pigs dug they brought up more rubbish. I erected a shute leading down from the garden to a wheelbarrow which I kept permanently stationed outside. After perhaps a day spent doing nothing else but barrowing rubbish away it was a matter of, two or three times every day, just going into the garden and putting such new rubbish as the pigs had unearthed for me on the shute, and every now and then emptying the wheelbarrow. For about a month rubbish was still coming up, but less and less. After a couple of months we felt it was time to move the pigs anyway, for their own sakes, and by then no more rubbish was forthcoming. Also, every perennial weed had been destroyed, the land had been dug down to several feet depth, and been heavily dunged by the pigs.

Sally made it her task to rebuild the fallen-down stone walls. The land anyway had been very stoney, and while I had been clearing the rubbish I had automatically flung every stone that came to my hand to the side. Sally, with great skill and determination, in little oddments of spare time, rebuilt the stone walls, and she did it so well that they stand there straight and upright to this day. All the stones were removed from the garden, and put to good use in the surrounding wall. I made a little gate out of split ash for it. Sally has made this garden her especial pride and joy. I limed it once (for our soil is short of lime) and slagged it once (for we are short of phosphate) but my guess is that it will never have to be limed or slagged again. For Sally, every year, barrows in loads of muck. It is immensely heavily manured. She digs it over very carefully with the spade at least every year. She seldom suffers a square yard of it to remain vacant for long. She has half a dozen cloches under

which she nurtures delicate things like melons in the summer, and hardy things like lettuce in the winter. It is a tiny garden, but it produces far bigger crops than my 'Long Garden' which I plough up every year with the tractor, and which is in such a lamentable state at the moment.

If you neglect a garden, or keep it in a state of semi-neglect, it is hell and will be a constant source of labour and anxiety to you. If you keep it under control though, and get the soil kind and friable by constant mucking or composting and constant cultivation, every task is easy and pleasant. Hoe weeds as soon as they appear. Some people will tell you that if you put a lot of compost on your land you won't have to hoe. This is rubbish—whatever you do you will have to hoe, unless you constantly douse your garden with toxic weed killers which will end up by killing you in the end. Put as much compost on your land as you can possibly get hold of: or as much muck, preferably muck from a variety of animals and not from just one species of animal. The more organic matter you can get in your soil the more easily you will be able to work it, weed it, plant it, and harvest your crops. Hoeing my Long Garden, which is new and has had very little working or manuring, is hell. It is like hacking at concrete. Hoeing Sally's Round Garden is a delight. The hoe glides easily through the kindly soil and the weeds come out easily. My Long Garden needs tons more ploughing, and tons more muck. In due course it will get right. The Round Garden never suffers from drought: the beautiful soil conserves moisture; the Long Garden dries out in a week. Plants in the Round Garden look fine and healthy and withstand any disease; plants in the Long Garden go down to anything. Look upon this picture and on this! All this comparison is to urge the new gardener to start with a bit of land small enough to manage in the time that he will have available, and then keep on top of it! Get the weeds on the run and keep them there. Do not let any weed seed. Suffer not the perennial weeds to exist. Couch grass, the curse of mankind, ground elder, bind weed, must be hit and hit and hit again until they give up through sheer exhaustion.

Jerusalem artichokes are a very good smothering crop to start off with in a new garden—better than the more usually chosen potato. Potatoes will suffer badly from ground slugs and from wire worm when planted on newly-ploughed-up grassland or weed land. Jerusalem artichokes will suffer from nothing. Lime the ground, if it needs it, and shove the tubers into the ground in February close together—in rows a foot apart and a foot apart in the rows. They will grow so dense and strong that it will be like the Burmese jungle underneath them and no weed can exist. Then in the autumn if you possibly can, shove pigs in. Keep the pigs in for a couple of months. Then plough or dig. Leave over the winter and dig with the fork in the early spring. Then plant your garden crops. At first the artichokes will start coming up again—incredibly the pigs haven't got the last little bit—hoe them out. Mulch with compost if you have it, or muck. The gardening books will tell you to muck at certain times of the year and to dig the muck well in. Muck at any time, and if you don't dig it in the worms will dig it in for you.

If you don't want to keep pigs then plough or dig and plough or dig again and again. Grow a good smothering green manure crop if you can wait that long: mustard is very good. Lime before you broadcast the mustard—a quarter of a pound of ground or burnt lime per square yard. Rake the lime well in, broadcast the seed thinly and rake again. Plant any time in the summer. Dig the mustard in before it flowers—when it just begins to bud: don't let it get too tough. If you sow your mustard very early, say in March, you can dig it in in May and set a late crop of potatoes, or later, say in July when you can plant haricot or French beans. Some gardeners, in digging up old grass, grow two crops of mustard in a summer, digging the first in in July and the last in September. This is to dismay the wireworm, which can be a menace after old pasture, and which don't like mustard. For a winter cover there is nothing to beat Crimson Clover, which being a legume, creates nitrogen. Dig it in in February.

If you keep any large farm stock you just don't have to go to the bother of keeping a compost heap. For example, if you have pigs out of doors, behind pig netting or an electric fence, if you have any sense at all they will be on land which you intend to garden or farm on. Just chuck every piece of waste vegetation you have to the pigs. They will either eat it and turn it into the finest compost in the world overnight, or they will tread it into the ground where, activated by their dung, it will rot and make humus. If you keep pigs in a sty just chuck all waste vegetation into their yard. That is your compost heap. If you keep cattle indoors do the same with them. If you stable horses clear the dung out of the stable when you have to, chuck it in a heap, and add your waste vegetation to the heap. If you keep hens by what I call the 'Balfour Method', after Lady Eve who invented it (See Chapter 8), throw your 'compost material' in the straw scratching yard. Ducks and geese will compost it for you too, in their night quarters, if they sleep indoors.

If you have none of these animals though, build two bins of the size that common sense whispers is necessary, out of heavy old timber (small pine thinnings ripped down the middle with a saw will do, if pressure creosoted, and can be got cheaply from the Forestry Commission in some places; old railway sleepers are marvellous), lay double rows of bricks on the ground in one of them to let the air in, or staggered railway sleepers, and put your waste vegetation in that. It is best to put it in layers of say a foot thick; sprinkle some activating material over each layer alternated with a sprinkling of slaked lime. The activator can be any highly nitrogenous material. A high nitrogen proprietary fertilizer is fine, or poultry manure, or fish meal, or piss, or manure of any sort. And of course any kitchen waste at all—although it seems a crime not to put that through a pig first! But compost needs some highly nitrogenous substance to make it rot quickly and properly. Lime also helps it, as does air. Some people leave some vertical posts in their compost as they build it up and, when then have finished the heap, haul the posts out. This leaves chimneys for air. The compost heap is in effect a bonfire, as that great and eloquent philosopher of the organic garden and the compost heap, Lawrence D. Hills, has so often pointed out. The only thing you can justifiably burn in your garden is wood, and that is better, surely, burnt on the fire in your hall where it will do most good. Some people say 'but ah—if you burn things you get potash!' Well you do, but the potash was there before you burnt whatever it is, and will still be there if you don't burn it. Let wood rot and it will release its potash just as well as if you burnt it—*and* you will get its nitrogen too and, more important of all, humus. When one compost bin is full—start on the other.

We will assume that we have at last got on the right side of our garden, and are ready to plant things we can eat.

This world is absolutely full of books on gardening. I imagine that they come second in sheer numbers to books on cookery: and if a cook were to cook every dish in just *one* cookery book it would take her years and she would bankrupt her husband. But, if you live in the British Isles, I would unhesitatingly recommend Lawrence D. Hills' *Down to Earth Gardening* and/or his *Grow Your Own Fruit and Vegetables*. Mr Hills is the most practical of gardeners, and yet he brings to the subject of gardening a high and questioning intelligence, and if he does anything, or recommends that anyone else should do it, he wants to know the reason for doing it. He writes delightfully, succinctly, and if a subject so complex and un-certain as gardening is can be instructed simply, he does so. And what I would recommend even more than Mr Hills' excellent books, is that you make friends with a good local gardener, and humbly and respectfully ask his advice about things, and do what he says. We came to Pembrokeshire full of book learning and three years at an agricultural college and we just make do. Garfield Howells, over the valley, grows onions like our melons and shallots like our onions, and I don't suppose he's ever read a book on gardening or ever will.

But this book is not a gardening book, any more than it is a cookery book, and so I will aim to provide a rough guide only for the year's gardening work of the self-sufficient gardener who wishes to grow enough of the most ordinary vegetables to feed his family. In fact I will only mention garden crops that we grow ourselves.

As for rotation, I would say that in the garden, as in the field, it is very important not to keep growing the same things on the same ground year after year, and when I say the same things I mean things of the same family: thus cabbage and all the things akin like cauliflower and Brussels sprouts are *brassica*, and therefore akin to turnips and mustard, and potatoes are *solanum* and akin to tomatoes This said the rules that should decide your rotation for you are pretty simple, and are these:

Potatoes do not like lime but they do like heavy dressings of muck or compost. In any case you should not put lime and muck on together, for the lime attacks the muck and wastes much of the nitrogen. Therefore plant potatoes after a heavy dressing of muck but no lime.

Brassica, one and all, like a lot of lime. If your soil lacks lime, therefore, grow brassica after potatoes, heavily liming first. The brassica will benefit by the heavy dressing of muck that the potatoes had, and the thorough cultivation and soil-stirring that the potatoes had, but the potatoes will not suffer from the lime because it will go on after they come out of the ground.

Legumes, meaning beans, peas and clovers, love lime too. So maybe grow beans and peas after your brassica, so that they can benefit from the lime you used for the brassica.

Maybe a root break could come after the peas or beans. Parsnips don't like freshly-mucked land, nor do carrots: it makes them fork. If you put them in after the legumes there will have been plenty of time for that heavy dressing of muck the potatoes had to have rotted away and they will do well.

After the root break, the lime will have dissipated enough to let you muck the land heavily and put in spuds again, and this is where we came in.

This rotation could be summarized: muck, potatoes, lime, brassica, peas or beans, 'roots' (parsnips, carrots, salsify, turnips, beet), muck, potatoes.

But gardening is very much a catch-as-catch-can process, and in practice you will find yourself scrambling a crop in on a piece of vacant ground when it suits you and not some theory. But it is as well to remember:

Brassica (all the cabbage, turnip and mustard tribe) like lime. They get club-root if they don't get it. They like nitrogen.

Potatoes (they get scab with fresh lime), carrots, celery, cucumber, marrow, seakale, rhubarb don't want lime. They like muck and potash.

Parsnips, carrots, salsify don't like fresh muck. They like phosphates and potash.

Onion tribe likes muck, lime and potash. Not too much nitrogen.

Legumes (meaning clovers, beans, peas, lucerne) love lime and phosphate. They don't want applied nitrogen, as they make it themselves.

Celery loves muck—hates lime.

If you find yourself left with a piece of land which has no crop on it, green manure it. That is grow a bulky crop and dig it in to rot, such as mustard in the summer, or crimson clover for summer-sowing and a good winter cover to be dug in in February. Clover seed is dear but you can grow your own —and why not? Grow all the seed you can. Onion seed is quite easily grown at home. Brassica is more difficult, as strains may not keep pure. Keep seed from the finest plants only, and leave to ripen as long as possible.

But to get back to that green manure, that muck, that compost, those loads of seaweed fetched home from a summer holiday, that cart-load of leaf mould fetched from the woods: the whole object of the organic gardener should be to increase, constantly, the humus status of his soil. Humus is a kind of indefinable substance made from rotting vegetation. Good soil is a living medium. A cubic yard of soil has an enormous population of living creatures, bacteria, protozoa, viruses, fungi, worms, insects: the soil of the agri-businessman is nearly sterile. Fresh vegetable matter dug in to richly organic soil, or merely left on top of it, is very quickly broken by a myriad organisms to useful humus on which the greater plants can feed. This is a matter of opinion (I don't want to get chucked out of the Soil Association!) but I see nothing wrong whatever in applying a little 'bag nitrogen' if I think a particular crop needs it, and I have no hesitation whatever in slagging land that is short of phosphate, liming land that is sour, or putting some potash on my potatoes or onions. I prefer to use 'organic manures' in these cases, because they are slower acting, last longer in the soil, and probably don't disturb the soil flora and fauna so much as 'chemicals'. In using the word 'chemical' I am perfectly aware that all matter in the Universe is 'chemical', but I am using the word in a way that nine people out of ten will understand. Fish meal as a source of nitrogen in this context is not a chemical: sulphate of ammonia is. But a *little* sulphate of ammonia applied to young cabbages just at the right time may well get them over a difficult period; grow them on quickly so they can get away from the ravages of, say, a caterpillar attack. Sally uses no 'chemicals' in her Round Garden because there is absolutely no need. She has achieved such a high humus status there—the general fertility of the soil is so high—that to shove in 'chemicals' would be like taking coals to Newcastle. That is the soil condition to aim at. I dug down two feet six in Sally's garden yesterday. For the whole of that depth the soil was kindly, friable, obviously fertile. You could have used any of it for a potting compost. Just outside the hedge the soil is a boulder clay, right to the surface, and filled with stones. Useless for anything.

What I intend to do is simply to go through a typical year in our own garden, month by month, and detail what we plant. I will not mention harvesting, for that is a matter of common sense: when things are ripe harvest them. Nor will I mention after care such as hoeing or weeding. That too is a matter of common sense: no crop in the world will flourish in the face of weed competition, and every crop in the world wants the soil loosened up around it, if possible.

*January.* We plant trees in January, and fruit bushes. We prune trees and bushes. Some people spray fruit trees with tar wash. We don't bother but we should. We cut pea and bean sticks. It's no good waiting until the leaves grow on them and then cutting them.

*February.* We sow celery seed in boxes indoors. It needs fine-spraying with warm water every day. We sow lettuce seed in boxes indoors. We set the First Early potato seed in trays to sprout. They don't want heat—just light. They don't want frost though! We sow parsnips on deeply dug unmanured land. As the seed takes such a long time to come up we sow radish with it. The radish will come up quickly and show us where not to hoe, and when it has done its job we will eat the radish. Radish then we will go on sowing, every week or fortnight, in tiny odd corners. Turnip lovers (which we are not) can drill early turnips. We plant shallots. Plant rhubarb, God bless it.

*March.* We put out onion sets. We buy these and they are pretty good. If we have autumn-sown onions we plant these out now. I am not going to give 'planting distances' because nine times out of ten they are common sense. After all, how much room does an onion need? Obviously leave the rows far enough apart so you can get in and weed, and weed you must, very often, for weeds seem to adore onion beds and onions simply hate weeds. The ground must be very firm for onions—roll it or get all those Hippy visitors who have come to drink your home brew to tramp it down.

Sow the brassica seed bed. This will contain: two or three sorts of winter cabbage, sprouting broccoli, self-protecting broccoli, red cabbage, Brussels sprouts, cauliflower, curley kale. You are thinking of next winter now; nobody wants to eat a lot of cabbage-stuff in the summer time, and note this, you cannot have—and never will have—enough Brussels sprouts. Get the ground for your brassica seed bed very fine, very firm, and plant in rows thinly. Keep hand weeded. Dust with anti-flea-beetle powder if little spots appear on the plants.

Drill early peas. To do this we scoop out a little trench with a hoe and sprinkle the peas in pretty thickly. Two or three peas in an inch. If the land is poor you want to dig a trench first, fill it up with muck, compost or leaf mould, bury it, and put your peas on that. Soak your pea seed in paraffin if you don't like mice, or if your mice do like peas. *You can't have enough peas.* Plant one row of early chitted spuds at the beginning of the month and another at the end.

Sow leeks in a seed bed.

Indoors plant celeriac in heat, melon in little pots in heat. March is a good month for planting out grape vines.

Sow lettuce and radish. Plant globe artichoke suckers.

*April.* A good month for establishing your asparagus bed. Buy three-year roots if you can afford to and never let them get dry! Get them into the ground straight away—no lying about in drying winds. Plant them in three rows on a raised bed, half earth and half muck, the rows a foot apart and the plants a foot apart in the rows. Plant four inches deep. A good plan is to build walls of planks or sleepers each side of the rows and keep the bed covered with six inches of seaweed if you can get it, straw or bracken if you can't. This will suppress all but perennial weeds and a tiny sprinkle of some fell weed killer will kill the perennials that poke their heads above the straw. The asparagus will push its way up in due course. Don't cut it the first year. Don't cut it after the first of June any year. It is very welcome in the early summer when there is not much else about. It likes salt.

Sow carrots. Sow thinly, and when they come up thin if you have the time. After thinning draw the soil up to the carrot rows with the hoe to prevent carrot fly which are attracted by the smell. Thin in showery weather for the same reason. Lawrence D. Hills recommends sowing your carrots between the onion rows to 'jam' the scent message for both carrot and onion fly. Or sprinkle with whizzed naphthalene or sand soaked in paraffin. We don't get much trouble so we don't do any of these things.

We dig our celery trenches, a foot deep or more, a spit (spade's width) wide, and four foot between centres. We dig plenty of manure into the bottoms of the trenches. No lime. We leave.

We plant salsify. We drill more peas (you can't have enough peas). We sow sweet corn, cucumbers, gherkins under cloches, or under glass. In Suffolk we just used to sow sweet corn outside, in May, and we used to get enormous crops every single year. Here we have to sow under glass a month earlier to get any crop at all.

Plant out leeks and, on a wet day, if our brassica seed bed looks ready for it, we start planting out brassicas. These will take up half the garden at least. The ground needs to be well ploughed, but firm. If it needs lime it should have been limed. Brassica need, above all, space. Brussels sprouts grow like small trees, and need three foot between each plant—more on good land. The others all need at least two foot-six in the rows—and maybe three foot-six between the rows. Leave enough room between the rows to get a garden cultivator down easily, if you have one, or a horse and a hoop-hoe if you have that. Give them far more room than you think they ought to have. They look tiny now—but wait 'til they grow! There is no hurry to plant your brassica though. As long as they are growing nicely in the seed bed you can leave them. Hills recommends waiting until the first lot of peas have been harvested and planting them after that. We need far more brassica to last us through the winter for the little that we could put on old pea-land to make much difference. I suspect a lot of suburban gardeners grow a few token cabbage-tribe plants—and buy nine-tenths of their vegetables from the shop. Sow lettuce and radish, and set out plants.

*May*. If you are on dry land sow New Zealand spinach. If on moister land sow Prickly or Perpetual.

Sow lettuce and radishes.

Sow more peas. Now you have an orgy of sowing all those things that are frost-tender, hoping that you will not get that nipper-frost on the first of June that we once got in Suffolk. Sow: runner and French beans (on previously dug and manured and limed trenches), marrow and pumpkin and squashes on muck heaps or rich land. Plant out outdoor tomatoes, sow sweet corn in the open, or plant out the sweet corn that you have been nurturing indoors, also melon plants.

More peas. You will never have enough peas.

*June.* Plant out your celery plants in the previously prepared trenches, after mid-month though. As they grow you will need to earth them up. I know all about self-blanching, and putting drain pipes over them and all the rest of it—but there is nothing to beat the old-fashioned *earthing up.* And it is less trouble in the end: most of these labour-saving gimmicks make work and don't save it.

Plant out more French beans, runners and dwarf beans.

Sow corn salad if you like the stuff.

Sow lettuce and radishes.

Stop eating asparagus in June and let it grow.

*July.* You may well still be engaged in planting out your brassicas. It's not too late. Keep on with the lettuce and radish sowings of course. Sow a seed bed with spring cabbage. (See September.)

*August.* Go on sowing lettuce and radishes, if you have the heart.

*September.* Plant out your spring cabbage plants on your harvested potato land. You will absolutely bless these spring cabbages come next April, when your family will be hungry for green stuff. Don't plant them as far apart as winter cabbages: twelve inches apart is plenty. They won't be giants.

Plant lettuce plants out under cloches for the winter.

Sow onion seed on a very well prepared seed bed if you are one of those brave hearts that grow their own onions from seed (and why not?).

*October.* Now a surprise. Sow your broad beans. Most books recommend sowing them in the spring—we never do. Sow them in the spring and the aphids will eat them. Sow them in October and you will have fine healthy plants that will laugh at the aphids and give you a heavy crop.

*The rest of the year* you can spend muck-carting, digging or ploughing, clearing up and feasting—the latter with a clear conscience.

# 15
# Fruit and Nuts

*A man who refuses apple dumpling cannot have a pure mind.*

COLERIDGE

It is one of the many disadvantages of the landlord and tenant system that there are so few fruit trees in English cottage gardens. No landlord is going to plant trees for his tenants, and no tenant is going to plant trees for his landlord. 'No man,' wrote that great prophet of the soil, Philip Oyler, 'unless he is a saint, can be expected to give the land the same care (the care it needs) if he is a tenant or an employee as he would as an owner.' That is so obvious that one would not think it necessary for anybody to say it, but it is necessary. He also wrote: 'We should accept it as fundamental that each individual has a right to a plot of the earth on which he was born—to as much as he and his family can farm well.'

Assuming that our self-supporter does own the land he is living on: his rightful share of the earth's surface shall we take it?, he will obviously wish to plant fruit trees. If there are any old neglected fruit trees on his land he will be wise to leave them in a year or two and see if they can be got to fruit well by heavy manuring, pruning (just cut a lot of the branches out of it) and winter washing. If the old tree still doesn't bear try root pruning, that is digging down and cutting a lot of the roots with a sharp spade. Bark-ringing is another method that has the same effect: remove a strip of bark right round the tree a quarter of an inch wide. More may kill the tree, but a quarter of an inch is not too much for the bark to jump again in a year or two so that the tree can go on growing. Bark-ringing and root pruning give the tree a nasty shock, which may be just what it wants to start it fruiting again. You can't do this with stone fruit by the way, only apples and pears.

*Planting.* Meanwhile, whether you have old trees or not, you should be planting new ones. Do this any time when the sap is down, i.e. in the winter, although November is supposed to be a pretty good time to plant. Go to a neighbouring fruit grower (if there is one) or a local nurseryman, and get from him the best varieties to plant on your soil. Get early varieties as well as late, so as to spread the eating season (late store better than earlies: the latter should be eaten at once) and also get various kinds of trees, i.e. some cordons or espaliers, some half-standards and some standards. The reason for this is that your cordons or espaliers, being small and kept small, will fruit several years before your bigger trees, and thus will begin to give you fruit fairly soon. The half-standards will come into fruiting next, possibly when your family or community is increasing and you need more fruit, and the standards will come last, but will go on and keep you in fruit for a lifetime. They have the enormous advantage that animals can graze beneath them. Three-year-old trees are best to buy, although you might try to put one or two older trees in, with enormous care, hoping that they won't die. I have seen ten-year-old apple trees planted, and they survived, but it was done by an expert.

As for varieties: this book is not long enough even to discuss this subject. Either gen yourself up on this, or go to a local expert. Make sure he knows about *stocks* too. It is most important that your chosen variety is grafted on to the right stock, i.e. a dwarfing stock for small trees (such as Malling No. 9 with apples), a non-dwarfing stock for large ones. If your 'expert' doesn't know about stocks, find one that does.

Keep the roots of your little trees moist when you bring them from the nursery. Dig large holes for each tree. Plant in good, well-drained, deep soil. Water-logged soil will simply kill them. Chuck some builder's rubble in the bottom of your hole if you have any (it helps drainage and provides lime in years to come), dump in a barrow-load of muck, shove in some soil, and then spread the roots of your tree nice and evenly on the soil, so that the roots stay in their natural shape and yet are all well in contact with the soil. Adjust it so that the tree will be an inch or two deeper than it was before. Put more good soil on the roots, tamp it down well; have sympathy with the tree that you are planting, imagine what *you* would feel like if you were a tree and being planted, how you would like your roots disposed of. It is that imaginative sympathy that some people have got and others haven't that is called 'green fingers'. Firm the soil well, but don't break the roots in doing so. Put a little lime with the soil and when you have filled the hole put a pound of lime on the ground around the tree. Mulch it well too with muck, old straw, cut nettles or bracken, or anything. The mulch keeps the soil from drying out, suppresses weeds and creates humus. All fruit trees, so far as I know, like lime. Stone fruit *must* have it (stone fruit are cherries, plums, peaches, etc.).

As for spacing, remember that the trees will grow! It is a very good plan to plant with the idea of using the land for something else besides big fruit trees. For example, plant wide apart rows, say 24 feet apart, with standards and 20 feet apart in the rows, and for years you will be able to grow two rows of soft fruit between the rows of big trees. When the standards spread somewhat only grow one row of soft fruit. When the standards reach maturity don't grow any. And here we might as well point out that the beauty of growing standard trees (the biggest), in spite of what most books on fruit growing tell us (they all say grow little trees for speed and space-saving), is that when they are fully grown you can graze large animals underneath them. The trees are high enough for the branches to be out of the reach of grazing animals (who would otherwise rip them to pieces—animals *love* fruit trees). There is no more productive use of land *possible* than a mature orchard of standard fruit trees with grass and clover underneath and animals grazing on it. All stock go well under fruit trees, and do well, and do the trees good with their manure, and their keeping of the grass short. Pigs (which have to be ringed so that they don't damage the roots) will eat the windfalls. But rotate your stock under the trees, as you rotate stock on all land: never keep the same species of animal on the same land for too long. Never make hay in orchards—it starves the trees.

Until your trees are, say, five years old, keep the ground just around their trunks bare. Either by mulching, or by mattocking or hoeing, keep the turf away from their trunks. And it doesn't matter how much muck you dump round those trees every year. People will tell you that heavily manured trees sometimes grow too fast and will not crop. I would say let 'em grow and good luck to them—they will crop one day, and be the better trees for it. Try pruning them harder, particularly in summer, and, when they get really big, if they still don't crop root-prune them.

*Pruning.* Pruning is all a great mystery, and everybody has his own idea about it. I know a man who says never prune at all, just leave the trees to nature and they will give you fruit. We have always pruned though and it seems to work.

Summer pruning is necessary for cordons and espaliers and trees being trained up walls. It is also good sometimes for a young tree which is growing too fast but shy about coming into bearing. Winter pruning is much more general.

Immediately you have planted a tree, prune it to the sort of shape that you are going to want. That is: cut the branches out of the centre of the tree, to some extent, so as to keep the tree open in the middle and let the light and air in. If two shoots are too near to each other cut one out. Aim to have four or five evenly spaced branches, and these branches, that you have left, must be shortened. Cut about two-thirds of the last year's growth off the branches that you are left with. The branches will shoot again from the last bud that you have left before your cut—so cut about half an inch from a bud that you wish to grow. This will probably be on the under side of the branch, for you wish to encourage the tree to assume an open-centred cup-shape, with spreading branches. It is important to prune hard this first year, because the branches of the tree should balance the roots, and by transplanting you have given the roots a pretty good shock, so you must give the branches one. Two wrongs make a right, in fact.

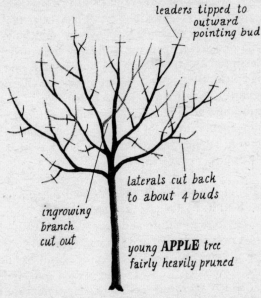

*leaders tipped to outward pointing bud*

*laterals cut back to about 4 buds*

*ingrowing branch cut out*

*young* **APPLE** *tree fairly heavily pruned*

In the second year you must distinguish between *leaders* and *laterals*. The leader on each branch is the shoot which comes from the end bud and makes an extension of the branch. Laterals grow from the branch behind it. You should shorten the leaders by about half their length, cutting again to a bud from which you want the new leader to grow. Laterals you should either cut off completely, if you don't want them, or more often cut them off to about three to five inches. Three inches for a weak and flimsy lateral, five for a stout one. These truncated laterals will then, in time, form fruiting spurs. For the next couple of years do much the same thing, but take less off the leaders until you are just tipping them. By now you should have a nicely-shaped tree, not overcrowded anywhere, nice and open in the middle, with plenty of well-spaced fruiting spurs.

After this, prune much more lightly. If they make very slow growth prune harder—cut away half the leaders. If they make too much growth don't prune. It has been said that they are like us: 'to those that hath shall be given, and from those that hath not shall be taken away'. This is, for fruit trees, how it should be if they are to thrive. I'm not so sure about ourselves.

*Pears* treat like apples. But they are a more delicate tree, and do best in sheltered positions, up against south-facing walls and so on. They need better treatment.

*Plums* like all stone fruit suffer from silver-leaf disease, which creeps into them by way of cuts. Except for the winter in which you plant them they should not be winter-pruned therefore, but pruned in May or June. They can then heal the cuts more rapidly and keep the disease out. Once they are shaped well leave them alone, the less pruning the better. Cherries and peaches the same.

*Spraying*. Spraying should be kept to a minimum in the organic orchard (when one meets commerical growers who have to spray *fifteen times* a year one can only wonder why they don't find an easier way of making a living!). But some spraying is necessary. Winter-washing, with stuff called Morteg, is worth it, or some other tar distillate. It kills the lichen and moss on the trunks of the trees, under which insect pests grow, and kills the eggs of aphids and other horribles. You must not winter-wash after the end of January for plums and pears or February for apples, or the strong tar will kill the buds. Summer sprays are much more complicated affairs and we don't do them unless we absolutely have to (a bad caterpillar attack, for example, when we spray derris) and if you must use them you must get expert advice. But if you are only growing for your own delight, and not to make a fortune, I don't advise much spraying. Spraying kills pests it is true—but it also kills the creatures that prey on pests. Once you start interfering with the balance of nature you may find yourself like a dog chasing its tail.

*Greengages*. Don't forget the humble greengage. I can remember as a boy when most cottage gardens had their greengage trees at the bottom of them, heavily laden with fruit in the late summer, and what a marvellous flavour they were! And what fine pies and puddings were made from them. Under their shade the cottager kept tame rabbits in home-made hutches, the hinges of the doors made from strips of leather, and the kind of cottager I liked best to associate with had ferrets too. Greengages need a Victoria plum tree somewhere near them to pollinate them.

*Peaches*. Lawrence D. Hills, who knows more in the lobe of his left ear about fruit growing than I know in my whole carcase, says a three-year-old bush Peregrine peach tree planted in September or October or February should have any fruitlets it grows in its first year picked off, be allowed to rear a dozen peaches the second year, forty the third year, and enough to make you ill the fourth year—with new cider! You should thin the fruits until they are eight inches apart. The only peaches we have grown have suffered from leaf curl. This because we did not spray them with lime-sulphur in late January and again perhaps in February. Alas—no peaches.

*Cherries*. Cherries should be pruned, if at all, in mid-June, and paint the wounds against silver leaf. But cherry growing in England, where we have practically exterminated our hawks, is a battle against birds.

*Walnuts*. There is a sawmill owner in Shropshire who buys every piece of good enough land that he can lay his hands on, and plants it up with walnuts. He does this, he explains, because *his* ancestors planted walnut trees for him to fell—now he wants to repay them by planting walnuts for his grandson. They will be ready to fell in 130 years' time. But meanwhile they will give an awful lot of walnuts and what in the world can be nicer than walnuts?

*Blackcurrants.* There is one soft fruit that every self-supporter should have, and that is blackcurrant. This is because black-currant has by far the biggest load of vitamin C, which is the vitamin that very many people are short of, in spite of the constantly reiterated statement that people eating an ordinary modern diet get enough vitamins. They get enough to stay alive and not get scurvy and that is all.

Plant the blackcurrants 4 feet 6 inches apart or five foot if you've got room. Prune so that the shoots come up from a stool at near ground level. Every year, in the winter, cut all the old, black wood out: the wood that has already fruited. But do not prune the new wood, that has not yet fruited, at all. For it is this that will bear the fruit next year. Plant plenty of blackcurrants: we have a dozen bushes but would like a dozen more. Manure very heavily every year with muck. Pull weeds out as they grow. One day your blackcurrants may get big bud; enlarged buds looking like Brussels sprouts but the size of a big pea. Put these buds on the fire. One day they may get 'reversion' and the leaves will look like nettles. Grub the bushes out and carefully burn them. But before they get that you should have planted more. You can grow more from healthy cuttings; stick six-inch-long cuttings in the ground in a row in November when you prune the old bushes. Leave them to grow for three years before planting them out into your new blackcurrant bed.

Red and white currants look beautiful but won't really feed the multitudes. Prune them like apple trees, not like blackcurrants which are completely different. You can let grass grow between soft fruit if you keep it short.

*Gooseberries* you should prune also like apple trees—but hard. Give them plenty of potash—wood-ash is fine.

*Raspberries* are very useful and well worth growing. Plant the stems that have grown up from the creeping roots of somebody else's raspberries; cut the stem about eight inches long with a bit of root attached about the same length. Plant in October in rich land not too deep, a foot apart in the rows and six foot between the rows. At each end of each row drive in a post and have two parallel wires between the tops of the posts and make the growing canes grow between the two wires. In the autumn cut out some of the old canes, right from the bottom, leaving not more than half a dozen good young canes per plant. You'll have to dig like mad every year alongside the rows to cut out the creepers which will cover your whole garden if you don't look out. Muck like mad—they're a greedy fruit. Our soft fruit garden was a piece of waste land which when we came here was practically devoid of soil: a little pocket of stones and gravel dumped here in the ice age. It is now deep black soil, and we get very heavy crops of both raspberries and blackcurrants, although the gooseberries, alas, aren't much cop.

*Strawberries* are a luxury and nothing more, but if you want them cadge good runners off your neighbours, or buy from a nursery, plant them in August in rich soil but no lime. The strawberry is a woodland plant and woodland soil is acid. Plenty of leaf mould is fine. Plant them shallow, with the roots spread wide. Weed them like the devil. You can't really hoe them because you would cut the roots. Mulch them well with bracken, straw or leaf mould. Spray sluggit or bait for slugs. The strawberry is a walking crop: it will not crop for many years on the same land, so establish a new bed every year, and every year (after you have got going that long) dig up a three-year-old bed. You can use your own runners for a while, but get in fresh blood every few years as your stock will lose virility.

*Tomatoes.* In Suffolk we used to grow Moneymaker and Harbinger tomatoes out of doors, and of these Harbinger were better although in very good seasons Moneymaker had a bigger crop. Being idle we used to buy the plants from a nursery, plant them out in late May or even June on very good ground against a south-facing wall, give them sticks to be tied to, and pull off the little shoots that grow from the angle between the stem and the branches and also shoots which sprang up from the ground. When tomatoes begin to grow you can feed the plants, like old-fashioned gardeners used to do, with the delicious liquor from a barrel filled with water and muck. Tomatoes suffer from blight in exactly the same way as potatoes do (the two plants are very closely related) and if you fear blight spray with Bordeaux mixture (see Ch. 15) or the proprietory Bulsol, and spray several times. If blight hits them—you've had it. Unlike potatoes the part you eat gets affected, and the fruit will simply turn brown and decay. Don't grow tomatoes twice on the same bit of ground without a rest. They build up Lord knows what dreadful infections.

If you insist on growing your own plants from seed, these should be sown on a mixture of $\frac{1}{3}$ sifted loam, $\frac{1}{3}$ leaf mould and $\frac{1}{3}$ sharp sand, in gentle heat, in March. Growers often soak this compost with boiling water a week before sowing to kill creepies. Sow $\frac{1}{4}$ inch deep in rows of one inch apart. Thin out as soon as you can to $\frac{1}{2}$ inch apart in the rows. Water moderately with tepid water—do not overwater. When they have made two leaves transplant to other boxes—two inches apart. End of April transplant plants again this time to 4 inches apart. You will need more patience than I have got. Tomatoes don't like lime.

Consider the idea of three-dimensional farming. In Mallorca I have seen large areas of very good land sparsely planted with food-bearing trees with good grass underneath on which animals grazed. The trees were exploiting the subsoil—bringing up minerals and trace elements from down below where the grass roots could not get. The grass was feeding the animals which in turn were manuring the trees. Many of the trees were locust bean, producing a heavy crop of high-protein stock feed. If we could find a tree that produced a high-protein food in the British climate we would be well on the way to self-sufficiency.

# 16

## Storage of Vegetables

*It is very hard to imagine, indeed, what anyone should want
ice for, in a country like this, except for clodpole boys to
slide upon, and to drown cockneys in skiting-time.*

WILLIAM COBBETT: Cottage Economy

From which remark one gathers that Cobbett would not have
been a great exponent of the deep freeze. We have a deep
freeze now, but personally I think it is a misuse of this instrument to use it for the storage of vegetables. The reason for this
is that, in the British Isles at least, it is possible to have good
fresh vegetables from the garden all the year round, and it is
far better to 'enjoy the fruits of the earth in their season' than
to try and prolong the seasons of vegetables by freezing them
into some horrible mush in plastic bags in a freezer. The reason
why asparagus tastes so marvellous when you first get your
teeth into it late in April or early in May, when you have just
begun to get sick of spring cabbage, is that you have not tasted
it for eleven months. If you had it every few days out of a deep
freeze it would be old hat—there would be no freshness about it.
This applies to peas, too, which I am told 'freeze well'; fresh
they are a great gastronomic experience (if they are garden peas
—not blue bullets from the greengrocers), and it is a crime
to keep nibbling peas all winter, thus doing yourself out of the
great treat of eating them in the summer time when they
come ripe as a fresh experience. I am not talking about dried
peas, which are an entirely different kettle of fish.

*Runner Beans.* People freeze runner beans. They are crazy in
their heads. I have eaten frozen runner beans and they are not
a patch on salted ones. Runner beans are things you can quite
justifiably store, because if you have planted them properly

you will have such a glut of them that you will eventually get tired of them, and they store so cheaply and easily. Pick them when they are young and green (not old and stringy), slice them (we do it with a little bean slicer that screws on the table), lay them in layers in a big crock with 1 lb. salt to 3 lbs. beans and pack tight to exclude air. When the crock is full cover it up. If they go bad you have not put enough salt in them. When you want runner beans, some time in the winter when the weather is foul and you don't feel like going out into the snow to pick Brussels sprouts, pull a handful out of the salt, wash under the tap for an hour and then boil. You can hardly tell the difference between salted runners and fresh. I know this goes against the 'fruits of the earth in their season' philosophy, but I think an exception should be made in the case of runner beans. It is good always to have some green vegetables available no matter what the weather.

*Root vegetables* of course should be stored, for the idea of the swollen root (or stem as it is in some cases) is just that—to store the summer's goodness for the winter time. We have discussed clamping under potatoes, but I will recapitulate it here. Pile any root vegetable in a long pyramidal heap, cover the heap well with straw or bracken (a foot thick at least), cover that with earth which you pat on hard with a spade. Leave straw sticking out at the bottom about every two yards to let air in, and little straw chimneys sticking out of the ridge at the top every two yards to let the air out. Most roots don't like frost, and the clamp protects them from it. If you have a good dry root cellar, or really frost-proof out-building, you might use them instead: less work than clamping. Potatoes don't like light (it makes them green and inedible). Parsnips don't mind frost—in fact they taste better after having been frosted: leave them out where they grow and dig them as you want them. A disadvantage of the root cellar or indoor store is that you can get a build-up, after a year or two, of spores which attack the roots you keep there. Clamps avoid this trouble, and personally I prefer them.

*Dried peas, beans or pulses.* These must be properly harvested. They must be allowed to ripen absolutely in the haulm, gently pulled, left in the sun and wind for some time, turned occasionally, then, if you have the room, hung up in bunches from the roof of a shed. If you don't have room like this to spare, and have a lot of peas or beans, make a rick of them and keep the rain out. Thresh with a flail and keep in dry bins or crocks. Soak for at least twelve hours before cooking, and add a little milk to the water when boiling.

*Onions* should also be properly harvested. When they are quite ripe it is a good plan to bend their tops over for a week or so. Then lift them out of the ground and lay them on their sides, bottoms to the sun, for a week or two, turning them occasionally. The best way to store them is to hang them in strings, which is quite simple. Just hang four strands of bailer or binder twine down from a hook, and plait the short tops you have left on your onions in to the strings—weave them in like the warp and weft of a cloth. Nothing looks nicer than a dozen or so fat strings of onions hung under the eaves of your house on the southern side, or else hung in an airy shed, or a big kitchen. To pickle onions: soak in brine for three days, wash, dry and put in boiling vinegar.

*Celery* is better when it's had a frost on it, and is that valuable thing—a winter fresh vegetable. Leave it in the garden, well earthed up, and eat it sparingly. Like peas and Brussels sprouts you will never have enough. In very severe weather cover the rows with straw or bracken.

*Tomatoes* can be bottled when ripe, made into chutney green, or each one wrapped separately in tissue paper and put in a drawer. Some can be laid, green, on a window-sill to ripen, but they'll probably go rotten like this. We used to lay them in draper's wadding, in drawers, not touching each other. If you live in a hot country, like Spain, you can hang them, ripe, in bunches in the sun. They'll shrivel up and keep good.

I think we should experiment in England with doing the same thing with artificial heat. Spanish dried tomatoes have a marvellous flavour. When picking tomatoes for dry-storing leave the stems on and do not bruise. To bottle tomatoes, wash in cold water, place in bottles, fill bottle with brine made with $\frac{1}{2}$ oz. salt to 1 quart water. Put the screwtops on the bottles but do not screw them tight because, obviously, the steam must escape or the bottles will burst. Place the bottles in a large kettle of cold water, with the water covering the tops, and bring *slowly* to 190° F. (88° C.). Keep it there for half an hour. Remove bottles from water and screw tops tight immediately. Another way is to scald the tomatoes first in boiling water for ten seconds, pull them out and drop them in cold water then you can remove the skins. Pack the fruit tightly into the jars with no added liquid, but if you add a teaspoonful of salt and half a teaspoonful of sugar to each pound of fruit it is said to improve the flavour. Then heat and seal the jars as for tomatoes in brine.

*Bottling.* I will here say a word or two about bottling in general. We have always used kilner jars, which are proprietary jars with screw tops holding down a glass disk on a rubber ring. The rubber rings need renewing occasionally (every few years—or as soon as they stretch) and the metal parts of the tops should be well rubbed with vaseline before you use them, otherwise they will rust. Store rubber in the dark. There are other proprietary bottling jars: they all have one thing in common: they cost money. Our forebears used to preserve things by putting them in stoneware jars, or pottery jars, or old glass jars, sterilizing by boiling as we do, then sealing by running hot fat, hot wax or other air-excluding substance over the material to be bottled. The principle of bottling is simply this. You destroy all the micro-organisms which might cause decay by heating them, while the material is still sterile; then you seal it from the air so that no more micro-organisms can get in. Canning is the modern industrialized way of doing the same thing.

For bottling it is very good to have a bottling boiler, which has a false bottom to stop the glass jars from standing directly over the source of the heat, and a hole in the lid for a thermometer. You can buy a special bottling thermometer. If you haven't got a thermometer you can achieve the same result by filling your bottles with hot syrup or brine, plunging them into hot water, heating until the water is simmering and keeping it simmering for half an hour. The idea, though, of the thermometer method is so that you do not have to heat the stuff you are bottling more than absolutely necessary to sterilize it, for over-heating kills the flavour, and, with that, the vitamins. If you haven't got a bottling boiler any old receptacle will do, provided that it is deep enough for you to be able to stand the bottles on a metal plate or grid or something (even a thick cloth) just to keep their bottoms from touching the source of heat.

If you grow outdoor tomatoes most of them won't get ripe. Such of these, as are not blighted, as you don't think will ripen in drawers, make chutney of:

Take 1 lb. of green tomatoes, cut them up; chop up half a pound of onions, put in 1 oz. of salt, 2 teaspoons of cayenne pepper, 1¼ pints of vinegar, ¾ lb. brown sugar or honey, ½ lb. raisins; simmer in a saucepan until it goes thick. Bottle hot in hot sterilized jars, and you don't need to heat the jars again. Don't cover with metal covers or the vinegar will eat the metal. Greaseproof paper is good enough to cover chutney, like jam.

It is well worth going to some trouble to preserve tomatoes. If you can grow a few tomato plants in the greenhouse, and some out of doors, you will have fresh tomatoes for a good many months of the summer and autumn, but after this you must have them preserved. Tomatoes make all the difference to good cooking, and, further, they are the third richest source of vitamin C that we have available (blackcurrant being the highest, lemon next).

Another use for surplus tomatoes is tomato juice. To make this you simmer the tomatoes and then rub the pulp of them through a fine sieve. Add to it ½ pint water, 1 oz. sugar, 1 teaspoonful salt, ½ teaspoonful pepper. Bring to boil immediately (you must not leave it in the air or it will go brown), pour into hot bottles, stand for ten minutes in boiling water and seal.

*Fruits.* Other things well worth bottling, particularly if you have children in your community, include blackcurrants, blackberries, raspberries and their kin, gooseberries. Put into bottles, fill bottles with a syrup of 8 oz. sugar to 1 pint water, boiled and then cooled, put on caps lightly, place bottles in bottling boiler, fill with cold water over the tops of the bottles, bring slowly to 165°F. (74°C.) and keep there for ten minutes. Haul the bottles out and tighten tops hard immediately. And here is a tip about tightening tops of bottles. After the bottles have cooled, unscrew the metal tops and pick the bottles up by the glass discs. If there is a proper seal there will be a vacuum inside and you can do this. If the glass tops come off then you must boil and seal again—you haven't got an airtight seal. After testing, if successful, replace the metal screw-top and screw on hard. Shove the bottle in a shelf and forget it until the darkness of the winter. It is very satisfying to walk into your larder and see shelf after shelf of bottled fruit in the early part of the winter: particularly if you know you have got a Jersey cow or two to milk and will have plenty of rich cream to go with it.

Soft fruit freezes quite well, and if you have a deep freeze you will probably find yourself using it to preserve your soft fruit and not going to the trouble of bottling. Pack in polythene bags of course.

People bottle all sorts of other things, like apples, but personally I think it is a waste of time.

Apples, if they are keepers, should be laid out on clean shelves (no spores from last year's fungus to decay them), on paper if you like, *not* touching each other, in an even temperature well above freezing and with ventilation. They should thus keep the winter through. If you have doubts about them dry some apple rings. Slice your apples into discs, core them and thread them on a string, dry them at from 120° to 150°F. (50° to 65°C.) for five hours, hang them in the cool for twelve hours, then pack in cardboard boxes and store in a dry place. If you don't want them to go brown put in the fumes of burning sulphur for ten minutes before you dry them.

Pears can be quartered and put in brine of 1 oz. salt to 1 gallon water for a minute (this stops them discoloring—you can't use sulphur with pears because it spoils the flavour). Dry the quarters on trays starting at 100°F. (38°C.) raising to 150°F. (66°C.) for five hours.

Prunes can be made of any plum or damson, and they are a rich source of vitamin A. Dip the plums into a lye made of 1 oz. caustic soda in a gallon of water for a few minutes. This softens the skins. Wash very well in cold water, dry on trays over your stove at 120°F. (50°C.) raising to 160°F. (71°C.) very gradually or the plums will burst. Keep in heat for two days. Soak prunes in water for 12 hours before using.

Any fruit juice can be made (if you have small babies to think about) by boiling fruit for half an hour, then strain juice through strainer, let it stand for a day, boil it for half an hour again, skim, add 1 lb. sugar per gallon of juice, boil again, skim again, pour hot into hot sterile bottles, stand bottles in boiling water for ten minutes, seal. Blackcurrant is very good like this.

*Mushrooms* are marvellous dried. Thread on strings and hang over stove, 120°F. (50°C.) is right, until dry. They are best crumbled up to a powder and stored in airtight jars or cans. Marvellous for flavouring soups or stews.

All herbs can be dried. Pick just before they flower and hang in bunches near your stove.

*Chutneys* can be made of nearly anything. The principle is simmer your fruit or vegetable together with onions and spices (the more spices the merrier in my opinion and onions are essential) in vinegar. When it has boiled down to a thick goo bottle and cover with greaseproof paper. You don't need recipes of ⅝ oz. of this and ¾ oz. of that if you just use common sense. Of course you need salt and pepper.

*Pickling*. To pickle anything cut it up, lay it in salt for a day, rinse and cover with cold vinegar. Gherkins are well worth pickling. Leave these in a brine of 1 lb. salt to 1 gallon of water for at least three days (weeks if you like), pull them out of the brine and drain, pour hot spiced vinegar over them, cover and leave for 24 hours, drain vinegar off, boil it again and pour it over the gherkins. Do this twice if you like—it improves the colour. Bottle and store.

To pickle onions leave in brine of 1 lb. salt to 1 gallon water (don't skin the onions first) for at least 24 hours—months if you like—the longer the better. Drain, put in jars, fill with cold spiced vinegar.

*Freezing of fruit and vegetables*. You can freeze tomato juice or other fruit juice by pouring it into cartons, putting it in the freezer until solid, taking out of the cartons as small blocks of ice, putting in plastic bags and back into the freezer.

All vegetables, if you *must* freeze them, plunge into boiling water first, bring the water back to boil and boil for three minutes, plunge into cold water, drain, pack in plastic bags, seal bags, label, and freeze.

Soft fruit you can put straight into plastic bags, seal, freeze; except gooseberries, which you should crush, sprinkle with 1 lb. sugar to 3 lbs. fruit, bag and freeze.

*Sauerkraut*. If you live in a land where no greens grow in the winter time because it is deep in snow, make sauerkraut. This is done by fermenting shredded cabbage sprinkled with salt in deep bins until you want it, which is done this way:

Rub clean the inside of a wooden tub (crock would do) with vinegar. Line it with cabbage leaves. Shred 12 lbs. cabbage, mix with 8 oz. salt, pack in tight, cover with whole cabbage leaves, stir occasionally for first three weeks and then leave covered until you want it. To cook it, drain, put in boiling water and boil for 2 hours.

*Sweet corn*: boil well on the cob, dry cobs in slow oven overnight, break kernels off cob, store in closed jars. Sweet corn will freeze well too—take it off the cob of course and stow in bags.

We lived for eight years in Suffolk without a deep freeze, and we lived very well indeed. We hardly ever bought any food and we never felt the lack of anything. We bottled a lot, made jam a lot, dried a lot. We were never short of vegetables nor of fruit. The only difference now that we have got a deep freeze, as far as vegetables and fruit are concerned, is that we freeze soft fruit and fruit juice and don't bottle them. I have a feeling that they were nicer when we bottled them.

# 17
# Fish

*. . . . flowers, and showers, and stomachs, and meat, and
content, and leisure to go a-fishing.*

IZAAK WALTON: The compleat Angler

## FRESHWATER FISH

The industrial working man's sport of catching fish out of
fresh water canals, lakes and streams, weighing them, and
throwing them back again, is as puerile as pulling wings off
flies, but I suppose it is better than watching hired men
playing football, for at least it gets its devotees away from a
crowd. The men who do it will solemnly assure you that these
fish are not edible anyway, and further that if they throw them
back it will keep the stocks of fish up so other anglers will
have a chance to catch some. They are wrong on both counts.
There is no freshwater fish that lives in England that I know of
that is not excellent to eat. And to crop, or harvest, the fully
grown fish is good for the stocks, in that it gives the younger
ones a chance to live and thrive. It is very good for the health
and welfare of a stock of fish in any piece of water to remove
the full grown fish that have had a chance to breed once or
twice and allow the younger generations some room.

I have eaten most kinds of English freshwater fish, very
many kinds of African ones, and in the Burma jungle during
the war we used to kill far more fish with our hand grenades than
we did the enemy. I have never yet found a freshwater fish
that was bad to eat. Some people manage to persuade themselves into thinking that freshwater fish taste 'muddy'. This is
a folk lore handed down from granny to granddaughter like
the other one that wild sea duck taste 'fishy'. Well *sole meuniere*
tastes 'fishy' but we still eat it. I must refer the reader back to

the excerpt from *Cottage Economy* which we have inserted at the top of Chapter Five of this book. But in sober fact freshwater fish do *not* taste 'muddy' and nor do wigeon taste 'fishy'. It is all in the imagination. If there is still anxiety on this score, however, freshwater fish from muddy places can be let to swim in clean water overnight or longer before cooking, as is done in France sometimes with carp.

We cannot in this book go in for advice to anglers, and angling in the accepted sense anyway is a sport which may give a by-product of something to eat rather than a way of getting food. There are plenty of ways of taking fish far more effectively than by 'angling' but most of them are against the laws of this country. As they are not against the laws of every country though it is quite permissible to describe them in this book and—who knows?—maybe the laws of *this* country might change one day; the laws of Man are not immutable, if those of God or Nature are. We will therefore discuss some methods of taking the better edible freshwater fish, fish by fish.

*Salmon.* The salmon is the king of freshwater fish and that nobody would try to dispute. He spends most of his adult life at sea and is in far better condition caught at sea if mature and off his homeland, for he is at his prime, clean and full of vigour. The monofilament net with a mesh of 5½ inches has made the taking of salmon at sea practical, and shown that there is a greater stock of salmon at sea than had ever been thought. The salmon comes into fresh water to spawn. In an ideal world, if the true welfare of salmon were really considered, I believe he should be netted at sea and left severely alone while in fresh water, for he is there strictly for breeding. The spawning rivers would, of course, have to be kept clear of obstruction and unpolluted, no doubt by the State, for a major incentive to do so would be lost.

But nevertheless we do catch him and eat him when he has entered the rivers, and the sooner after he has entered the fatter and better he will be. In countries where there is no law against it, netting is the best way of taking fresh-run salmon. The new monofilament nets of man-made fibre are perfect for this. If put across a stream at night (the salmon lay up in the day, move upstream at night) salmon will swim into it and gill themselves. For salmon a net of 5½ inches is used (4½ inches is better for small salmon and sewern, or sea trout), six meshes deep, mist green colour, hung on head rope of 1½ mesh for two (which is a way of saying the net is bunched up on the head rope—not pulled tight). The head rope contains plastic floats just sufficient to keep it up and the foot rope just sufficient small leads to keep it down.

Gaffing is the method of taking fresh-run salmon most used by poachers in this country. No doubt it is wicked to break the law, but it is a very good way of catching salmon, and has often been described. The gaff is a hook about 3½ inches across the mouth and has a barb on it. A gaff with no barb is no good—you will simply wound fish, which is unforgivable. It is not fixed permanently to a stick but concealed in a pocket, and it has a line attached to its eye. The poacher walks slowly along the river bank gazing intently into any deep water near the bank. Under overhangs, under rafts of sticks, under submerged roots of trees are the places. He must gaze intently and long into one place, for a salmon is very hard to see. Many poachers wear polaroid glasses and these are an enormous help for they cut out the glare of the sky on the water. A salmon hardly shows up at all—just a long black streak over the bottom, the only thing moving the tail, which gently stirs to and fro: sometimes the line of the mouth is the only thing you see to give him away. When the poacher sees his fish he goes and cuts a light stick the right length, lashes his hook to one end of the stick with its own line, takes the loose end of the line (which has a loop in it) up to the other end of the stick and puts the loop on his wrist. Very carefully he leans over, pushes the gaff into the water, and gaffs the salmon in its middle. He lets go of the stick, the line unwinds and releases the stick from the gaff and the poacher is left with his salmon on the hook and the hook tied to his wrist by a long line. He hauls the fish in, gets him high up on the bank, and bashes him on the head with a priest if he has one (a priest is a small club — it 'administers the last rites'), or with a well-aimed blow from the foot. He then conceals the gaff in his pocket again, conceals the fish in the undergrowth and starts to worry about how to get it home without being seen. Of course if he has a fishing rod with him, and has a licence, he just carries the salmon home openly and says he caught it on a 'Butcher's Glory' or some such artifact and gaffed it to get it out of the water. The *drivver*, or *pritch*—a Neptune's trident or fork with barbs—is even better than a gaff.

Some poachers poison rivers by liming, or cyanide, or other disgusting substances. I would send all such poachers straight off to Siberia. Such practices are absolutely unforgivable, for they kill every fish in the water, great and small. To take the odd salmon with the net or the gaff may be against the laws of Man but it is not against the laws of Nature or of God. To poison water is nothing less than blasphemy, and a deadly sin.

Now having caught your salmon (legitimately, with a fly of course, no poaching methods for us) you have to cook it. If you want it cold, put it in a pan, cover with water, vinegar, and olive oil in equal parts, add bay leaves and pepper and salt, bring to boil, simmer for ten minutes per pound of fish. Let it cool in the cooking liquid.

To smoke *Salmo salar* (and this is what you should really do with it because there is just nothing like real smoked salmon. The 'smoked salmon' you buy nowadays is often not *Salmo salar* at all but a distant relative that is imported from Japan in enormous frozen blocks then half smoked and dyed to make it look like real salmon. Also, smoked stuff can never be deep frozen and still taste any good):

Fillet but leave the lug bones on (common sense will tell you what these are).

Remove ribs; this is difficult but if you get your salmon you will soon see how to do it. You have to trim the flesh away a little and pull the ribs out with a pair of pliers. String through the shoulder. Carefully score through the skin at the thickest part so the salt can penetrate. Lay fillets on a layer of fine salt skin-side down and put ½ inch of salt on cut surface. Start with ½ inch at thickest part—taper off to hardly any salt on tail.

Leave in salt 12 hours for a 1½ lb. to 2 lb. fillet, 18 hours for a 3 to 4 lb. fillet, 24 hours for a 5 lb. fillet or over. These times are terribly important. But if the underlying flesh (the flesh under the surface) still feels soft give more time in the salt. Wash the salt well out of them and dry. Smoke for 24 hours at 70°F. (21°C.), then for 12 hours at 80°F. (27°C.) in light smoke.

The fillet should lose 10 per cent of weight in salting and 10 per cent in smoking.

Some smokers rub on molasses, others brown sugar; some sprinkle saltpetre, some pour rum on. I prefer to pour the rum down my throat and wipe the fillets lightly with olive oil both before and after smoking. Both rum and oil do more good that way.

*Trout.* There is little to say about trout, beyond that any country boy in the trout areas of Britain knows how to tickle them and I have a friend who pokes them out of holes under tree roots or rocks with two sticks which have an onion net between them. They fly out into the onion net.

To smoke trout: gut and clean well; soak 1 hour in 80 per cent brine; pierce through eyes with a metal speat and prop belly open with a match stick; put in smoke still wet at 90°F. (32°C.) for half an hour; give them two hours at 180°F. (82°C.). They are then 'cooked smoked' and should, like smoked salmon, be eaten cold and raw.

*Eels.* Eels are the most underestimated fish in Britain. They are highly prized in every country of the world that I know of except Britain and Norway. The Japanese fish-farm them, importing live elvers for the job from the River Severn; so do all of those Eastern European countries whose rivers do not run into the Mediterranean; they fly elvers from the Severn to stock their rivers, for the Black Sea and the Caspian have no natural supply. The old Zuider Zee (now the Ijselmeer) is given over to eel fishery, and the eel weirs of the Baltic form a serration of fences out to sea from every suitable piece of shoreline. The eel is perhaps the most delicious and nutritious of fresh water fishes.

Eels, by the way, can be taken in 'hives', which are torpedo-shaped baskets of withies with inverted funnels in one or both ends of them which are sunk below the water and baited. Nowadays most people make cages of fine-mesh wire netting to do the job instead. Fresh chicken guts make a good bait, so do sea-water shrimps or their heads. Eels can also be caught with the long-line: that is a long line with many hooks along it. Bait the hooks with worms and leave the line down over-night. I have filled many a tin bath up with eels by *babbing*. To do this you collect a bunch of worms, thread each worm on a piece of knitting wool, tie them all up in a knot or 'bab', tie them on the end of a string and hang the string from a short stick. Go out in a boat in the shallow of an estuary and lower the 'bab' to the bottom. After a minute or two bring it over the boat (and the tin bath), give it a sharp shake and you will shake the eels that are clinging to the bunch of worms off into the bath. But the eels you want for smoking are the big fat silver eels that are on their way off to sea after their seven or eight years in fresh water to lay their eggs in the Sargasso Sea. Eel traps on the weirs of watermills used to catch these, and many a miller paid his rent with his eels, and many a mill owner still could, if he smoked them before he sold them. To cook fresh eels: half skin, stuff, and pull the skin back to hold the stuffing, hold eels with a rag.

To smoke eels: gut (do not skin), clean, lay in dry salt for 12 hours; hang on sticks and dip in boiling water for a few seconds. This makes them open out; smoke at 140°F. (60°C.) for from 2 to 4 hours according to size.

For the cooking of all other freshwater fish I will refer you to *The Compleat Angler*, the recipes in which make one drool at the mouth. After his ecstatic recipe for pike, Izaak Walton says: 'This dish of meat is too good for any but anglers, or very honest men; and I trust you will prove both, and therefore I have trusted you with this secret.'

*Fish farming.* The way in which freshwater fish can make a really important contribution to the self-supporting community is by fish farming. An acre of fish farm in the tropics will yield five tons of fish per year (half a ton of beef is a good yield off an acre of the very best grassland), and the fish farms in cold East Germany yield 242 kilograms per hectare per year. In days gone by fish farming was a very important branch of animal husbandry in Britain. Lent and Fridays were meatless days anyway, meat was always in short supply and towards the end of the hungry gap (in Lent that is) people could stomach no more salt junk and had not tasted fresh meat for months, the sea was far away, and so freshwater fish was the only answer. John Taverner, writing in 1600, recommends making big shallow ponds, keeping the ponds flooded one year and dry the next. When dry, plough and seed their beds with clover and then graze with cattle: 'their dung and stale together with the natural force of the Sunne . . . will breed flies and bodes of divers kindes and sortes', which the subsequent fish will fatten on. You should drain your pond to be dry about the first of November. Take the best fish thus exposed by draining the pond to your stew pond, which is a small, deep pond for storing fish for the winter: deep so the frost won't kill them. They will keep there until you want to eat them. The smaller fish you put in the pond that you have newly flooded and which has had cattle grazing on it all summer. They will thrive in this and grow and fatten for next winter. Taverner says the ponds should be under six feet deep and on boggy land, fit for nothing else (but 4 feet is deep enough). He advises only to handle fish in cold weather. The fish he recommends are carp, bream, tench and perch, but he has reservations about bream because they spawn too freely and overstock the pond. If you have pike you can afford bream—the pike will keep them within reason. He recommends feeding fry with oatmeal. A carp will commence eating when 1 inch long. Old carp, he says, are to get: 'sodden barley and mault steeped in water and sodden pease'. He liked to have cattle feeding near the fish ponds, geese to keep the grass short and as 'good watch dogs', and ducks to do good by keeping weeds down and manuring the water.

Taverner's methods are obviously a good example of proper husbandry: interaction between different crops and animals and interdependence. The fish fertilized the subsequent grassland, the cattle fed the subsequent fish. Modern fish-farming practice is heading back for this sort of husbandry, and all Taverner's recommendations are modern practice.

Carp are the classic stew-pond fish. They don't need running water, live well in small ponds,. and are very good to eat. They must have half the food they eat natural pond food, so you must encourage the natural organisms of the pond by throwing in muck or compost. Any kind of animal manure will do and can simply be tipped into the pond but not, of course too much; only enough so that the bacteria of the pond can cope with it comfortably. You can then add a considerable amount of artificial food: oatmeal, barley, corn of any sort. If you put 100 lbs. of trout fry in you can expect to get 450 pounds of fat fish out in three years' time. Schaperclaust (*Die Karpfenteich-swirtschaft in der Deutch Demokratischen Republik*) says that ponds which have sewage effluent running into them near Berlin are yielding 10,000 kilograms of rainbow trout per hectare per year! Trout need running water according to this writer, from five to ten litres per second into a pond of 100 square metres. They want at least five feet of water. Only rainbow trout can be fed on sewage effluent—brown or brook trout need clean water. You can stock up to five trout per square metre of water surface. Trout are carnivorous and must be fed on finely ground meat or fish. You can buy proprietory trout food in England. You can buy young trout from trout farms, or breed your own in indoor tanks by squeezing the roe from an adult hen and squeezing into it the milt from an adult cock.

I have never done fish farming, but simply write so much about it in the possibility that it will arouse interest in someone with more energy than I have. An excellent book on this subject, from which I have drawn much of the above, is *Fish Culture* by C. F. Hickling (Faber and Faber) and another is *Fish and Invertebrate Culture* by S. H. Spotte (Wiley, New York). (For method of controlling water in ponds see illustration below.)

But anybody can improve the carrying capacity of a trout stream by building some small dams to cause deep 'holding

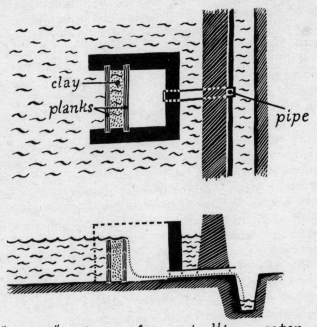

*"MONK" device for controlling water level in fishponds*

pools', or adapt an old mill pond by letting loose some fish fry in it and encouraging them by throwing in some crushed corn from time to time, or fish meal or meat meal for trout. From there it might develop into something more systematic and scientific in the true sense of the word. There is a lot of swampy land which could only be drained at a prohibitive cost but which, with the help of a bulldozer or mechanical digger, could cheaply be turned into big shallow fish ponds, which could be laid dry every alternate year to provide good grazing for cattle in the summertime. When laid dry it should be heavily limed and dressed with phosphatic manure and sown to clover.

All fish will deep freeze, but do not delude yourself that deep-frozen salmon or trout, for example, bears any relation to fresh fish. And never commit the atrocity of freezing smoked products of any kind.

## SEA FISH

The sea is never more than a few hours from us in the British Isles, provided we use mechanical transport, and of course if you live near the sea it is madness not to make use of sea fish. All you need to catch these is a small boat and some gear. The full-time professional fisherman has to go out in all weathers, and scrape about trying to pick up a few fish when there really aren't enough to bother with. He is forced into this by the fact that he has to earn a living for twelve months of the year. The man who has other work to turn to can, however, when fish are scarce, or the weather is bad, avoid going to sea. He need take very little risk and should have a good catch every time he goes out. For if the weather is not fine, or looks the slightest bit unsettled, he has plenty of work to do ashore. And, if he strikes his sea harvests right, a very few days fishing in the year will be enough to keep him and his family, or his community, in fish the year round.

*Herring.* The herring is the acknowledged king of the sea. There is no finer fish and they are excellent for preserving. They come to British shores at various times of the year in various places, but in many places the summer sees the start of them.

At first they may well be small fish with immature roes, but the time will come (about October or November on the east coast, perhaps December in Wales) when huge shoals of big fat herring packed with roe or milt come close inshore. Those are the boys to go after. Don't waste time after the others, and above all don't catch spent fish—they are worthless. Spring herring are generally spent.

The best thing for catching herring is the drift net. The new nylon nets are streets ahead of hemp or cotton, and herring drift nets can be obtained ready made up and hung from Bridport Gundry, Bridport, Dorset. They are expensive but you only need about fifty yards. If you hit lucky such a length will give you all you need. Don't go out at all until you have heard that other fishermen have been getting them in quantity. Let somebody else go out night after night prospecting. When you know the fish are there—out you go, and shoot your net close to the shore, or wherever you think the fish are. Shoot it in a straight line so that it hangs like a wall in the water; hang on to one end of it in your boat and play cards, drink rum or go to sleep. But keep a watch and occasionally cast the boat off from the net and row along a little way and haul some net up to see if there are any fish in it. If not—back to the end and hang on again. The net and you will drift with the tide, hence the name drift net. If the fish really hit you you will know immediately because all the corks of the headline, which is all you can see of the net, will sink. Haul the net up immediately. Pay it into the bottom of the boat, fish and all, don't try to shake the fish out of the net on board. Then row, sail or motor back to port, spread a large sail on the sand beside your beached boat, and overhaul the net over it, shaking it hard to get the fish out into the sail.

We find we need three hundred herring to salt down every year for our family. If we had more we wouldn't eat them. Instead of lashing out money for a boat and a net you might consider just buying your herring direct from a fisherman in a time of glut. My boat is round the south coast this year and so I bought from a man in Fishguard two hundred and fifty small herring for a pound. And if that isn't cheap food I don't know what is! But eschew middlemen, at all times.

Having caught your herring you salt them. We head ours so they don't take up so much room, but professional 'Klondykers' leave the heads on. We scrape the scales off, cut the heads off, put the roes in the deep freeze, whip the guts out (pig bucket of course, although heads and guts we often boil first), wash the fish well, and pack them down in a barrel with dry salt. Enough salt really to cover the fish. You can use an earthenware crock just as well as a barrel of course. Naturally you will cover whatever it is.

We have two ways of eating our salt herring. One is in the way in which herrings are eaten at every street corner in Dutch cities having been sold from those colourful booths which fly the Netherlands flag at every corner, and which advertise in large letters *Nieuw Haarring*. They are advertised as new to give the customer the impression that they haven't been in the salt since Noah cast a drift net from his Ark, but as most of the customers have a hangover anyway they wouldn't notice, for the 'new herrings' are the sovereign remedy for this complaint. How the Dutch merchants make them I do not know, but we make them by soaking the salt herrings overnight if they are still only a week or two old but for twenty-four hours if they have been in the salt longer, skinning the fish and then filleting them. We try to pull the ribs out of the fillets unless we are very hungry and can't wait. Then we just eat them. They are very good indeed, and particularly good on bread and butter, on toast, or as 'snacks' at parties.

Our other great remedy is to make rollmops of them. Soak them as above, lay each fish flat on its tummy on a board and press hard down on its back—kneading hard down all along the backbone. Now you can turn him round and pull out the backbone with most of the ribs with it (pig bucket). Now you can just dump the fish into a jar with vinegar and bits of onion, but if you have time and patience it looks prettier to roll each fish up, with a few chips of onion in it, and stick a sharpened match stick through it. Put some pepper corns in the vinegar, and a chilly if you like, cover and put away for a week. Next time you go to a shop enquire the price of rollmops! They will keep about a month, or a bit more.

When the herring are fresh in the salt, say not more than a week in it, I pull them out and hang them in the chimney. I have various cronies whose delight it is to sit around my fireside, late at night, and sop up the home brew they have been drinking by taking these herrings out of the chimney and throwing them on the hot ashes of the fire. After a few minutes they are done and we eat them with our fingers and they are good beyond any telling of it, but then we are probably pretty barbarous people.

The Scottish islanders, and such as live on salt herring for a great part of their diet, I believe soak the salt out of the herring and simply boil them with potatoes. We find them so delicious eaten in the three ways I have described above, and we have so much other meat to eat anyway, that we have seldom experimented with this basic method of cooking. Information on the treatment of salt fish in this country is sorely lacking. There are a score of books which will tell you how to salt fish, but not a single one that I can find that will tell you what to do with them after you have salted them beyond selling them to the Italians. They just know. There is one point I must make about salting herrings: professional salters never head the fish, but 'gib' them: that is with one skilful movement of the knife they whip out the gills, the long gut and the stomach, leaving the roe inside the fish. I used to watch the 'Scots lassies' doing this at Lowestoft and they did it like lightning. Probably you get a better salt fish this way, for you do not lose the rich oil in the heads, and the fish retains the flavour of the roe. We like herring roe *per se* though, and since we have had the deep freeze we indulge this taste to the full. Before the deep freeze days we ate roes for days after our little private 'herring voyage', and a sprinkling of salt on them would make them keep, in the cold larder, for several days. Vinegar on them would make them keep longer.

*Mackerel.* If you live near a part of the coast where mackerel come you are very lucky. They come to us in Pembrokeshire about July and keep on, off and on, all summer, ending with a fine flourish with the 'harvest mackerel' in September. We catch them with 'the feathers'. Actually I use a modification of the feathers—'the fish fag', which is an invention from Norway. The principle is the same, and if you live near any part of the coast where mackerel come you have only to ask the first person you meet where to get 'the feathers' and how to use them, and he will tell you. You can often catch three or four hundred mackerel in a day like this, and so one day's fishing will stock you up with salt fish for the year. One year the mackerel stubbornly refused to come here, and as I was going for a voyage in my little boat to the south coast of England I was desperate to catch my quota before I left. Alas, by my sailing date I had not caught one, so I sailed away leaving my poor wife and children mackerelless. But as I was rounding Strumble Head I just thought I would try a line overboard. Two hours later I sailed into my first port of call, Porth Gain, with 260 fat mackerel. I telephoned to Sally, she came over in the horseless carriage, and the mackerel were in the salt 'ere midnight. Treat them, in every respect, as you would herring. There is nothing you can do with herring that you can't do with the mackerel. You can freeze mackerel, but not, to any advantage, herring.

To make the various kinds of smoked herring (or mackerel) in the proper professional manner:

*Kippers.* Split down the back. Soak in 70–80 per cent brine (say 3 lbs. salt per gallon water) for an hour or two. Smoke for six hours at 85 F°. (30° C.). (I would say simply leave them in the chimney all night.) They will keep a week in cold weather— the harder you smoke them the longer they will keep.

*Bloaters.* Don't gut them at all. Leave them in dry salt all night. Smoke them for four hours at 80° F. (27° C.). Again, I just hang 'em in the chimney and forget 'em. I have a neighbour here who used to be beaten as a boy for pinching the herrings from the *simnai fawr* until it was discovered that an owl had been flying down the chimney and it was this that was responsible for pinching the herrings!

There is a difference between what are known in the trade as *cold smoked* and *cooked smoked* fish. In the former the temperature of the smoke must never be allowed to go over 86° F. (30°C.).

*Buckling* are cooked-smoked. They stay in brine for a couple of hours, gutted but unsplit (but leave roe), then hang for an hour in smoke at 90°F., then 180°F. for an hour. If it goes up to 250°F. (121°C.) it doesn't matter.

In other words they are being cooked at the same time as they are being smoked. You must get them soft. They won't keep long, and like other smoked things are ruined by being put in the deep freeze.

Mackerel freeze quite well (but should be eaten before three months are up). Herring don't freeze at all well, and I don't recommend it.

*Sprats* come to our shores all round Britain, and considering what a delectable fish they are, are woefully neglected. After the first mad rush they sell for ridiculously low prices. You buy them at the peak of the glut, or catch them yourself with a drift net of the right mesh (again Bridport Gundry).

To make *Kielersprotten*, a common German remedy, soak sprats in 80 per cent brine (as for kippers, see above) for fifteen minutes. Stick them on a speat (sharpened stick) through their gills. Put them, still wet, in smoke at 90°F. (32°C.) for half an hour then at 180°F. (82°C.) until they are soft and a delicious golden colour. If you put any smoked fish in jars and cover with olive oil or peanut oil they will keep for some time, and if you sterilize before sealing up by heating for half an hour they will keep much longer, and you will have something very like anchovies.

A method of treating salt herrings which a Dutchman told

me, but which I have never tried, is to soak the salt herring in fresh water overnight, slice the fillets very thinly, soak in vinegar for an hour, smoke in dense hot smoke for half an hour, and pack in olive oil. It keeps for a couple of months in the winter, and it sounds delicious.

If you get sick of fresh mackerel during the mackerel campaign try this: heat some chopped parsley and a chopped onion in olive oil in a frying pan, shove in the mackerel, fry for five minutes, add three sliced tomatoes, salt and pepper, some thyme and garlic, cover the pan up and let it simmer for five minutes. It gives mackerel-eating another lease of life.

*Pilchards* may one day visit these shores again, and in fact they do sometimes approach the south-westerly coasts. In the days when Cornishmen drank a toast to 'Tin and Pilchards' before they thought of toasting the King the method of dealing with pilchards was thus:

They were caught in enormous quantities—when they were caught at all—with the seine net (nowadays the gill net or drift net would suit the self-supporter better). The pilchards were laid in plenty of dry salt layers to a height of five feet. They were left thus for a month or six weeks. The oil ran out in great quantities—into gutters, from whence it went into an underground sump where it was stored. The fish were then packed into barrels and often pressed with powerful presses to get the last drop of oil out of them. They were then sent off to the Mediterranean where the people must have been hungrier than the Cousin Jacks were because they would eat them. The oil was then used for lamps, for curing leather, for making soap and for many other purposes. It, and whale oil, were the chief sources of oil in this country for centuries. I merely mention this process here in case any self-supporter wishes to experiment. I have no doubt that either herrrings or sprats would yield oil in the same manner. And if the squashed fish were found not much good to eat, and the Italians didn't want 'em, at least they would make excellent fish meal for fertilizer or for pigs or poultry.

*White Fish.* If the homesteader wishes to catch white fish he has three courses open to him: hand lining, long-lining and trawling. Hand lining is fun, but only occasionally very productive. Long-lining can be extremely productive of such things as conger eel, hake, cod and codling, haddock and whiting. Trawling is the only method by which you are likely to catch soles, and any quantity at least of plaice or other flat fish. You can buy little beam trawl nets from Bridport Gundry: they sell one small enough to be towed behind a 20-foot open boat with a Seagull engine. You can make up a long line yourself, but I recommend that you buy swivel hooks. Professional long lines may have a thousand hooks or more on them, but if you have a hundred you will catch quite a lot of fish—that is provided there are any fish there. The usual thing is to shoot them at night and pick them up in the early morning. In the summer you probably don't get much but dog fish (marvellous for pig food) but in the winter you should get other fish. I cannot go into detail about either trawling or long-lining here, but there are sure to be professional fishermen near you somewhere, and if you do as they do you will fare all right. There is a very good book, *Inshore Fishing* by Stan Judd, published by *Fishing News*. I have been long-lining with Mr. Judd and we caught half a ton of conger eels so he seems to know his job.

Now for preserving your white fish when you have caught them. Flat fish are best put in the deep freeze where they freeze quite well, but don't keep them too long: perhaps three months is long enough. Everything loses its flavour in time in the deep freeze.

Thick fish, such as cod, ling, haddock and whiting, can be salted. Split the bigger fish, such as cod, and rip out the backbone except the tail which you keep as a handle. Pile in dry salt and let the juice run away (compare with oily fish such as herring, where you do not let the juice run away but leave the fish in their 'pickle'). After a few days with small fish, but 15 days with big cod, pull the fish out of the salt and expose on racks to the air and the sun—but *not* to the rain. A more

scientific way is the Gaspé cure. Fill a tub with 7 lbs. salt (if it be winter—9 lbs. if summer) and 100 lbs. split fish. Leave in brine for 48 to 72 hours depending on size of fish. Pull them out and stack them for six hours. Dry in sun and wind.

This sort of fish will keep indefinitely. You can cook it how you like but you should soak it for at least 36 hours before you do so or you will have a thirst that the waters of Niagara will scarcely quench.

Smoke haddocks, after half an hour in brine, for a few hours in cool smoke, or hot smoke to make 'smokies'.


*Lobsters, crabs and crawfish* may be taken in pots (see your local fishermen). The 'parlour pot' much used in the north east coast is best for the occasional fisherman, for it can be left down a week or more and the lobsters are unlikely to get out. Also the bait will not be eaten and will go on working. It has a 'parlour' at one end of the pot into which the lobsters can crawl and thus leave the bait chamber. Salt herring make good bait for lobsters but crabs like fresh fish. Whisper it not in sporting circles but a tin of Kit-e-Kat with a few holes punched in it will bring 'em in.

The new-fangled tangle net, or ray net, is the best way of catching shell fish though, and will catch anything else that happens along. It is a killer, and if used indiscriminately will denude our coasts. A short length of it for a self-supporting family or community is quite justifiable though (Bridport Gundry).


*Skates and rays* should be 'winged', that is the head part cut right out with a semi-circular cut of the knife, and the tail part and guts served the same. This leaves the two 'wings' tied together by the middle. Hang the wings up in the wind for a few days before you cook them. Scald the wings in boiling water for a few seconds to skin. Haul the thorns of thornback off with a pair of pincers. Cook by frying in milk and butter, pepper and salt and what have you.

*Conger Eel.* Dorothy Hartley gives this recipe for conger eel in *Food in England*, but I have not tried it. Take the whole middle out of a big conger, rub inside with a cut onion, wipe over with a little dry mustard. Stuff with a good well-flavoured force-meat and sew up strongly. Cut an apple in two and use each half to plug the ends. Tie up with tape like a packet. Roast it with dripping and cider, basting often. Eat with samphire pickle.

*Sole.* To skin a sole, scale its bottom by scraping. Skin its top by nicking the skin near the tail and pulling forward—but following your pulling hand with your other hand to hold the flesh down, otherwise you will rip it off.

*Oysters* can be preserved: steam for half an hour; soak for five minutes in brine of 2 lbs. salt in 1 gallon water; dip in olive oil; lay on wire trays and smoke in hot dense smoke (180°F.) for half an hour. Turn them once during this treatment.

Pack in jars, fill up with oil, sterilize in a pressure cooker at 15 lbs. pressure for 15 minutes, or for half an hour by standing the jars in boiling water. Seal. I have never done this but got it out of a book.

*Potting.* The east coast fisherman pot mackerel or herring, and we do too. Cut your fish up into chunks (three or four from a fish), salt in dry salt for twelve hours, wash the salt out, put them in an earthenware pot and cover with vinegar. The usual bay leaves, pepper corns, a chilly, and whatever common sense suggests. Cover with greasproof paper and put in a slow oven overnight. Take out, make sure it is well covered, and it will keep until mackerels come again. Don't mind if a little mould forms on top of the vinegar. Eat cold, late at night when you come home from the pub and your wife has nothing to welcome you with but tongue pie, cold bum and the copperstick.

# 18

## Bees, Wild Food, Wine, Wood, Smoke-house, Seaweed

*Every farmer will understand me when I say, that he ought to pay for nothing in money, which he can pay for in anything but money.*

WILLIAM COBBETT: Cottage Economy

### BEES

The pre-Industrial Revolution manner of keeping bees would not commend itself to the officers of the R.S.P.C.A., because the bees were 'put down', as the latter would term it, every autumn. The hive with precision-cut moveable frames had not been invented, and the only way in which the honey could be extracted was to burn a little sulphur underneath the hive and liquidate the bees. The picturesque straw skeps were treated in this manner, and in Africa and most parts of Asia today this is still the manner of keeping, and ceasing to keep, bees. In Central Africa one frequently sees hollowed-out logs hung in the trees: these are the equivalents of the medieval bee skeps in England. There are bee keepers in dear old England today who, whisper it not, do this very thing. They put old orange boxes or other crates and receptacles around the backs of their houses, where the neighbours can't see them, and put a few old bee frames with a bit of wax on them and the smell of bees inside them, and either hope that some bees will arrive from somewhere (and if bees have been kept in that garden for a long time you can be fairly sure some will) or else go out and capture a swarm and put them in the box. The busy little insects fill the box completely with honeycomb and honey, but all jammed in there higgledy-piggledy, and there is absolutely no way known to man of extracting that honey without killing those bees. But there, the economics of the thing, from Man's point of view, are perfectly sound. The bees, by the autumn, have done their work. They have made their honey. If the man is going to keep them alive all winter it either means that he has got to leave a large part of their honey with them for them to live on, or else feed them with sugar. In a country with a high proportion of woodland and forest, and therefore of wild bees, there will always be plenty of fresh swarms in the spring, and a swarm of bees in May is worth a load of hay, and worth none the less because you didn't have to feed it and look after it all winter.

It was the discovery of the *bee space* that made this yearly butchery unnecessary though. The bee space is the exact space in which a bee will build its comb and yet leave a space for itself to crawl about in. Thus the frames of a modern beehive are exactly the right distance from each other so that the bees will build the combs out from them to the correct size of combs but yet leave a bee space between the combs. If the frames were a small fraction of an inch further apart the bees would start building 'wild comb' between the frames and thus fill the whole space in; if they were a fraction nearer the bees would not be able to build out from both frames, because there would not be room for them to work. Therefore, with this discovery of the bee space, it was possible to construct beehives with such precision that the bees build their combs as we want them to, on frames that we put there for them, frames that can be removed to extract the honey without disturbing the bees too much, and be put back again for the bees to start filling with honey again. The stock of bees can be kept from year to year, which is more humane, and also enables the bee keeper to start early in the season with strong stocks of bees in all of his hives. He doesn't have to wait for the Lord to send him 'a swarm of bees in May' because he's already got several good swarms of bees tucked up in his hives in January.

The feeding of a little sugar to the bees to keep them alive in the winter and to enable the beekeeper to rob them more thoroughly in the autumn has developed, among many modern beekeepers, into feeding them on sugar all the time exclusively. Bees will not bother to go and look for nectar if there is plenty of sugar available, and some commercial beekeepers buy stores of cheap sugar condemned for human consumption, and feed it direct into their hives, and the bees just turn it directly into honey. Which is why so much honey today tastes something like honey, and yet not *quite* like honey. The honey that comes in from underdeveloped parts of the world like Mexico, however, generally really tastes like honey, because the beekeepers in such lands cannot afford to buy the sugar to feed the bees: it is when labour is dear and industrial sugar is cheap relative to labour that beekeepers shove in the sugar.

But the keeping of a few colonies of bees is an obvious ploy for the self-supporter. The initial outlay necessary on modern hives and equipment is fairly high (you have to have an extractor, for example) but once you have the equipment there is a very valuable harvest to be taken every year for the rest of your life. You don't need to buy any sugar, condemned or otherwise, to feed the bees on. We have not so much kept bees as had bees around for the last sixteen years, and most years we have got some honey from them, and we have never fed them on any sugar. We merely abstain from robbing them too severely in the autumn.

Of all the arts and crafts of the countryside, beekeeping is the one that least lends itself to being taught by a book. Also to give any idea of the subject would take a book at least as long as this one. Therefore, I must merely recommend the novice to join his local bee group, if he has one (and he probably has), or at least put himself under the tuition of some good master. Also, buy a book on the subject. There are many. We have two hives, but not enough 'supers' for them (that is stories to add to their height and make more room for honey), but this year we took nearly a hundredweight of honey without going to much trouble and leaving plenty of honey to keep the bees through the winter time. A day a year is really all you have to devote to your bees. All I would advise is, do not make the mistake that we have made and get hold of components from two different sorts of beehive, also get a really bee-proof rig to wear when you are working with your bees. Nothing is more likely to diminish your love for these little insects than having a few score of them buzzing about inside a leaky veil trying to get *out*, while a few hundred of their sisters outside dive-bomb angrily at you outside trying to get *in*. And remember bees, when they alight on you, crawl upwards. They won't crawl *down* into Wellington boots but by God they will climb up your jumper if it isn't well tucked into your trousers. And the presence of a dozen or two crawling about your midriff, and occasionally stinging you, will not increase the calmness and efficiency with which you are likely to carry out your operations. If you are completely bee-proof you can be very cool and efficient, and cool and efficient you have got to be.

If you had enough bees, and looked after them well enough, you would not need to buy any sugar at all. Two hives, managed in a professional manner, would be enough. I lived for years in what was then called Barotseland, in what was then called Northern Rhodesia, in what I believe is still called Africa, without ever tasting sugar. There was plenty of wild honey. Once you have got used to it honey is fine in tea or coffee, and on porridge if you must eat the stuff. In fact there is no good purpose for which honey is not better than sugar. It is not in any way bad for your teeth, as sugar is, nor does it lead to all the other evils now being put down to refined sugar. It is a lot dearer than sugar—if you have to buy it, but if you don't have to buy it as we don't, it is, quite simply, free.

## WILD FOOD

It goes without saying that the kind of wild food that you will get will depend entirely upon where you live. As an example, when we lived in Suffolk, pheasants, hares and wild duck made up a very large proportion of our meat intake (particularly pheasants and hares); we ate, of fungi, parasol

mushrooms, ceps, shaggy ink caps, saffron milk caps, puff
balls, field mushroom; there were plenty of blackberries,
some nuts, plenty of elderberries, sloes, plenty of wild plums
every three years, mussels down on the estuary. In Pembrokeshire we find no pheasants, no hares, very few fungi except a
few field mushrooms, tons of the finest blackberries, most
years plenty of hazel nuts, elderberries and sloes, and cran-
berries on the mountains if we have time to pick them, which
generally we have not. Small sea mussels, cockles and razor
fish are there for the getting.

*Pheasants.* The self-supporter, unless he is just doing it for a game
like Marie Antoinette playing shepherdess, will scarcely wish
to indulge himself in shooting driven pheasants with twelve-
bore cartridges at tenpence a shot. But there are cheaper and
more effective methods of taking pheasants, and, if you have
a game licence, you are quite within the law shooting pheasants
on your own land unless the right has been reserved by a
previous owner when he sold the land. You can't own a rifle
without a police permit, but if you have this then a .22 is a very
effective weapon for killing pheasants, and 'short rifle' am-
munition is very cheap.

In the first place, if a man occupies even a small piece of
land, and his neighbours have pheasants, he can *also* have
pheasants. There are certain crops which pheasants just
cannot resist. One is the Jerusalem artichoke that we have
already discussed several times in this book. A row or two of it
won't make much difference, but a stand of, say, a quarter
of an acre will bring pheasants from far and wide. They like
the cover and they like the artichokes.

Buckwheat is a marvellous crop for attracting pheasants.
Kale is not bad but only so-so. Maize is good. Sunflower is
absolutely splendid—as good as Jerusalem artichoke, which
it so closely resembles. But I would say the latter plant plus
buckwheat are the ones to plant.

Dogs will catch pheasants. Many a gypsy man has a lurcher
dog (a cross-bred with greyhound or whippet in his ancestry)

which will take a pheasant on the ground. It is unforgivable of course to take a hen off the nest, and no decent poacher would do it. If it did happen by accident he would collect the eggs and put them under a chicken hen to bring them off.

But if you do get any pheasants, or partridges, hang them up, guts and all, by their necks (*not* their legs like chickens) in the larder, and leave them there for at least a week in the winter before you cook them. You hang them by their necks to keep the blood in the body, and also to keep the guts from tainting the breast meat.

*Pigeons and other birds.* Pigeon would be fine if they didn't cost so much to shoot. I used to shoot wild geese but don't any more since I discovered that they mate for life. We all may get fed up with our husbands and wives from time to time but we don't want them shot. Wild ducks don't though, and are noble food, so are most of the waders. Curlew, lapwing, golden plover, red shank were once considered grand eating, but they are protected birds in Great Britain. They all want hanging for a few days, at least.

*Rabbits*, if they ever come back, can be picked off with the .22 in the early morning or the evening, driven into a purse-net from their holes by ferrets, driven into a long-net at night by a dog or two. The long-net is set, very quietly, between the feeding grounds of the rabbits and their holes. It is set on sharpened pickets sloped into the ground, but very baggy. Then one operator takes the dog and walks round the feeding grounds and drives the rabbits into the net, while the other crouches down at one end of the net and runs along it to take the rabbits out and 'show them London' by breaking their necks in the manner I have described for killing chickens. I used to go long-netting with a deaf man, and as we had to be very silent (it was gamekeeper country) communication between us could be hazardous. A countryman will 'hulk' a rabbit (paunch it) and 'hock' it (cut behind the gam string of one leg and shove the other leg through so that it can be hung on a stick or on the handlebars of his bicycle) without using a knife. He uses the sharp claw of the rabbit's own foot. Gut or 'hulk' rabbits as soon as you catch them, but not hares.

*Hares* can be caught with a good lurcher. We had a very small lurcher named Esau who would run down a hare very often if he had the chance, and I remember taking him for a walk over the marshes when we already had too many hares in the larder and coming back with three more hares. A lurcher can be trained to keep out of sight, and never to come near his master if a stranger is in sight. Don't hulk hares immediately. They are game, while rabbits are not. Hamstring a hare, hang her up in a cool larder by her hind legs for a week (or a fortnight if you like game hung well) then skin her carefully before you gut her, then hulk her (a stinking and disgusting job—but don't be put off by the whiff, it doesn't matter); always save the blood to put in the sauce. Hares are absolutely delicious and there are many ways of cooking them besides jugging them. A hare a week throughout the winter is not too many.

*Fungi*. Most fungi are edible and some, notably parasol, shaggy ink cap, and cep, are absolutely delicious. But I positively refuse to start describing which fungi are edible and which are not, for without very good photographs this course might lead to disaster. You must either get somebody to show you, or get a very good book. It is absurd though that only the field mushroom generally gets eaten, when there are so many other excellent ones. We have a good book, and try any fungus that we can identify as edible at least once. Some are edible but pretty tasteless.

*Mussels*. Mussels are fine if they come from genuinely unpolluted water but can be very dangerous if they do not. In any case do not take the advice of most cookery books and only steam them long enough for them to open their shells. This is very dangerous. They should be boiled, or thoroughly steamed, for at least twenty minutes. And make absolutely sure that you use none that were not tight-closed before you cooked them.

*Cockles* can be raked out of sand-beds at low tide with a steel garden rake. Professionally they are raked into a little hand net and swished about in shallow water over the sand to get the sand out. I have seen four men rake out a ton of them on one low tide. In such cases the fish are generally loaded straight into the holds of smacks which have been stranded on the sands at high water, but in Kent there are men who load them on to old bicycle frames, and in Wales women who load them on donkeys. Boil them for twenty minutes in sea water.

*Razor shells*, or razor fish, are delicious to eat: a kind of clam. You may see their blow-holes in sand right down at the water's edge at very low spring tides. If you walk backwards over the sand you will see them spurt water after you have passed. Either dump a handful of salt on the hole, in which case they will come out and you can get a spade under them, or use a 'razor-fish-spear'. This is a slender steel spear with small barbs on it. You push it down the hole, the razor fish closes on it, and you pull him out.

*Limpets* can be eaten, and I have eaten them raw. To get them off the rocks kick them quickly before they know you are there, or they will cling down hard and you won't get them off. They are better cooked.

*Salt.* If you don't like buying salt—take a large vessel down to the beach one fine summer's day, send your children looking for plenty of driftwood, light a fire under the vessel and keep pouring buckets of sea water into it. Make sure you draw your sea water from where it is fairly deep and has no sand in suspension. If you keep doing this all day you will have enough of the very best sea salt to last you for table use throughout the year, although not—of course—enough for curing fish or ham.

# WINE

Now 'home-made wine'. Grape wine should be pure juice of the grape, with nothing added, and nothing taken away. This is because the ripe grape is very rich in sugar, has enough water in it so that it doesn't need any more, and carries its own yeast spores on its skin ready to ferment it. But the 'wines' most country people make in Britain are really little more than solutions of sugar—ordinary beet or cane sugar (sucrose) in water, flavoured and reinforced with the juices of some fruit or vegetable, and fermented with added yeast.

I know a village in Worcestershire (a county of mighty wine-makers) in which at least three farm-working gentlemen have sheds in the bottoms of their gardens purely devoted to the making and drinking of wine. These three gentlemen share this in common: half of their gardens are devoted to the culture of the rhubarb and the other half to that of the parsnip: their wives can whistle in vain for anything else. They each own two sixty-gallon barrels. In the winter they each brew sixty gallons of parsnip (this root should not be used until the frost has been on it) and in the summer sixty gallons of rhubarb. They are apt to 'go on the barrel' as they aptly call it, all gathering in the shed of one or other of them, and I have on occasion, 'gone on the barrel' with them. It is an experience.

We make elderberry (a glass a day, in the winter, keeps the 'flu away, and if it doesn't then an occasional glass, hot, with a teaspoonful of honey in it, gets rid of it); elderflower, which is a most delicate wine and quite delicious and also, I believe, has therapeutic properties; blackberry, which is a full-bodied rather port-like wine; blackcurrant, which is absolutely excellent; mead, which we make from the cappings of the honeycombs which would otherwise be wasted anyway; sloe wine, which is a very good port-like wine; and a few others. People make 'wine' out of absolutely ridiculous things: lettuces and tea leaves and hell knows what. This is simply fermenting sugar and water and flavouring it with some unlikely vegetable matter. Throw your pea-pods to the pigs, they'll do far more good.

But the principles are always the same. Get your juice by whatever means is suitable (boiling, steeping, crushing, soaking your material), keep it as far as you can from contamination with the wrong sort of organisms, make up its sugar content by adding sugar to it, introduce yeast into it when it is the right temperature (blood heat), keep the vinegar flies out of it, and leave it to ferment. When it has fermented it is wine. If it is red wine leave it a year at least if you are able for it to mature; if white a few months. And remember that it will probably be far stronger than grape wine.

Really all wine making is pure common sense, once you realise that about three pounds of sugar is all you are going to get to ferment into alcohol in a gallon of water, you must use clean containers and you must keep the vinegar flies out. One generality is that the larger quantities you make at once the more chance you have of success. My old friends who make wine in sixty-gallon casks never get a failure. It's the amateur who makes dribs and drabs of this and that who—although he possibly gets a lot of fun out of it—also spoils a lot of wine. My Worcestershire friends have never even *heard* of special wine yeasts nor of Campden tablets nor hydrometers and things like that. But none of them could even remember having had a failure in their wine, and I can vouch for it that it is always superb of its kind.

I am not running down science. I would advise any beginner in the art to get a good little book about wine making (there are scores of them), to get a hydrometer, to use special yeasts if he finds in practice they are better; but I would have my reservations about Campden tablets. They are made from a chemical which inhibits unwanted yeasts and you hope they won't inhibit the yeast you are using. I use them to sterilize bottles sometimes but have never put them in my wine. I am fussy about what goes in my stomach. I don't like eating off dishes washed with detergents and then not very thoroughly rinsed, nor do I like drinking mains water, which is full of chlorine. And I don't like consuming sulphur dioxide in my wine.

Here follow a few recipes for making some of the more sensible kinds of home-made wines.

*Parsnip.*

 4 lbs. parsnip
 3 lbs. sugar
 1 gallon water
 some lemons or citric acid
 yeast

Cut the parsnips up and boil 'em but not too soft. They should just be easily prickable with a fork. Boil a couple of lemons up with them if you've got them. Strain off the liquor, stir in the sugar while its still hot so as to melt it; some people put some raisins in too; put in some lemon juice or citric acid; put in a vessel and ferment with your yeast. Of course you must wait until the temperature has gone down to about blood heat before putting in the yeast. Like all other wine, ferment under a fermentation lock, or a wodge of cotton wool in the neck of the vessel, to keep the vinegar flies out and let out the $CO_2$. Rack it well a couple of times (that means pour it gently off its sediment into another vessel; we *have* had difficulty clearing parsnip—but I think we boiled it too long) and then keep it as long as you can lay your hands off it.

Now the citric acid and/or the lemons in the above recipe was to give the yeast enough acidity to feed on, parsnips being lacking in acidity. With anything that common sense tells you is not very acid—shove in some lemons or some citric acid.

*Rhubarb.*

 15 lbs. rhubarb
 2½ lbs. sugar
 1 gallon water
 yeast

Chop up rhubarb, pour on the water boiling and mash the rhubarb. Don't boil any more though. Leave it to soak until next day, strain off your liquor and press the 'fruit' to get as much out as you can. Stir in the sugar and bung in the yeast. Multiply everything by sixty and that is how my Worcestershire friends make it.

*Elderberry.*

>  4 lbs. elderberries
>  3 lbs. sugar
>  1 gallon water
>  yeast

You are supposed to get all the berries off the stalks but I have shoved stalks in and all and not found any difference and, after all, if you can save a lot of work by departing from slavish convention why not do so? Pour the water on boiling, mash hard with a potato masher, and leave to soak for 24 hours—but cover it up. Put the yeast in and let it get on with it. The longer you keep it the better. Of course when it has finished fermenting you will wrack it into bottles or other containers, so as to leave the sediment behind. You will do this with all wines.

*Redcurrant or any other berry wine:*—just as for elderberry.

*Mead.* As much comb cappings, and odd bits of 'wild comb' that you couldn't put in the extractor, and perhaps some pure honey stolen from the main storage pot when your wife isn't looking to supply what in your estimation is about three pounds of honey to a gallon of water. Melt the honey in the water and ferment. Honey is deficient in acid, so put the juice of two or three lemons in a gallon or some citric acid if you can't get lemons. Mead also likes some tannin to feed the yeast. Apples supply tannin, so some crushed crab apples are a good idea. Last time I dumped some rose hip syrup that the children decided they didn't like into my mead, which wasn't fermenting very well, and it started to ferment like blazes. I have heard of people putting tea in mead to supply tannin. Mead goes on fermenting for a long time, so don't hurry it, and if you can leave it in bottle for a few years so much the better. But can you? Some people spice mead well, and it is a good idea.

A *metal* (not a wooden) corking tool is a good buy, such as you knock on the head with a hammer. You can then cork your bottles professionally and leave the wine to mature in bottle much longer and more safely. Boil the corks before you use them and use new ones.

## WOOD

There is just one other natural product which we must discuss, although it is not something that we can eat. And that is wood. But we cannot manage our little self-supporting estate unless we know something about this.

Nobody should ever cut a tree down without planting several to take its place, and the question is what trees to plant.

If it will grow at all on your soil the tree to plant before all others is the sweet chestnut. It has absolutely every advantage and, so far as I know, no disadvantage. For a hardwood tree it is quick growing; it makes the finest fence or gate posts of any tree; it will *rive* (split straight—a most important achievement); it is magnificent firewood (if anybody could bring themselves to use this splendid timber for such a purpose); it is straight grained; it is hard and lasting. The long fairly straight trunks rive as sweet and true as a nut, and the resulting posts, driven into the ground, will last until *you* are in the ground. Just why the Forestry Commission has been allowed to blanket the countryside with millions of acres of Scots or Corsica pine, or Sitka spruce, when they could in many cases have been planting this magnificent tree is a mystery that I suppose will never be solved.

The softwoods, unless you like the look of them, are of practically no value on the estate whatever. They don't even make good firewood. You can pressure creosote them until the stuff meets in the middle and they still won't last many years in the ground. They were good for pit props—until the pits went over to steel—and are now good for pulp. Unless you intend to make pulp, or run a coal mine, don't grow firs and pines.

*Ash* is a splendid tree to grow. It grows fast, rives well, makes the best firewood there is ('seer or green it's fit for a queen') and it looks beautiful. But it won't last long in the ground. I have been using small pickets of ash for fifteen years now for holding up electric fencing, but they are never in the ground for more than a few months at a time, and when they are out— if it happens that I am having a creosote boiling at the moment —I boil them. The principle of boiling stakes in creosote incidentally is to boil them in it—and let them cool in it. It is when they are cooling that the contracting air inside them sucks in the juice. A big oil drum with the top out of it perched up on some concrete blocks is fine, with a fire under it— but *beware—seven times beware*—letting the stuff boil over onto the fire because it is highly inflammable. I once set fire to a jeep by making this mistake and I'm still paying for it. You should buy it by the 44-gallon drum, to get it in penny-packets will break you. Green wood will take in very little creosote. It is when you use posts twice that you should boil them. But boil them green too—even the little they do absorb helps.

I made a dozen gates of split ash when we came to Wales six years ago, and excepting one which disintegrated they are all still as good as new. I rived the ash as soon as I cut it down, nailed the members together with well-clenched nails, drilling holes for the nails first for otherwise they would have split the wood. I went to the trouble of dolloping creosote into the nail holes before I drove the nails in, for that is where rot starts. Hinges I found lying about. I used little bolts for the main joints which, like the nails, I did have to buy. But I don't suppose each gate costs me half a crown. They look very good and do the job well. If I could have got sweet chestnut instead of course I would have used that: ash was a *faute de mieux*. I wash them with creosote every three years or so though.

*Oak* (which is very closely related to the sweet chestnut) will rive too, but nothing like as easily and sweetly as chestnut. You cannot easily make small members of it by riving. If you have a rip saw you can rip it down of course, and most professionally-made gates in this country are of sawn oak (*never* buy softwood gates). Heart of oak makes the best posts—as good at least as chestnut, and many an oak post is still holding up a gate after sixty years in the ground. The sap wood, though, which makes up most of the volume of a young oak, is not much good at all. Dried oak makes magnificent firewood. Oak is traditionally the best wood for smoking fish or meat—but it doesn't matter all that much.

*Birch* is a long-lasting wood indoors but no good for posts outside. When really dry it is a very hot and good firewood.

*Alder* is a tree-weed, and is good for very little. It makes indifferent firewood when it is dry. We burn a lot of it *faute de mieux*, and because we want to get rid of it.

*Willow* is good firewood when it is really dry. If you plant a willow post it will grow into a tree. Not a bad way of holding fences up. We have planted about a hundred basket-withy willow on boggy ground.

*Elm* and *Beech* I have had little to do with, for we have never had any. *Sycamore* is fine for turning and surely the ability to make *treen* (turned and carved implements and objects) would be a good one for the self-supporter to possess.

*Larch* is a good tree. Larch posts are quite good in the ground, particularly if well creosoted when seasoned. It's a good firewood, 'though spits, and if you can't kindle a fire with the brittle dry twigs that a larch keeps shedding you can't light a fire with anything.

The trees I should plant are, in this order, sweet chestnut, oak, ash, larch, walnut. The latter would be an investment for my posterity.

## SMOKE-HOUSE

To make a smoker for bacon or fish. An old outside lavatory is perfect and in Suffolk that is what we used to use. Any construction inside or outside the house about that size or shape will do. Put a big old enclosed stove (the Forester is fine, because it's made for wood burning, but any stove that will burn wood will do) *outside* the 'little house' and poke the chimney pipe straight through a hole in the wall. You thus get fairly cool smoke going straight into your smoke-house. If you want hot smoke, supplement this by lighting a smoulder-ing wood and sawdust fire *inside* the smoke-house on the floor. An obvious economy is to have the smoke-house up against the outer wall of your house and the wood-burning enclosed stove inside. Thus you warm the house as you are smoking the bacon. But there is nothing to beat the good old open fireplace, with pipes put across at various levels according to what heat you want. Oak is the best smoking wood—but it is not all that important which you use.

## SEAWEED

*Samphire* (*Crythmum maritimum*), an edible seaweed, beloved of the Fenlanders, can be pickled thus:

Fill a jar with it, add peppercorns and some horse radish shavings, pour over it a boiling mixture of dry cider and vinegar (50–50), infuse it in the oven for an hour and seal. You can also just boil it fresh. It is stringy, but you pull it through your teeth so as to leave the succulent flesh in your mouth.

*Sea Holly* (*Eryngium maritimum*). Eat the flowering shoots like asparagus, and roast the roots. (I've never tried it.)

*Laver Weed* (*Porphyra vulgaris*). Soak for a few hours in fresh water. Dry in slow oven and powder in mortar. Boil for 4 hours, changing water. Drain. Fry. Serve with bacon.

# 19
# Last Word

*Some did their work thus: they sat and sang and drank,*
*And helped plough the half-acre with 'Hey trolly-lolly'.*

WILLIAM LANGLAND: The Vision of Piers Counsel

And the established homesteader gets a surfeit of people coming along, and getting their feet under his table, and helping the work of the holding on with 'Hey trolly-lolly' usually accompanied by a large guitar. Piers Plowman had the right reply to these warblers:

*Now by the Prince of Paradise says Piers in his wrath,*
*If ye rise not straightway and hasten to work,*
*No grain that grows here shall gladden you at need,*
*No, though ye die for dole, devil take him that cares.*

Not that there is anything wrong with 'Hey trolly-lolly' in its place, but its place, or time rather, is in the evening after a hard day's work, sitting on the grass under the big oak tree in summer or around the roaring log fire in the winter with the home-brew flagon making its rounds.

The homesteader cannot afford to carry passengers, and many of the 'Hey trolly-lolly' boys just have no idea of what the word work signifies. They think that if they have done an hour or two of messing about with a hoe they have earned a day's food. They have *not*. They also think that if their host grows his own food it is free. It is *not*. It is as well to impress on all guests and would-be helpers that three square meals a day cost six and a half hours of hard and continuous labour for *somebody*. And why should it always be you? If they get that straight in their minds right at the start relations with them will be much easier.

I have not intended that this book should be advice on how to live, nor an exhortation to live in any particular way. I have merely endeavoured to explain the way to do certain things connected with producing your own food from the land and the water. Few people would ever want to do *all* the things I have listed above, although Sally and I have done very nearly all of them: in fact if I have described anything we have not done I have tried to say so. Most of these things we have done constantly for many years now, and are continuing to do with undiminished vigour. I would impress again, though, on the reader, that for one couple to attempt all this and pay off a mortgage too is a great strain. It is too much. But you don't have to produce such a great variety of food. People live very well on much simpler diets than the one that would include all the things I have described how to produce in this book. And somebody living, even, in a bed-sitter in a huge city can go out and buy a sack of wheat, for example, and have a coffee grinder to grind it into flour, and bake his own bread and have it for a fraction of the cost of shop bread. Nobody has to do *everything*. People are constantly saying to me, very agressively, things like: 'But you don't do what you recommend—look— you're using a typewriter —you're wearing a machine-made tweed.' Etcetera, etcetera. My answer to this sort of thing is that it's no damned business of their how I live. I can take what I want from the rest of civilization (if I can pay for it) and leave what I don't want. Sally and I don't make any fetish of it. It just seems very silly to work for eight hours a day in an office (and I can't stand air-conditioning) to get the money to pay for things that we can produce so much better and more pleasantly ourselves.

The trickle of dropouts coming from the cities into the country-side is increasing year by year. One can almost say now that it is becoming a small flood. Unfortunately these people don't seem to have the slightest idea what to do when they get into the country. They cannot find a job: they have no skills. Some of them get temporary work doing seasonal work on farms. Nearly all of them are on National Assistance for much of the time. Some of them scratch about trying to make 'handi-crafts'. Some of them try to grow some of their own food. 'Of course we're going to produce all our own food,' they say, pointing to three square yards of ground half dug up and planted with dying cabbage riddled with flea-beetle.

Some of them collect into communities of one sort or another. There is a register of such communities now that numbers several hundred in the British Isles, and there are many thousands in the United States. (The School of Living, Free-land, Md. 21053, U.S.A., is in touch with thousands of home-steaders and communiteers, and in this country the Commune Movement, Secretary, Nicolas Albery, 141 Westbourne Park Road, London, W.1.) I have seen with interest several attempts of this sort. I don't think any of the ones I have seen will succeed. All they will ever be are repositories for people living on National Assistance or 'the Health'.

This is very sad and I don't think it need be. I realize that these escapers from the city have lived possibly all their lives never having had to do what I would call work, and their fathers before them. But I think they could get back to it if they really wanted to and knew how to do it. After all, the Israelis, who were perhaps the most urbanized and sedentary people in the world—city-dwellers *par excellence*—got back to the land in one generation and have done wonderfully well.

I don't think personally that the hugger-mugger community in which everybody loves each other and nobody ever tells anybody else what to do because it's not democratic will ever work, anywhere. I have never seen any sign of such a thing working. But I do think that groupings of people living near each other, each with his own holding and dwelling space, co-operating in some things and living under some sort of an organization, would work very well indeed.

There are, in this country, many great houses, mansions and the like, for sale and they sometimes sell at ridiculously low prices. I have seen a fourteen-bedroom mansion going, with twenty acres of land and plenty of outbuildings, for £25,000. Now a house such as this could easily accommodate five good-sized families (because more bedrooms could be improvised), with communal use of some of the main rooms, with a good garden for each family, and perhaps communal use of part of the land. Thus each family would pay £5000 each—and what sort of a house would anybody get for £5000 in some dreary suburb of a city? If you searched further in Eire for example you could find much better values than this too. Five such families could split up food production marvellously—'A' keeps cows and runs the dairy and keeps us all in milk butter and cheese, 'B' keeps sows and supplies most of the other members with piglets to fatten in their gardens; 'C' is a handyman and runs a carpenter's and a blacksmith's shop and goes fishing; 'D' grows corn, mills wheat and malts barley. And so on. Each family will run its own enterprises privately, and sell what it can off the estate—to bring in some foreign exchange as it were. Each family will have a money-getting enterprise as well: some might even have 9 to 5 jobs. The exchange of produce between families could be done with money, but I would favour at least an experiment with a private currency, which would only be used between members: a token currency. The Communist slogan: 'From each according to his ability, to each according to his needs' is all very fine—but who decides what these needs and abilities are? I might have quite a different idea of my needs from the other members of the community. Successful monastic communities have always had strict government, and I suspect the best *kibbutzim* are not really anarchic. The kind of democracy of a Scottish fishing boat— the crew elect a skipper—*and then do what he says*—is the best sort of democracy.

There are an infinite number of ways in which communities such as I am suggesting can be created. They will vary from almost completely self-supporting communities to ones which buy most of their food requirements with their 'foreign currency'. Some will be completely integrated communities— some loose leagues of individuals. The planning laws in Britain make all development in rural areas very difficult. Any industrialist can get planning permission to put up a chemical factory bang in the middle of a national park. But just you try to get permission to build a house on a bit of land so you can start a smallholding. One day this will have to be changed. One day the huge empty farms will be broken up again, and homesteads will grow up on them, and the land will become populous again and people will live as they were meant to live, close to Old Mother Nature, for surely this is the course suggested to us by that other Old Mother I have referred to many times in this book: Old Mother Common Sense.

Just as we cannot, for ever, go on keeping hens in wire cages, or pigs in total darkness, or supressing every species of life on the land except one money-making crop, so we cannot go on for ever ourselves living in human battery cages and more and more distorting our environment.

It's all going to collapse. Either the oil will run out, or the grub, or the uranium-235, or the power of Man to withstand the unutterable *boredom* of it all, and Mankind will have to find a different way of life. And he will not go *back* as so many people think he will. He will go *forward* to something very much sounder and better than has ever been before. And it is then that I hope that this book will prove useful.

# Index

Aberdeen-Angus, 46
Acidimeter, 71
Africa, 117, 140, 229
Alder, 240
Alfalfa, *see* Lucerne
Apples, 186–91; storing, 202
April in the garden, 183
Artichoke, globe, 183
Artichoke, Jerusalem, 176; pioneering new ground, 123; suppressing weeds, 131
Artificial insemination, 47
Asparagus, 183, 185
August in the garden, 185
Ayrshire cattle, 46

Bacon, 77, 83, 89
Barley, 149–51
Beans, 168–70, 180 (*see also under* Broad, French, etc.)
Beef, 109–116; illustrations, 113
Beer, 151–60; small, 158
Bees, 226–9
Beet, 167
Belsen houses, 97, 100
*Biltong*, 117
Binder, 138
Birch, 240
Blackberry wine, 237
Blackcurrants, 193; wine, 237
Blight, potato, 165
Bloaters, 219
Boar, 76
Bottling, 200–3
Brassica, 180, 182, 184
Bread, 134–5; baking, 143–7
Brine, 115
Broad beans, 185
Broccoli, 180, 182
Brucellosis, 56
Brussels sprouts, 180, 182, 184
Buckling, 220

Butter, 57–61

Cabbage, 170, 180
Calves, 49
Calving, 47
Cambridge roll, 33
Carrot (in field), 168; (in garden), 180, 182
Carrot fly, 183
Cattle, 42–54
Cauliflower, 180, 182
Celeriac, 183
Celery, 180, 182, 185; storing, 198
Ceylon, 129, 140
Chapatis, 147
Charollais, 45, 46
Cheddar, 69, 71
Cheese, 61–74
Cherries, 192
Churn, 59
Chutney, 203
Clamping roots, 166, 197
Clover, 121; for gardens, 176, 180
Cockles, 233
Cod, 222; salting, 222
Combine harvester, 138
Communities, 244
Compost, 177–8
Conger eel, 225
Corn, Indian, 163
Corn-on-the-cob (*see* Sweet corn)
Corn salad, 185
Cow, 42–54
Crabs, 224
Crawfish, 224
Cream, 57
Creosoting, 239
Cucumber, 180
Cultivators, 31, 40
Curlew, 231
Currants, 193; wine, 237

Dairy, 55–74
Deep freeze, 95, 196, 204
Diesel, 30
Digging, 27, 34
Dipping sheep, 106
Distilling, 159
Drainage, 24–6
Dried peas, 198
Duck, 102
Dwarf beans, 185

Eel, 210; smoked, 211
Elderberry wine, 237
Electric fence, 78
Evans, George Ewart, 33

February in the garden, 182
Ferguson, 29
Fish, 206–25; farming, 212; sea, 215; salting white fish, 222; salting oily fish, 217–18
Flea beetle, 182
Flour, 134, 142
Fluke, liver, 24
Folding sheep, 105
Forestry, 238–40
Freezing (see Deep freeze)
French beans, 184, 185
Friesian cattle, 45
Fruit, 186–95
Fruit juice, 203
Fungi, 232

Garden, 172–85
Gaspé cure for cod, 224
Geese, 101
Globe artichoke (see Artichoke, globe)
Goat, 107
Goose, 101
Gooseberry, 193
Grass, 121–8
Grazing, 121, 124
Greengages, 192
Guernsey cattle, 45

Haddock, 222
Ham, 90

Hare, 232
Harness, 34
Hartley, Dorothy, 115
Harvesting corn, 137–9
Hay, 127–8
Hens, 97–100
Hereford cattle, 46
Herring, 215–18; potted, 225 (for kipper, buckling, etc., see under headings)
Hills, Lawrence D., 178
Hog, see Pig
Horse, 32–41
Howard cultivator, 31

January in the garden, 181
Jersey cattle, 45
Jerusalem artichoke (see Artichoke, Jerusalem)
July in the garden, 185
June in the garden, 185

Kale, 170, 180, 182
Kilner jars, 200
Kipper, 219

Lambs, 105
Land, 14–26, 130
Larch, 240
Laver weed, 241
Leeks, 184
Legumes, 179
Lettuce, 182, 184
Limpets, 233
Ling, 222
Liver fluke, 24
Lobsters, 224
Lucerne, 170, 180

Mackerel, 219; potted, 225
Maize, 163
Mallorca, 195
Malting, 152–4
Mangolds, 166–7
Manuring, 18, 22, 122, 175, 180
March in the garden, 182
Marrow, 180, 184
May in the garden, 184

Mead, 237–8
Meat, 109–20
Melon, 182
Merrytiller, 31
Milk, 55–7
Milking, 49, 54
Milling, 133–5, 142
Mowing, 127, 138
Mushrooms, 203
Mussels, 232
Mustard, 171, 180
Mutton, 116–18

Nuts, 192

Oak, 239
Oats, 161–2
October in the garden, 185
Onion, 180, 182; storing, 198
Oyster, 225

Parsnip, 180; wine, 236
Pasteurising, 56, 57
Pasture, 121–8
Peaches, 192
Pears, 191; storing, 203
Peas, field, 168–9; garden, 180, 182; storing, 198
Pheasant, 230
Pickles, 204
Pig, 75–82, 176
Pigeon, tame, 108; wild, 231
Pilchards, 221
Planting fruit, 187–9
Plough, 32–4, 130
Plums, 191
Pork, 95
Potato, field, 163–6; garden, 180, 182, 197
Potting, beef, 116
Poultry, 97–102, 177; slaughtering, 118–20
Prunes, 203
Pruning, 189–91
Pumpkin, 184

Rabbit, tame, 107; wild, 231
Raddish, 184

Rape, 171
Raspberries, 193
Razor fish, 233
Red currants, 193; wine, 237
Rennet, 65, 118
Rhubarb, 180; wine, 236
Roller, 33
Rollmops, 217
Root crops, 166–8; storage, 197
Rotation of crops, 123, 179
Runner beans, 184; storage, 196
Rye, 162–3

Salmon, 207–10; smoked, 209–10
Salsify, 180, 184
Salt, 233
Salting: beef, 115; white fish, 222; oily fish, 217; runner beans, 196
Samphire, 241
Sauerkraut, 204
Sausages, 92–5
Scythe, 127, 138
Sea holly, 241
Seakale, 180
Seaweed, 180, 241
Seeds, grass, 124–6
September in the garden, 185
Shallots, 182
Shearing, 106
Sheep, 102–7
Sheep fly, 106
Shorthorn cattle, 46
Sickle, 138
Silver leaf disease, 191
Skate, 224
Slaughtering: pig, 83–9; ox, 110–16; sheep, 116–18; poultry, 118–20
Smoking: eel, 211; Biltong, 117; bacon, 90; herring, 219; salmon, 209–10; sprats, 220
Smoke-house, 241
Soft fruit, 193–5
Sole, 225
Sowing, 137
Spade, 27, 34
Spinach, 184
Sprats, 220
Spraying fruit, 191

Spring cabbage, 185
Squash, 184
Strawberries, 194
Suckling calves, 52
Suet, 112
Sweet corn, 184; storage, 205
Sycamore, 240

Thatching (rick), 139
Thoreau, 11
Threshing, 141
Tomatoes, 184, 194; storage, 198
Tractor, 28–31, 40
Trout, 210
Tuberculosis, 56
Turkey, 102
Turnips, field, 166; garden, 180, 182

Veganism, 20
Vegetarianism, 19–21
Vinegar, 159

Walnuts, 192
Weeds, 131, 175
Welsh Black cattle, 46
Wheat, 129–43; varieties, 135
Whisky, 159
White currants, 193
Willow, 240
Wine, 234–8
Winnowing, 141
Winter in the garden, 185
Wood, 238–40

Yeast, 147
Yoghourt, 56